WHEN TO HIRE—OR NOT HIRE—A CONSULTANT

GETTING YOUR MONEY'S WORTH FROM CONSULTING RELATIONSHIPS

Linda M. Orr
Dave J. Orr

When to Hire—or Not Hire—a Consultant: Getting Your Money's Worth from Consulting Relationships

ISBN-13 (pbk): 978-1-4302-4734-0

ISBN-13 (electronic): 978-1-4302-4735-7

President and Publisher: Paul Manning
Acquisitions Editor: Jeff Olson
Developmental Editor: Robert Hutchinson
Editorial Board: Steve Anglin, Mark Beckner, Ewan Buckingham, Gary Cornell, Louise Corrigan, Morgan Ertel, Jonathan Gennick, Jonathan Hassell, Robert Hutchinson, Michelle Lowman, James Markham, Matthew Moodie, Jeff Olson, Jeffrey Pepper, Douglas Pundick, Ben Renow-Clarke, Dominic Shakeshaft, Gwenan Spearing, Matt Wade, Tom Welsh
Coordinating Editor: Rita Fernando
Copy Editor: Carole Berglie
Compositor: Bytheway Publishing Services
Indexer: SPi Global
Cover Designer: Anna Ischenko

Distributed to the book trade worldwide by Springer Science+Business Media New York, 233 Spring Street, 6th Floor, New York, NY 10013. Phone 1-800-SPRINGER, fax (201) 348-4505, e-mail orders-ny@springer-sbm.com, or visit www.springeronline.com. Apress Media, LLC is a California LLC and the sole member (owner) is Springer Science + Business Media Finance Inc (SSBM Finance Inc). SSBM Finance Inc is a Delaware corporation.

For information on translations, please e-mail rights@apress.com, or visit www.apress.com.

Apress and friends of ED books may be purchased in bulk for academic, corporate, or promotional use. eBook versions and licenses are also available for most titles. For more information, reference our Special Bulk Sales–eBook Licensing web page at www.apress.com/bulk-sales.

Any source code or other supplementary materials referenced by the author in this text is available to readers at www.apress.com. For detailed information about how to locate your book's source code, go to www.apress.com/source-code/.

To Makayla, Isabella, Victoria, and Christian.

Contents

About the Authors

Linda M. Orr, Ph.D., is an Associate Professor of Marketing at the University of Akron. Her specialties are sales, sales management, and data analytics. She is the primary author of *Advanced Sales Management Handbook and Cases: Analytical, Applied, and Relevant*, and a co-editor of two other books: *Direct Marketing in Action: Cutting Edge Strategies for Finding and Keeping your Best Customers*, finalist for the American Marketing Association's Berry Book Prize for the Best Book in Marketing (2009), and *Marketing in the 21st Century: Volume 3: Company and Customer Relations*. Dr. Orr has also published in several refereed journals. In addition, Dr. Orr served as assistant marketing director for Warner Bros. Records in Nashville, and in a variety of managerial capacities in the restaurant and finance industries. She has served as a consultant in numerous Fortune 500 companies and smaller companies in many industries.

Dave J. Orr has worked in process improvement, technical sales, engineering, product development, operations management, and quality roles for over fourteen years. He has served the healthcare, automotive, appliance, military, consumer product, and aerospace industries. Dave is a certified Six Sigma Master Black Belt from Kent State University. He earned his MBA from Robert Morris University and has a BS in Plastics Engineering Technology from Penn State University. Currently working to help improve the care delivery and administrative processes at Summa Health System, Dave is contributing author of one book, *Advanced Sales Management Handbook and Cases: Analytical, Applied, and Relevant*. In addition to his work in healthcare, Dave is a lecturer for operations management at Kent State University. Dave brings unique insight to this book by having hired and worked alongside consultants throughout his career and by analyzing the value they have and have not brought to companies. On the other side of the business, Dave has worked as an internal and external consultant in order to use his experiences to help improve companies.

Introduction

Why Write a Book on Whether or Not to Hire a Consultant?

If you don't like what's being said, change the conversation.

—Don Draper, *Mad Men*

Consultants can be both grim reapers and angels at the same time. Some people hate them; some people love them; and some people are indifferent. While specific, run-of-the-mill examples of failed consulting engagements are hard to find, due to their private nature, there abound urban legends of consultants who simply were ineffective to those who were flat-out unethical.

Example A (the unethical consultant): The Enron/Arthur Anderson scandal. In 2000, Enron paid Arthur Anderson $25 million in auditing fees and $27 million in consulting fees essentially to cover up its fraudulent reporting practices.[1] Anderson's collusion in Enron's fraud ultimately led to Enron's bankruptcy, the destruction of $60 billion in shareholder wealth, $2 billion lost in the pensions of long-serving employees, and the first-ever criminal conviction of an accounting firm. Enron and Anderson's agreement to steal money from millions of people is perhaps one of the most famous examples of unethical consulting.[2]

Example B (the incompetent consultant): The McDonald's "hot coffee lawsuit." Nearly everybody has viewed the McDonald's coffee-spill lawsuit in the context of overzealous litigation. However, the basis of the case lies in bad

---

[1] FindLaw; http://fl1.findlaw.com/news.findlaw.com/cnn/docs/enron/senpsi70802rpt.pdf.

[2] Ibid.

consulting advice. Documented in court transcripts, legal documents, and online summaries, the case involved a woman who had bought coffee at a McDonald's drive-through and then spilled it on herself, incurring third-degree burns. She sued McDonald's and was awarded over half a million dollars, though the amount was significantly reduced in later appeals.

What many people do not know is that, at the time of the incident, McDonald's guidelines dictated that coffee be served at a temperature between 180 and 190 degrees Fahrenheit.[3] In fact, liquids at this temperature will cause third-degree burns of human skin in just two to seven seconds. In contrast, coffee served at home and at other restaurant establishments is typically 135 to 140 degrees Fahrenheit.[4]

A consultant had recommended the high temperature as a way of maintaining optimum taste and, more important for McDonald's, of increasing return on investment.[5] According to legal transcripts, the real reason for the high temperature had nothing to do with a higher-quality product; instead, it was to slow down consumption of the coffee, thereby reducing demand for free refills. Apparently, more than 700 claims had been made against McDonald's, and many of the victims had suffered third-degree burns similar to the widely publicized incident.[6] Yet the company had refused to change its policy, supposedly because a consultant said that it was better for business and had backed up his advice with some return-on-investment analyses that showed how the savings in coffee refills exceeded the projected legal expenses.[7]

Now let's look at how consultants can help businesses.

Example C (the revenue-increasing consultant): If done right, consulting can lead a company to great success. In one such experience, a small manufacturer of automotive components sought credible advice on increasing the capacity of its sales force. We worked with this manufacturer to create a sales training program that had a total cost of slightly over $20,000. A large component of this training focused on handling buyer objections and selling value. The sales force learned that price is seldom a legitimate objection and were able to counter any hardcore negotiators objections with quality and value responses. Not only were buyers no longer able to haggle with sales reps until they reduced prices, but the company actually was able to increase prices across

---

[3] The famous/infamous "McDonald's Coffee Spill Lawsuit"; www.slip-and-sue.com/the-famous-infamous-mcdonalds-coffee-spill-lawsuit-r.

[4] Ibid.

[5] The Lect Law Library, "The Actual Facts About the McDonalds' Coffee Case"; www.lectlaw.com/files/cur78.htm.

[6] Ibid.

[7] Consumer Attorneys of California, ATLA Fact Sheet, 1995, 1996.

the board by 10 percent! An investment of $20,000 in consulting yielded the ability to increase pricing across the board for a company with $12 million in total sales. That is a significant return on investment.

Example D (the skill-building consultant): When a small injection-molding firm had problems with inconsistent process control, the general manager decided to research consulting firms that could help build internal capability. He selected RJG, Inc., of Traverse City, Michigan, to develop a training plan geared toward teaching engineers and technicians the process of scientific molding. Although neither consultant nor company calculated an ROI for the work, RJG created a new skill level within the organization.

This increase in capability, along with some process-improvement techniques like Lean Manufacturing and Six Sigma, additionally reduced internal waste and improved customer satisfaction. This ultimately contributed to greater profitability because the molding company could prove that it had a higher skill and more consistent quality than many similar firms. Salespeople were able to convince potential customers to give more work to the company.

Why We Wrote This Book

Although almost all business leaders interact at some point with consultants, many regard the interaction as a routine convenience, on a par with dropping off the dry cleaning. It's supposed to be simple, quick, and not require special tools or skills to enter into and manage the relationship. Yet nothing could be further from the truth. The decision to hire a consultant is in many ways harder than that of hiring, retaining, reviewing, and compensating employees. Sound decisions should mobilize all human resources skills, strategic mindsets, root-cause analyses, and statistical abilities—to name just a few of the factors affecting the executive–consultant relationship that we examine and teach in this book.

Similarly, many organizations become dependent on consulting relationships—to the point of its being an addictive relationship. Resistant to building internal capability and dedicating full-time resources, they choose to overpay for external resources that will ultimately still require internal resources. Indeed, this is one of the hidden costs of a consulting relationship. The skills and experience to execute culture-changing activities often exist within the organization; however, managers who hire consultants either do not know about those internal abilities or do not believe that the skills are robust enough to employ in the change effort. This approach is like having a reliable and well-maintained car in your garage, but deciding to call a taxicab every time you want to go somewhere.

In contrast, no organization that makes a decision to downsize its workers in order to improve profitability should justify the external consulting expenses to do so. This is especially scary when experienced people are available in house and would likely do a better job of sustaining gains than could anyone offering external advice. Many companies suffer what should be called "consultant addiction." Ultimately, it reflects a conscious decision to do what is bad for the company. This addiction is damaging in both the short and long term. Yet we have found that organizations do this all the time, and desperately need the help we can provide managers in deciding to end this addiction.

It became apparent to us that there is no good book providing guidance to managers on how and when to work with consultants. There is also no adequate book on how to quantify and correct the many costly misconceptions about the consulting relationship. The absence of books on how to use consultants effectively is conspicuous and strange, especially given that the $149 billion consulting industry in the United States is increasing the number of consultants at an astonishing rate of 83 percent a year.[8] The books that focus on consultants either help individuals to become consultants or, frequently, bash those who have entered the field.

In short, this book is for business leaders wanting to improve profitability and efficiency, whether that's through consultant use or not. Between us, we have two decades of experience both working independently as consultants and also working alongside many other types of consultants. This book provides a unique prospective to the market. Although we both occasionally consult each year, neither of us makes our living in the consulting industry. We are a full time professor and a full time executive. Thus, we are writing this book to benefit ourselves In particular, we have spent our time helping companies become better companies and want to pass this knowledge along to you.

How We Wrote This Book

In writing this book, we combined our own experiences with qualitative research on the popular press books and academic journal articles on the subject. Our aim is to provide managers and executives both insight into the consulting industry and a pragmatic guide with flowcharts and decision-tree worksheets on deciding whether to hire a consultant.

We undertook our qualitative research because much of the academic research on consulting, which was conducted in the 1970s and 1980s, is not applicable to today's business environment. We developed a survey that asked

---

[8] Arlene Dohm and Lynn Shniper, "Occupational Employment Projections to 2017," *Monthly Labor Review* (November 2007): 86–125.

open-ended questions designed to avoid predisposing respondents to implicit assumptions. Despite the unconstrained nature of the answers, nevertheless we found significant commonality among responders. We surveyed 61 executives in various industries (including healthcare, utilities, tele-communications, food service, retail, and manufacturing), at various levels (ranging from CEO to business analyst) and in various departments (including information technology, strategic development, and human resources). The respondents had an average of 15 years' (between 1 to 30 years) experience in their field. Of these 61 executives, 44 were from companies that focus on business-to-consumer sales, and 17 were from companies that focus on business-to-business sales.

In the group of executives, 37 were from companies that provide services and 24 were from companies that sell goods (9 of which sell durable products and 15 of which sell nondurable products). The companies ranged in size from 1 employee to 350,000 employees, with an average of 23,000 employees. The firms also had operations in a multitude of countries, including but not limited to the United States, United Kingdom, India, Saudi Arabia, and Cameroon. Our sample was skewed in favor of Fortune 500 companies rather than small firms, which reflects a greater use of consultants by large firms. (Large firms often have more resources to devote to consultants, and therefore, the large firms use them more often.)

Of the executives, 22 (36 percent) worked with IT consultants; 8 (13 percent) with operations consultants; and 7 (11 percent) with project management consultants (Figure 1-1). The statistical breakout in Figure 1-1 of the expertise areas of the consultants used by our respondents is fairly representative of the overall composition of the consulting industry, as we show in Chapter 2.

By validating that this sample of qualitative responses represents similar proportions in the overall consulting industry, we assume that the responses are useful in explaining the challenges organizations face when deciding to work with consultants. The average length of the consulting experience (in months) was 16.25 (roughly 1.5 years). Of the consultants they used, 57 percent were from small consulting firms, and the rest were from large consulting firms.

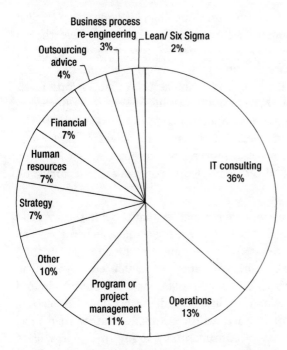

Figure 1-1. Types of consultants used by the executives surveyed in the qualitative study.

The Outline of the Book

We reference this qualitative study throughout this book to help support some of our conclusions and opinions. Because this is a comprehensive guide, we start in Chapters 2 and 3 by describing the current state and history of the consulting industry, referencing the work of some other authors who have done research in this area. This background is necessary for a few reasons. For example, say your first consulting relationship was with someone hired to help install an enterprise resource planning (ERP) system in your organization. This initial experience would be drastically different from an experience with a business management system or business process engineering consulting firm. So, the more you know about the consulting industry, the more you can make productive use of consultants and not run down blind alleys or led astray.

By explaining the industry, we also hope to lay the foundation for the rest of the book, describing different consulting models. As part of the history discussion, we also explain what it takes to become a consultant. It may be surprising to some readers that it requires little in the way of credentials to begin consulting.

After the foundation is set in Chapters 2 and 3, we start discussing how to make decisions about when to use a consultant and how to hire one. In Chapter 4, we show how to calculate the potential return on investment associated with a consulting relationship. Our research and personal experience reveal that many organizations do not calculate ROI, either in selecting a consultant or in evaluating the outcome. It seems simply irrational to make a business decision without conducting an ROI, yet this seems to be the norm with companies who hire consultants. This is why a whole chapter is devoted to this subject. We also provide worksheets in the Appendix for doing such calculations.

In Chapter 5, we examine the situations in which you should *not* use consultants. As you'll see, companies often hire consultants for the wrong reasons, leading ultimately to project failure. These unsuccessful consulting relationships taint the image of the industry overall. If you search for "when to use a consultant" online, for example, you will receive a host of blog-type pages, written by consultants that make it seem as though consultants are needed for just about any business decision or process.

We do not wish to present the impression that all consultants are bad. Consultants hired for the right reasons can be highly effective tools for driving performance improvements. In Chapter 5, we provide a decision tree to help you decide rationally whether you should or should not use a consultant for a given purpose. Our goal is to help you understand when to use or not use a consultant, and how to use one when you decide to go ahead. In Chapter 6, we explore the positive aspects of the industry and define the conditions under which you can benefit by reaching outside of your organization. It is just as important to understand the reasons to hire a consultant as it is to understand the reasons to avoid hiring one. Such knowledge will help ensure the success of projects.

In Chapter 7, we examine how to select the right consultant and set up the best relationship for success, including the nuts and bolts of the hiring process and the negotiation of contracts. In Chapter 8, we focus on techniques for managing these consulting relationships and troubleshooting common problems, such as project schedule slippage, no buy-in from staff, lack of communication, and inadequate review processes. You will see that proper review processes need to be applied at every point to ensure a project's success.

Finally, in Chapter 9, we consider the alternative principles and methods for deciding whether to use consultants. The Appendix provides many items, including project checklists, a Request for Proposals template, a contract template, and a sample confidentiality clause.

When you have read this book, you will have gained a deeper understanding of the consulting industry, the criteria for deciding when to hire a consultant and for picking the right one, and the tools for successfully managing and benefiting from a consulting relationship.

The Industry

The Growth of Consultants and the Consulting Industry

Consulting: If you're not part of the solution, there is a lot of money to be made in prolonging the problem.

—Despair.com

Consulting is one of the fastest-growing professions in the United States. The Bureau of Labor Statistics (BLS) projected in 2007 that employment in this industry would increase by 83 percent over the next decade.[1] Also, salaries for the industry are among the highest paying of the groups that the BLS tracks. According to the U.S. government, there were 719,000 consultants in the United States in 2010, and the number of consultants is expected to grow to 993,000 by 2020.[2] Forty percent of all MBA graduates attempt to enter the consulting industry.[3] This figure becomes a daunting statistic, considering the growth rate of MBA programs. The number of MBA degrees awarded annually has increased from 26,000 in 1970 to 168,000 in 2009.[4]

Once upon a time, in the 1960s through the 1980s, MBA programs were management training grounds for large Fortune 500 companies. It seems that now, instead, they are large breeding grounds for consultants. Figure 2-1

[1] Arlene Dohm and Lynn Shniper, "Occupational Employment Projections to 2016," *Monthly Labor Review* (November 2007): 86–125. Vol. 130, No. 11.

[2] Ibid.

[3] P. K. Milne, "Consulting Career Choices"; March 2009, http://ezinearticles.com/?expert=Pk_ Milne.

[4] Ronald Yeaple, "Is the MBA Obsolete?," *Forbes*, May 30, 2012, http://www.forbes.com/sites/ ronaldyeaple/2012/05/30/is-the-mba-obsolete.

shows the worldwide growth of the consulting industry since 2007 while Figure 2-2 shows the recent growth in the United States alone.

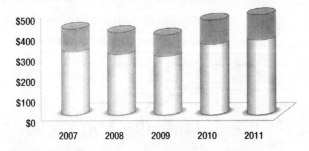

Just "Management" Consulting   Additional - Tax Prep and Accounting

Figure 2-1. Annual worldwide revenue of consultants (in $billions). The line segmenting the cylinder shows general consulting (below) and general consulting plus tax preparation and accounting. SOURCE: Plunkett Research, Ltd., *Consulting Market Research – Industry Trends* (Plunkett Research, 2010). http://www.plunkettresearch.com/consulting-market-research/industry-trends.

Nearly every employee and manager interacts with a consultant at some point in his or her career. It is hard to find anyone who has never hired, fired, or worked with a consultant. Yet consultants are in no way like "normal" employees. They are not hired in the same way, not compensated in the same way, and not subjected to the same review and retention processes as are regular employees. Negative and positive predispositions about consultants abound in the business arena. Some business leaders think consultants are worthless and unethical. Others go into consultant relationships with the blind belief that an external resource can save a troubled firm. Given the billions at stake, such costly decisions should never be taken blindly.

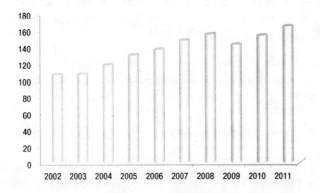

Figure 2-2. United States consulting spending (in billions). SOURCE: Plunkett Research, Ltd., *Consulting Market Research – Industry Trends* (Plunkett Research, 2010); U.S. Census Bureau, 2010 U.S. Census, 2010; http://www.census.gov/services/sas/data_summary54.html.

Why the Growth?

Business guru Peter Drucker said that there are two main reasons businesses hire consultants. The first is that management skills, techniques, and knowledge are best learned through exposure to and experience with many different companies in many different industries.[5] Typically, executives lack this wide exposure. They may work at only a few organizations—or even just one—throughout their career. In contrast, consultants continually get exposure and experience across organizational and industry boundaries.

The second reason businesses hire consultants is that executives value objective insights into their management problems. Because all businesses have problems, it is logical to believe that an expert who has worked with multiple businesses has been exposed to a problem similar to the one that the client is currently facing and, therefore, can offer some solutions that will work.

The research of Gattiker and Larwood from 1985 confirms that businesses turn to consultants primarily for three deliverables: new ideas, proficiency, and impartiality/objectivity.[6] Figure 2-3 shows a model that helps explain some of the other reasons the consulting field has grown.

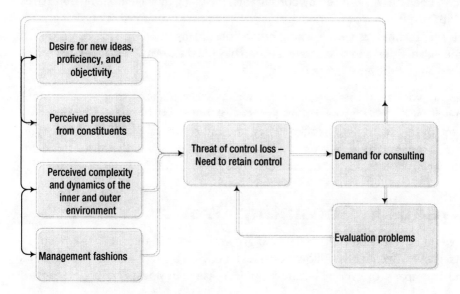

Figure 2-3. Factors leading to the growth in demand for consultants.

[5] Steven H. Appelbaum and Anthony J. Steed, "The Critical Success Factors in the Client-Consulting Relationship," *Journal of Management Development*, Vol. 24, Issue 1, (2005): 68–93.

[6] U. E. Gattiker and L. Larwood, "Why Do Clients Employ Management Consultants?," *Consultation* (Summer 1985): 119–29.

Another factor leading to an increase in the consulting business is the perceived pressures from constituents. The public nature of large companies forces them to focus on stakeholder needs and short-term growth, not necessarily on what is best for the company as a whole and for long-term growth. This limited, short-term focus drives many companies to seek creative solutions from external consultants as a way to promote quick, measurable growth. Likewise, the competitive environment, types of products, and customer demand are factors that change so rapidly that managers need out-of-box, up-to-date, creative thinking that external sources can best provide.

Also, for better or for worse, managers seek to keep up with fads and fashions. According to the work of Crandall and colleagues, "management fashion refers to popular programs used in organizations to improve performance."[7] The authors tend to categorize a management theory as a "management fad" based on how long it remains in the academic literature. For a theory to be a fad, generally, there is a huge amount of research on the subject all of a sudden, but then the research dissipates rapidly after three to five years.[8] The term "management fad" carries a negative connotation, implying that the organizational process changes are simply the "thing to do," not because there is real internal need. Numerous examples of management fads and fashions have been heavily utilized by consultants, including management by objectives (MBO), quality circles, empowerment, benchmarking, sensitivity training, sales closing techniques, and learning capabilities. Many of these fads come out of the universities, and so managers think they need external help from academics who advocate these latest trends.

Finally, with all of the pressures that executives are under, there is a constant need for help in many other aspects of business. Managers must satisfy employees, customers, stockholders, and the community at large. Simply put, the harder and more aggressive the competition gets, and the more turbulent the environment gets, the more help executives need.

Trends in Consulting Growth

Even though the consulting field has grown faster than many other industries, its growth frequently follows business cycles. For this reason, consultants must prepare for cyclical business. An increase in business prosperity leads to

---

[7] William Crandall, Richard E. Pembroke, and Mohammad Ashraf. "The Perilous World of Management Fashion: An Examination of Their Life Cycles and the Problem of Scholarly Lags," *Proceedings of the Annual Meeting of the Academy of Management* (2006).

[8] Leonard J. Ponzi and Michael Koenig, "Knowledge Management: Another Management Fad?," *Information Research* 8, No. 1 (2002), paper No. 145.

an increase in the demand for consulting services, while recessions often lead to a decrease in demand for such services.

This is an illogical trend if you assume that businesses hire consultants to help improve performance. Seeing this trend at a macro level, however, shows that many organizations hire consultants for the wrong reasons: they cut the budget for consulting services when money is tight, and they hire consultants when there is extra money on hand. This is ill advised. Consultants should be used in two broad instances: (1) when there is a need for a special product or service within a company (ERP implementation, ongoing sales training), and (2) when business is bad (sales training to counter a loss in sales productivity).

International Expansion

While consulting is growing around the world, it has grown at especially high rates in Asia, as businesses continue to prosper in those economies. In particular, Japanese companies use more consultants than do businesses in other Asian countries. This Asian demand has created a huge need for local consulting firms. Large consulting firms with international offices tend to fail, due to a general lack of cultural competency and international business acumen, leading to misunderstandings and unsuccessful relationships.

Any person who has traveled or worked extensively around the world has likely seen how easily people may be offended, or become less cooperative, when there is a basic lack of familiarity with the local culture. For example, a firm in Afghanistan realized it was in need of both strategic and IT consulting in order to grow and to better integrate its business with the rest of the world. They agreed to consulting services with a large consulting company from Sweden. The Swedes came in and started running meetings and making decisions, without consideration of the Arabic culture. The employees, luckily, were not offended; rather, they found it humorous to watch the consultants continually hit brick walls and not bother to think about why they were not succeeding and why the employees were not doing what was asked of them. Eventually, the consultants realized their mistakes and took time to learn the local culture, and they eventually succeeded.

Another problem can be a lack of understanding of the local language. In some areas, people who can speak English will nonetheless refuse to communicate in English. Asian attitudes regarding consultants differ tremendously. In Asia, hiring a consultant may be seen as a reflection of failure for a chief executive officer, leading to reluctance to reach out for help. This, of course, is in direct contrast to the United States, where use of consultants is part of the business culture.

Culture also plays a part in the available consultant pool, especially in Asia. When Asians are choosing careers, they often prefer engineering and medicine, which are more respected fields than consulting. Therefore, those who do pursue consulting may be less talented than their counterparts in North America. Due to this attitude, among other factors, and despite the apparent stigma associated with hiring a consultant, the demand for competent consultants in Asia exceeds the supply, and this international demand will likely continue. Given the consulting field's international growth potential, it is critical that consultants and executives alike recognize that hiring a consultant is like hiring an employee, and cross-cultural issues must be considered.

Size of Consulting Firms

The large consulting firms that dominated the industry in the 1980s and 1990s are becoming smaller. New, smaller firms and individual consulting businesses are growing. The exceptions are large consulting firms that possess a strong information technology (IT) department. IT consulting is growing as a reflection of the organic growth of technology and the reluctance or inability of managers to keep up with current technology. If you compare the services available from the top ten firms, those with strong IT backgrounds, such as IBM, SAP, or Oracle, continue to gain market share while those focused on the finance sector have only seen very modest growth.

Though the large consulting firms are slowly shrinking, ten large ones still dominate the industry with over one-third of the business (Figure 2-4). Nevertheless, as the industry continues to grow and the number of private consultants continues to grow, their percentage of market share will decrease. Companies are seeing the clear advantage that niche firms have over the large shops with no distinct specializations. The advantages and disadvantages of specialization are discussed in Chapter 9.

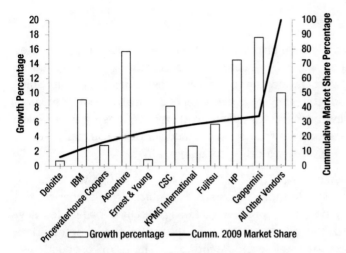

Figure 2-4. Top 10 Firms Growth. Source: Von Uechtritz, "Market Share Analysis: Top 10 Consulting Providers' Revenue, Growth and Market Share, Worldwide and Regional 2009," (Gartner Dataquest Research Note, 2010).

Types of Industries that Use Consulting

The types of businesses that use the most consultants say a lot about why consulting services are needed. For example, according to the data presented in Figure 2-5, the finance industry was the second largest user of consulting services in 2008 and 2009. Given the industry's continuing woes, the finance sector is likely to move to the third spot soon.

The rest of these industry categories are discussed in the sections that follow.

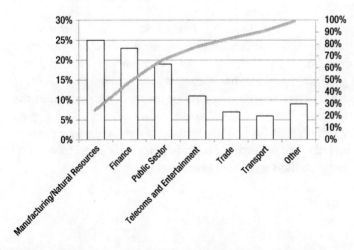

Figure 2-5. Global end users of consultants in 2008 and 2009. Source: Joe O'Mahoney, *Management Consultancy*, (Oxford, UK: Oxford University Press, 2010).

Manufacturing

As Figure 2-5 shows, the manufacturing and natural resources sector uses more consultants than any other sector. In manufacturing areas, speed to market or total product-development time are key metrics for companies that invent new products. They hire consultants to analyze the company's ability to develop new products compared with the abilities of their direct competitors. This is especially true for manufacturers of products that sell either directly to end users or to other companies.

The race here is to incorporate the best technology or design while staying ahead of the competition. In more customized manufacturing scenarios, the consultant focus may be on the process of taking purchase orders for new products through to the product-realization phase in the shortest time feasible without increasing total development costs. The term "product" may refer to a service that either is new to the market or has been introduced by a competitor. Often in a service industry, the work to develop the product includes more coordination, so that it is of high quality from the moment it is offered.

Another key consulting area in manufacturing may be to review techniques to maximize income. This may involve pricing, distribution channels, and customer demographics. Likewise, it could include ways to bundle services or products or to cross-sell into different markets. This category of consulting will likely grow in America, as manufacturing begins to return to America and companies work to grow to meet these new market needs.

Public Sector

As of 2008, the public sector accounts for around $57 billion of the world economy.[9] This figure mostly excludes healthcare, especially U.S. healthcare. However, in some countries, healthcare is so intertwined with the public sector that the figure does reflect healthcare expenditures. Public-sector spending on consultants has seen monumental growth. For example, in the United Kingdom, between 2002 and 2005, expenditures for consulting grew from £600 ($956) million to £1.58 ($2.52) billion.[10] There are many reasons for this increase, including cost-cutting objectives and attempts to combat resistance to change by public-sector workers.

---

[9] Joe O'Mahoney, Management Consultancy, (Oxford, UK: Oxford University Press, 2010).
[10] Ibid.

As we will discuss in chapter 5, consultants are often part of change management since they can be used as an excuse for the change. In government especially, it is helpful to "make a change" via having someone else to blame.

Healthcare

In 2008, the healthcare consulting industry was worth $34 billion, according to O'Mahoney.[11] As mentioned above, healthcare does not show up as a separate category in Figure 2-4 because it often gets lumped into the public sector. However, the use of consultants in the healthcare field helps drive reform; and as inefficiencies in healthcare continue to increase, so will the percentage of the consulting market that is devoted to this area.

Current regulations have helped support the growth in IT consulting area. For example, providers have used consultants to help conversions to electronic medical recordkeeping. In fact, compliance with electronic medical record-keeping has started a boom in healthcare IT firms.

Thanks to Obamacare, healthcare providers will be responding to changes in regulations and newer methods of care. As organizations scramble to catch up to these new standards, consultants will be offering services such as process improvement, IT implementation, care redesign, strategy development, and quality and patient safety initiatives. The need for hospitals to reduce cost per case, errors per case, length of stay, and over-utilization will drive the need for process redesign activities. Clinical workers who have transitioned to consulting guide some of the redesign work. Engineers who specialize in waste elimination and process design may facilitate other activities.

Universities have also jumped on board with new healthcare MBA programs and healthcare IT programs. Many of these new MBAs decide to become consultants, aware of the overwhelming market demand for their skills. As healthcare reform continues to progress, the demand for healthcare consultants as well as healthcare professionals in general will increase.

Telecommunications and Entertainment

At the turn of the 21st century, increases in broadband and 3G license sales helped lead to an increase in telecommunications marketing. There will likely still be a steady need for telecommunications and communications consulting in the future as the technology continues to progress in this field. It is likely that some of the same skills to support the demand for IT consulting will be

---

[11] Ibid.

used to meet this demand. Firms that have a technological edge are well positioned to participate in two major markets for consultants.

The entertainment industry's need for consulting has grown due to the growth of digital content, including films, music, and documents. The new digital world means that managers must keep up with the challenges. When the digital revolution began, it seemed most of the battles were going to be in the legal arena, in terms of copyright and other legal safeguards. However, Google very much rewrote the book in terms of how business is conducted by making it all free, with very few legal ramifications. Businesses once again scrambled, thinking that they were not going to be able to make money on any entertainment content. We know now that this is not true. Consumers are willing to pay for good-quality films, music, and books. However, the industry has unique marketing, advertising, and strategic needs that must be met to succeed in this rapidly changing world. Consultants will likely continue to be needed in this area.

Other Industries

Other industries also use consultants, but it is important to mention here that these other industries have increased their use of consulting for a few key reasons. One is new-product and new-process consulting—what products the organization should provide. Even the process that is used to create and innovate may be a focus of a consulting contract. Product life cycle and portfolio management are two other areas where executives reach beyond their company's capability. To meet these perceived needs, executives may hire consultants to perform market research, provide training, or perform competitive analyses.

Many consultants make money by offering cost-cutting methods. Skills such as Lean or Six Sigma are applied as cost-cutting measures. Though internal experts may have taken the training, relatively few have the varied experience to use these techniques successfully to implement enough change to meet cost-cutting goals. For this reason, after initially failing to save money through Lean or Six Sigma using internal resources, companies will often reach out to external experts in these tools. The experts can then guide business leaders through the Six Sigma processes and help them improve financial results.

Consortia of purchasing organizations offer to consult for members on how to manage suppliers to minimize purchasing expenses. The techniques offered include customized pricing analyses, data normalizing, memberships in group-purchasing organizations, reviews of current contracts, and on-site coaching for purchasing decisions. Some of these consultants tout themselves as experts within certain industries, thereby giving them greater credibility among employees when changes are required. Other consultants focus on a particular area of expertise, such as supply chain, which can span multiple industries. They serve to optimize warehouse layout, develop logistics, increase fill rates, and reduce variation in order fulfillment, all of which lead to more efficient shipping and receiving activities.

Types of Consulting

There are multiple ways to categorize consulting companies.[12] For example, consultancies can be considered either hybrid or pure. *Pure consultancies*, like McKinsey, Bain, BAD, and Arthur D. Little generate roughly 10 percent of the total consulting revenue. These organizations claim that, since consulting is all they do, they can be trusted to have better consulting skills. Even with this proclaimed advantage, however, these organizations are part of the industry that is declining in size and will soon be taken over by hybrid consultants. This decline is likely because you do not want a consultant who is good at consulting per se. Rather, you want a consultant who is good at fixing or improving business issues. In essence, the big consulting firms are large sales organizations that exist to sell consulting. Unless the firm is in a niche market (like ERP implementation or ISO auditing), these pure consultancies rarely offer true advantages.

Hybrid consultancies include firms like IBM, PWC, Accenture, KPMG, and Deloitte. They often have a core competency in a particular industry. This sometimes causes regulatory issues, however. The SEC has forced some of these firms to sell off their consultancy divisions, due to perceived conflicts of interests.

Consultancies can also be categorized as niche or generalist.[13] *Generalist consultants* like Accenture offer multiple services and have a network of independent consultants they call upon when specific skills are needed. Clients often benefit from the wide and varied experience accumulated by these consultants. The same disadvantage exists here as pertains to pure consulting firms, however: businesses want consultants who are good in their product/ service category, not just good at selling consulting.

Niche consultants offer specific services to specific markets. These consultancies are more reliable, and often more successful in their work, than generalist consultancies due to their concentrated experience. Some generalists bid for a consulting job, then hire people with the necessary skills. Due their greater versatility, generalists tend to have the upper hand when compared to niche

---

[12] Ibid.
[13] Ibid.

consultants, although if clients value the quality of their consultants, niche consultants are often a better choice.

Size is another categorization method. *Small consultants* represent 98 percent of all firms and 78 percent of all consulting employees. *Large consultants*, on the other hand, represent 50 percent of all the revenue. Small companies generally charge less and, therefore, generate less income per consultant.[14] Large consultancies obviously have stronger brands, allowing them to charge a premium for services that can likely be provided by a smaller company. Figure 2-6 shows the size of the overall consulting market by company size. As can be seen in this figure, the market is driven by small firms, which continue to gain market share from the larger organizations.

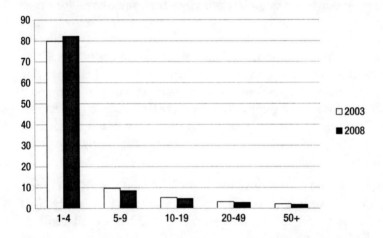

Figure 2-6. Market share by consultancy size (number of employees). SOURCE: Joe O'Mahoney, *Management Consultancy* (Oxford, UK: Oxford University Press, 2010).

Types of Consultants: Different Business Models

Traditionally, businesses hire consultants from outside firms to work on a project. However, there are several other types of consulting business models. *Internal consultants*, for example, are people hired by organizations to act as consultants within the organization. This could include hiring a project manager for a year or employing someone for a couple of years to implement a new management system. Organizations hire internal consultants if they have the specific need that those consultants can serve. Internal consultants cost less than external consultants to employ per hour, so if the need is

---

[14] Brett Howell Associates, *Financial Benchmarks: Management Consultants Survey;* http://www. a14bha.co.uk/control/product/~category_id=SURVEYS/~product_id=10000.

constant, this is a much better option than hiring a third-party consultant. There is also a greater commitment from internal consultants because they are, in essence, employees. There is a downside, too. *External consultants* may be incentivized by the promise of a performance-based bonus while internal consultants often are held to the same bonus programs offered to regular employees, which leads to less than optimum performance and a potential lack of drive.

Contractors and Interim Managers

Business executives often hire *contractors* to take on short-term assignments in order to provide them with specific skills. For example, some large clients might need basic work done for an IT project, but they do not want to pay a consultancy rate for the work. Therefore, they retain a contractor to work a couple of days per week to maintain an existing system. This might be more cost-effective than cross-training a current employee or hiring a full-time employee. This way, the company can have the skills it needs without hiring a full time employee.

Companies may also need staff for a short time, and contractors provide those skills without a long-term commitment. Recruiting for a permanent employee can cost as much as 30 percent of that person's salary; a business can avoid this expense by hiring a contractor. Other expenses, such as insurance, pension, 401(k) matching, sick pay, and holiday pay are also avoided by hiring a contractor. Contract relationships benefit the contractors, as well, because the pay rate is often higher than for a full-time position. A person making $113,000 per year as a full-time employee will gross $56.50 per hour, while a contractor may gross around $100 per hour.[15]

Finally, some companies bring in a consultant with the intention of hiring the person. This allows the company to test the consultant's skill levels and cultural fit before making a long-term commitment.

Interim managers are senior-management types brought in to fill a gap left by a departing executive. Temporary consultants, they are typically around for less than four months. They usually demand a higher salary due to the short-term nature of the assignment. Banking and finance organizations account for a high number of interim manager positions, although they are used in other industries as well, such as manufacturing or healthcare. The large banks used many interim managers in 2009 after they had fired a good portion of their staff and needed quick replacements during the recession-induced crises.

---

[15] Joe O'Mahoney, *Management Consultancy*, (Oxford, UK: Oxford University Press, 2010).

Types of Consulting

There are a few types of consulting firms that are hired to meet a variety of company needs. The largest of these is the management-consulting type, as described below, with other major types following.

Management Consulting

The term "management consulting" embraces many areas of the consulting industry. According the U.S. Census Bureau, this category includes IT, operations, strategy, actuarial, human resources, financial, marketing, and other fields.[16] Figure 2-7 shows the revenue in the United States for each of these areas from 2005 to 2010. As could be predicted, revenue decreased with the recession in 2009. However, the industry has since rebounded as companies have looked for ways to improve their revenues in a period of diminished sales.

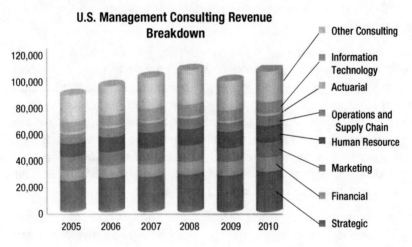

Figure 2-7. Management consulting revenue. SOURCE: U.S. Census Bureau; accessed 2010, http://www.census.gov/services/sas/data_summary54.html.

Information Technology

Information technology is one of the key areas in which consultants are used. Even companies that do not have their own consultants maintain relationships with consulting firms that specialize in the implementation of their products. Enterprise resource planning software companies, such as Oracle and SAP, use this model rather than having their own consulting divisions. Big

---

[16] U.S. Census Bureau; accessed 2010, http://www.census.gov/services/sas/data_summary54. html.

implementations often have software and hardware needs that may require hiring a consultant to manage the project. That consultant in turn may hire other consultants to perform tasks related to smaller portions of the project.

For instance, a company may hire a contractor to be an internal project manager to manage a relationship with an SAP implementation firm. As part of the SAP project, it becomes apparent that the company's warehouse needs to have a wireless net built. So, the implementation firm hires a consultant group to set up the warehouse's wireless network. The project manager may also realize a need for consultants to analyze the processes within the organization and will hire them. It is easy to see how one set of consultant skills may drive the need to get other consultants to implement successfully new business software.

Despite some setbacks, such as the dotcom bust of the early 2000s, IT consulting continues to grow. It is currently worth over an estimated $150 billion. IT consulting is now rarely about coding or systems analysis, although these are components of the market. More often, it is about integrating business units within the organization or between divisions of an organization.

There are a few key reasons to hire IT consultants. These include growing the business through the use of Internet tools, cutting costs through ERP or outsourcing, improving service through things like customer relationship management (CRM), and developing business intelligence tools. There are many other reasons, like developing faster communication channels and integrating companies. As various software and cloud computing solutions are employed to help businesses solve operational problems; the need for consultants to support these solutions will grow.

Some organizations own hundreds of discrete software packages, each to meet a specific company need. As these companies mature, they need to work with experts in data integration and normalization to have the disparate systems communicate with each other. This, then, allows companies to have an overall real-time picture of organizational performance.

Two examples of tasks associated with IT consulting are configuring ERP systems to parallel business processes and developing customization to meet business needs. Helping with data transfers or setting up system interfaces are other tasks that may be performed. When organizations put in large-scale software and try to avoid customization expenses, they tend to bring in consultants to share best practices across their specific industry and provide training on the software use. This shows that, potentially, IT consultants may not be technical in nature, but are truly able to work with people through training and business process analysis.

Program and Project Management

Companies often need to manage large programs, but lack seasoned internal employees with program or project management skills. *Program management* involves coordinating several complex projects that may be related to each other. Examples of program management include starting up a new company division or developing a new product line. Because projects of this scope are not a normal part of business for most organizations, they hire consultants that specialize in program management. A consultant program manager can provide a strategic benefit due to the scope of their influence and control.

Project management is about managing resources to ensure that the project is completed on time and within budget. It does not require strategic representation or decisions, but it does require experience and a specific set of skills to complete a project successfully. Project managers use tools such as Gantt charts and budgets; they often present themselves with project management professional (PMP) certifications and a portfolio of projects successfully implemented. This allows them to show that they are capable of doing what is necessary to manage a project. A project manager is paid much less than a program manager and works only within predefined specifications.

Operations

Operations consulting is a diverse category of consulting, including areas that transcend industries, such as business process redesign, process improvement, rapid cycle innovation, cost reduction, quality improvement, and customer relationship management. Other areas focus on specific industries, such as patient safety in healthcare, banking best practices, and manufacturing logistics. Operations consultants often have longer tenure than consultants within other areas. These consultants may be retired leaders from the business world, in contrast to career consultants who may have started working for a large consulting firm right out of an MBA program.

Operations consultants can be very helpful, especially when a problem is not clearly defined. To justify their fees, consultants likely do a baseline analysis of the company and identify target improvement areas. Because of the specific skills associated with this type of consulting, it is important to ensure the sustainability of their suggested improvements and verify any claimed successes.

Outsourcing Advice

"Outsourcing" can mean a lot of things and encompasses many different business strategies to control costs. *Business process outsourcing* (BPO) involves outsourcing standard company functions, such as human resources, payroll, and IT, as a means of avoiding the costly investment in infrastructure and skills required to perform these tasks. This is helpful for small to mid-size companies that may not have enough activity to justify dedicating resources to these functions. However, many large companies also use this method to turn fixed overhead into variable overhead, based on fluctuating staffing needs.

The outsourcing of IT infrastructure, and use of hosted solutions such as software as a service (SaaS) is called *infrastructure outsourcing*. For example, a company might not want to manage all its own servers, so it will hire a third party to manage the servers. *Application outsourcing* includes developing software, and then managing its operation and improvement; examples include some SaaS models. This is a growing market, thanks to the prevalence of cloud computing. SaaS works very well for organizations that do not want to spend capital funds and labor and infrastructure to maintain their own programs. Many organizations avoid this type of consulting, however, due to concerns for data integrity and potential downtime on their applications.

Many outsourcing companies bundle their services to offer a complete package, and this can be a lucrative business for consulting companies. Accenture, for example, receives over 20 percent of its income from running outsourcing operations. The market is so large that Accenture's CEO believes that this may eventually reach 50 percent.[17] As the economy continues to become more global, and IT infrastructure becomes more stable, the companies that currently avoid outsourcing some of these common services will likely reconsider. At that point, there will be enough history to track the security of the data and the robustness of the systems.

By having up to 35 percent of their staffs in Asia, companies such as IBM, EDS, and Accenture can offer Western firms access to cheap, and increasingly highly skilled, labor in India and China to answer calls, host IT applications, and run business processes. Even with potential lingual, cultural, and time-zone challenges, this is a good model for certain companies to maximize profits, although it eliminates local jobs.

In recent years, Indian companies such as Tata, Wipro, and Infosys have increasingly taken the battle to the West, building up massive outsourcing contracts and buying up skills and assets in the United States. Although this business continues to grow, with margins getting tighter and the competition becoming more intense, the outsourcing market is not as profitable as it was in the 1990s. The high startup costs associated with outsourcing keep most

---

[17] Accenture, Accenture Annual Report; accessed 2011, http://www.accenture.com/us-en/company/annual-report/Pages/annual-report-2011-ceo-letter.aspx.

consultancies from making entry into the market this late, which helps solidify the position of the incumbents.

Financial

Financial consultants are trained professionals with mastery of broad and diverse finance topics ranging from insurance to tax laws. They must possess a solid education and superior people skills to perform effectively. The education required is usually in the form of certified financial planner, CPA, or tax attorney.

These kinds of consultants are typically responsible for bringing in their own business. Thus, for a financial planner, sales skills tend to be more important than financial skills. In fact, many of the large financial firms are recruiting candidates from the few undergraduate-level certified sales programs in the country. We have personally spoken with executives in these firms, who feel that it is easier to train financial skills than selling skills. These types of consultants are typically very well paid, due to required skills and education, making this a desirable profession for many intelligent, financially minded professionals.

Financial consulting will likely remain an important area of consulting. People and companies are always going to need help in the area of finance. A financial planner we know once said, "You would not perform heart surgery on yourself, so why would you try to manage your own finances?" Finance is such an emotional and technical area, ridden with legalities, that it makes sense even in large corporations to have a trained, nonbiased third party analyzing the financial aspects of the business.

Strategy

In essence, strategy consultants started the whole "consulting industry" around 1900. They asked two basic questions: (1) Where should the client company position itself, or what is its strategy? and (2) How does the company get there? The answer to the second question is the company's strategic plan. In many companies, the development of strategy often fell to the executives. As a result, many strategic decisions were made at the last minute and were not based on careful analysis of the market.

All the major consultancies have developed strategic tools and frameworks, some of which are the Growth Share Matrix, Porter's Five Forces, the 4Cs, SWOT, and countless others. The biggest firms, such as McKinsey, Bain, and Boston Consulting Group, create their own frameworks. Though many of these frameworks are not based on solid research showing the effectiveness of the methods, but they have nevertheless been embraced by many businesses and MBA professors because of their practicality.

Even when organizations employ strategists, they may not have the resources or access to applicable data needed to develop effectively those strategic plans. It is important to realize that none of these frameworks should serve as an analytical or decision-making tool; rather, they are simply frameworks, which are helpful in organizing information about the company.

Strategy consulting is what many fresh MBA grads want to do. Michael Eckstut, a Booz Allen Hamilton former partner, stated, "The pure-strategy, big-picture stuff is over."[18] One reason for this is the increasing sophistication of business executives who have been successful, due their ability to navigate their industry. Another reason for the decline is that the realization that the tools created by the big consulting firms are, contrary to their use on many MBA projects, virtually worthless unless accompanied by an in-depth, statistical analysis of markets, competitors, and consumer trends. Without these tools, the "soft skills" learned in business schools provide little in the way of the analytical power that is useful in directing a business. Strategy is worthless without good data and statistical analyses. Consulting *should* move away from the "fluffy" strategic-type consulting.

Business Process Reengineering

Business process reengineering (BPR) became big in the 1970s and 1980s as companies thought they needed to move from vertical to horizontal. Total Quality Management (TQM) and just-in-time philosophies became popular around this time, contributing to the demand for this type of consulting. In its infancy, however, BPR was often done violently, through drastic operational changes that caused a fair amount of turmoil within the organization. This led to BPR's going out of style for a short period. Likewise, the dotcom boom of the 1990s presented consulting opportunities that took precedence over BPR. Companies suddenly focused on having an online presence and were not as concerned about inefficiencies.

With the beginning of the 21st century, BPR has experienced a resurgence. It is now being used to design data management systems, such as enterprise resource planning (ERP), and for defining tasks that can be outsourced rather than entire departments. Also, regulations and legislation such as Sarbanes-

---

[18] Melanie Warner, "The Incredible Shrinking Consultant: To Survive, the Big Three Strategy Firms Need to Make Big Changes," *Fortune*, May, 26, 2003, http://money.cnn.com/magazines/fortune/fortune_archive/2003/05/26/343083/index.htm.

Oxley have created the need for firms to implement process changes, opening up a new market for consultants with BPR expertise.

The healthcare industry is currently facing drastic changes due to the increasing costs and ineffectiveness of treatments. New legislation such as the Affordable Care Act (Obamacare) is forcing both administrative and clinical staff to reevaluate their processes and provide better care at lower cost. Organizations are currently scrambling to prepare for what industry experts feel will be the outcome of healthcare reform. For example, companies are developing patient-centered medical homes and accountable-care organizations to go from a fee for service model to a good health models. However, this requires significant process changes. Berwick and coauthors have laid out their vision for reform of the American healthcare system, describing it as the Triple Aim of Healthcare, which is "the simultaneous pursuit of three aims: improving the experience of care, improving the health of populations, and reducing per capita costs of health care."[19]

Government is still in need of drastic business process reengineering, since the costs of many government activities outweigh the benefits. A good example of this is the U.S. Treasury's decision to continue producing pennies and nickels when the cost of making this currency outweighs its nominal value. So, process reengineering consulting, in its many guises, will likely continue unless another priority takes precedence.

Human Resources

In the last five years, as many companies have faced economic uncertainty and increased competition, they have done everything in their power to get rid of as many employees as possible, usually through delayering, automation, and outsourcing. Human resource (HR) consultants help with the outsourcing and IT consulting, thereby meeting the demands of these companies. They also help with the turmoil that the reorganizing creates.

With good employees now job-hopping an average of every three years, much of HR consulting is directed toward finding, enticing, and motivating the right people. Companies are finding that they would rather invest the money in a consultant to make sure they find the best candidate for the job, than to hire a bad fit and reap the enormous repercussions.

Executives who have been in the workforce for quite some time do not understand the demands and needs of the younger generations as they leave college and work their way up the corporate ladder. For example, there are

---

[19] Don Berwick, "Don Berwick's Vision: The Triple Aim – Health Affairs Blog," http://healthaffairs.org/blog.2010/04/20/don-berwicks-vision-the-triple-aim.

roughly two jobs for every graduate of a four-year college with a major in sales, and the starting salaries are all near six figures. Executives listen to the news about unemployment and think there will be many recent grads to fill jobs. Nothing could be further from the truth, especially in the high-demand areas. On the same note, these college degrees are dramatically different today. It is important for executives to have helpful advisers to guide them through the rapid changes that have occurred in the employment market.

Environmental and Sustainability Consulting

Environmental consulting is a growing area that includes companies offering a variety of services. Recycling companies look to increase volume by teaching customers how to be more "green." Other organizations are concerned with a sustainability scorecard on their production of greenhouse gases. (This may be driven by the desire to report on the Global Reporting Initiative, as have over four thousand other organizations through 2012.) Consultants may be hired to provide analyses of the company's current position and to suggest the "low-hanging fruit" activities that can be implemented. Included in this analysis are measures centering on energy use, time of energy use, recycling programs, contracts with local suppliers of energy, logistics, and regulatory compliance, such as particulate matter and storm water compliance.

Sustainability consulting has grown as companies realize that being sustainable is often also cheaper. As a bonus, there is a public relations benefit to showing consumers a company that is operated in a sustainable fashion. Sustainability is the process of making your business more responsible in financial, social, and environmental measures. It is often used as a synonym with the environmental portion, but, in fact, it is a holistic approach to responsible business practice.

As organizations are asked by their customers to become more sustainable, the demand for this type of consultant will likely grow. For instance, from 2005 to 2010, environmental consulting grew in the United States by over 42 percent. Figure 2-8 shows the breakdown of services from 2005 to 2010. The largest growth areas were environmental assessments (62 percent) and waste management (67 percent).[20]

---

[20] U.S. Census Bureau; accessed 2010, http://www.census.gov/services/sas/data_summary54.html.

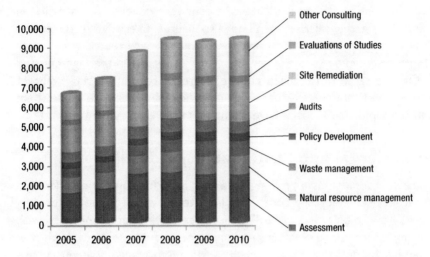

Figure 2-8. Environmental consulting. SOURCE: U.S. Census Bureau; accessed 2010, http://www.census.gov/services/sas/data_summary54.html.

Summary

Chapter 2 has provided an overview of the size, structure, and growth of the consulting industry. It is clearly a very large industry, and one that is likely to get much larger and much more important in years to come. Also, it is growing both domestically and internationally, and in categories of business that are experiencing rapid change, such as healthcare.

Information technology (IT) is the largest category of consulting and will likely grow even more in the future. This is because most companies have antiquated computer systems that do not allow separate parts of their operations to "talk" to one another. It will take a very long time for every company to implement an updated software system, thus keeping IT consultants in high demand for the foreseeable future.

Origins

The Origin of Consulting and Consultants

Research serves to make building stones out of stumbling blocks.

—Arthur D. Little, *Technology Review*

Chapter 3 focuses on two key areas. The first is how "consulting" came to be a legitimate profession. The second concerns how people become consultants. Both of these points are important. If you are going to spend large sums of money—thousands or even millions—on a consultant or consulting firm, you should understand things like how the consultant you are paying came to be a consultant. Is there a required accreditation? Is there a prerequisite degree? What about the big consulting firms—how did they get to be big? Why? Can you expect a successful engagement once you hire a consultant? How can you determine the success of the consulting relationship?

Few managers actually ponder these questions prior to hiring a consultant. While we examine unique situations in the remaining chapters, we will provide a little more history first.

A Brief History of Consulting

The industrial revolution marked a major turning point in history. This development began in the nineteenth century and happened over time as a result of major inventions, such as the steam engine, the cotton gin, and the telephone, as well as subsequent changes in manufacturing processes that led to greater efficiency in the production of goods. A prime example of process improvement was the invention of the assembly line at Ford Motor Company in 1913.

In the nineteenth and twentieth centuries, the sudden, sustained growth in population and income was unprecedented. Worldwide per capita income increased by ten times, while the world's population increased by six times.[1] By the early twentieth century, we had what we now term "businesses."

These early business operations often lacked the management and direction to focus their productivity and make steps toward improving their sales and marketing of goods. There were "managers," but they had yet to learn the value of human resources. Laborers were not thought of as a resource; instead, they were abused and exploited. Also, this time became known as the "Barnum and Bailey era of advertising." In lieu of rules or guidelines, marketers of products were able to sell anything by promising everything in an ad, much the way P. T. Barnum promoted "oddities" in his circus. And people tended to believe those ads. While consulting would have been helpful during these times, especially to avoid ethical and moral violations, no such consultants existed.

Arthur D. Little, the first real consultancy firm, was founded in 1886. The MIT professor that started the organization with his name, incorporated it in 1909.[2] Originally, Arthur Little specialized in technical research—namely, papermaking and its technical aspects. The company later grew into a general management consulting firm, and later became famous by establishing key changes in the strategies used for bringing products, like synthetic penicillin, to the market, as well as the much later developments of LexisNexis and NASDAQ.

The second major consultancy was formed in 1914 by Edwin G. Booz, a graduate of the Kellogg School of Management. Booz Allen Hamilton (though that name did not arise until 1942)[3] was the first management consultancy to serve both government and industry.[4] His first two large clients were the Canadian Pacific Railway and Goodyear, but the firm's clients have included other very well respected companies, including General Motors, the National Football League, and the U.S. government's Internal Revenue Service.[5]

---

[1] Angus Maddison, *The World Economy: Historical Statistics* (Paris: Development Centre, OECD, 2003), 256–62.

[2] Joe O'Mahoney, *Management Consultancy* (Oxford, UK: Oxford University Press, 2010).

[3] Christopher McKenna, The World's Newest Profession: Management Consulting in the Twentieth Century (New York: Cambridge University Press, 2006).

[4] Consulting Ideas, "The History of Consultancy"; accessed 2012, http://consulting-ideas.com/learn/the-history-of-consultancy.

[5] National Name Data Base, "Edwin G. Booz"; accessed 2012, www.nndb.com/people/588/000207964/.

Up until the end of the 1920s, businesses did not really need consulting services beyond help to deal with ethical violations. They grew rapidly because these companies were bringing products to a marketplace full of people who did not have those products. The prime goal of most businesses at the time was to be innovative—to invent products that consumers would need and that would make their lives better. It was a wild period with few consumer protections and was marked by excessive speculation.

As the country entered the Great Depression following the collapse of the New York Stock Exchange, multiple bank failures led to a loss of faith in the country's economic systems.[6] Through various acts of the New Deal, the federal government took steps to restore confidence. Among them was the passage of the Glass-Steagall Act, separating investment services from consumer banking services. Many types of businesses now needed to hone their activities to remain profitable while meeting new compliance standards. This situation gave rise to a demand for advice on finance, strategy, organization, labor relations, and implementation of the new rules. Additionally, many businesses needed to start growing again to meet increased consumer demand as the Depression waned. Demand for consultants grew steadily until World War II. Then the field experienced a brief slowdown until it really took off in the latter half of the 1940s and early 1950s.

Postwar Boom

The postwar growth in America and Europe from 1945 to 1960 was explosive. Consumers had money to buy automobiles, electric appliances, housewares, and more. Businesses had money to buy machinery, real estate, office equipment, and more. Affordable mortgages for returning soldiers caused a housing boom. The famous baby boom was happening at the same time, which ultimately contributed many more consumers to the market.

Big businesses started taking over family farms, leading to industrial production in agriculture and bringing a massive change in our nation's food supply. Food became a commercialized, processed, and packaged item, which of course led to huge growth in food-processing companies. In fact, more changes have happened to our food supply and the way we eat in the last fifty years than in the previous ten thousand years.

Other changes were occurring, too; American citizens migrated from cities to suburbs, as cars and single-family homes became more affordable. The invention of air conditioning allowed cities such as Houston, Atlanta, Miami,

---

[6] New York Times Law Library; accessed 2012, http://topics.nytimes.com/topics/reference/timestopics/subjects/g/glass_steagall_act_1933/index.html.

and Phoenix to grow. Transportation was improved through federally funded highway projects, which boosted the shipping of goods from one coast to the other and changed overall distribution patterns. Shopping centers multiplied, rising from 8 at the end of World War II to 3,840 in 1960. Many industries soon followed suit, leaving the cities for less crowded "industrial parks" in surrounding regions.

All these changes led to more businesses and more business needs and problems. And these problems created the need for consultants, so the consultants grew right along with the business growth. In the 1960s, the three leading management consulting firms in the United States—Booz Allen Hamilton; Cresap, McCormick and Paget; and McKinsey & Company—had reached the height of their power. Though not the largest consultancies, these three firms won the most prestigious assignments and referred to themselves, as did the American automobile oligopoly, as the "Big Three of Management Consulting Firms."

Like the Big Three automotive manufacturers, this elite club of consulting firms exercised significant economic influence and power. And as did the large law, accounting, and engineering firms, these consultants became a crucial element in the institutional infrastructure of the American economy. The leading management consulting firms continued to command greater respect and authority. When the country's leading corporations expanded overseas in the early 1960s, consultants not only transferred their American managerial models, but also established the American institutional system that had routinized the use of management consultants.

Many historians have written about this "Americanization" of business in Europe. Indeed, American management consulting firms set up offices in Europe and sold their organizational know-how to French, German, Italian, British, Swiss, and Dutch executives. Figure 3-1 shows how rapidly, one such firm, McKinsey, grew during this time. (Note that McKinsey now has about 6,500 consultants.)

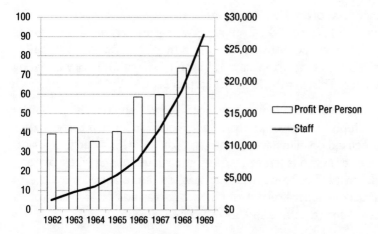

Figure 3-1. Profitability of McKinsey and Company. SOURCE: Christopher McKenna, *The World's Newest Profession: Management Consulting in the Twentieth Century* (New York: Cambridge University Press, 2006).

From the 1950s onwards, consultancies also expanded in terms of the categories of consulting they offered. The field of strategic marketing started as a result of the 1960s and 1970s activities of McKinsey, Boston Consulting Group, AT Kearney, Booz Allen Hamilton, and the Harvard Business School.

Changes at the End of the Twentieth Century

The consulting industry continued to grow in the 1980s and 1990s. In 1980, there were five major consulting companies, each employing more than one thousand consultants. In the 1990s, there were more than thirty such firms with more than one thousand consultants. The 1990s growth was caused by consulting firms specializing in subjects like culture and strategy, lean processes, and information technology.

The Harvard Business School influenced the industry further when Harvard professors founded the Monitor Group. This group had a major impact on the consulting and business arena by bringing Harvard theories into the business realm. Thus, management theorists spent much of the 1980s and 1990s analyzing "corporate culture," the unique culture of a company while more generally studying the culture of white-collar work with considerable success. Their scholarship on corporate culture, in turn, inspired other academic disciplines, with historians now tracing the regulation of big business, economists analyzing the relation of shared values to economic efficiency, and cultural critics studying the controlling influence of American capitalism on society and the arts.

However, research on corporate culture was not purely academic. Management consultants from McKinsey & Company, alongside academic theorists sponsored by McKinsey, popularized the concept of "corporate culture." It was not until the 2000s that organizations began to view the theory as having very little substance. This, in turn, led to a sharp decline in "culture consulting."

The late 1970s and 1980s also marked an increase in "lean consulting." Taiichi Ohno, who developed the principles of the Toyota Production System after World War II, focused on eliminating waste and using the knowledge of front-line workers. These methods led to Just-in-Time reductions in inventory and improved productivity. The Toyota method reached out to suppliers to create long-term, mutually beneficial relationships. Cross-trained employees led to a flattened management structure and fewer wasted resources.

The ten rules of lean production that were promoted by consultants can be summarized as: eliminate waste, minimize inventory, maximize flow, pull production from customer demand, meet customer requirements, do it right the first time, empower workers, design for rapid changeover, partner with suppliers, and create a culture of continuous improvement (Kaizen). This mindset quickly became popular in America as the Big Three automakers struggled to compete with Toyota and other Japanese automotive imports.

Outside of production systems, the nation's corporate hierarchies and models needed to change to adapt to leaner, more efficient systems. So, lean consulting philosophies expanded from mere production to corporate processes.

Along with corporate production and management changes, consultancies have had to deal with cultural changes in the workforce. For example, baby boomers, or people born between 1945 and 1964, are said to live to work, rather than work to live. They tend to hold top positions in most companies, although this is changing as they approach retirement age. In fact, in the 1970s, the term "workaholic" was coined to describe the baby boomers' work ethic. According to one author, baby boomers invented the phrase "Thank God, it is Monday," along with the 60-hour work week.[7] While these mindsets keep workers at work, and in their offices, it does nothing in terms of productivity and efficiency. In fact, workaholism actually reduces efficiency.

Now, add to the workplace mix the influx of Generation X workers (those born 1965–1977).[8] These workers tend to be driven by "free-agent

---

[7] W. V. Govitvatana, *Generation Gap in the Workplace between Baby Boomers and Generation X*. Doctoral dissertation, University of Wisconsin, 2001.

[8] B. Tulgan, "Generational Shift: What We Saw at the Workplace Revolution"; retrieved 2003 from rainmakerthinking.com.

inclinations," or a self-serving, but a high-efficiency mentality.[9] In addition, as they begin to enter the workforce, Generation Y (post 1977 births) people are bringing even greater changes to the workplace culture.

These opposing views of work have created inherent waste and conflict in the workplace. Even though most managers know about lean principles, the waste continues, especially in very large businesses, due to conflict between the "work hours" and "work efficiency" mentalities. Consultants now serve to focus on workplace relationships and help companies bridge the generational gap.

In addition to organizational culture and lean operations, IT consulting grew as innovations and computing power exploded. In the second half of the 1980s, the big accounting firms entered the IT consulting segment. The industry stagnated in 2001 with the dotcom bust, and then started recovering after 2003. Current trends suggest continued and even more targeted growth for consultancy through the twenty-first century. Companies are especially seeing a need for system-wide implementations of enterprise resource planning (ERP) and customer relationship management (CRM) programs. Even though the technology has been around for a decade or two, the bulk of companies are just now starting to see the necessity of ERP and CRM systems.

The Twenty-First Century

The collapse of Enron in 2001 made the field of management consulting visible to the world. Unlike the other corporate failures after the "New Economy" stock market crashed in 2000, Enron's bankruptcy was followed by late-night shredding of documents by Arthur Andersen employees. The story captivated the public in a way that no other corporate bankruptcy had, largely for its consultancy connection. In 2002, for example, the *Wall Street Journal* highlighted the fact that more than 85 percent of the Dow Jones Industrial (DJI) companies "paid their auditors more for consulting, tax, and other services than for the company's audit."[10]

It was no coincidence, therefore, that Congress wrote into the Sarbanes-Oxley (SOX) Corporate Reform Act (which followed the collapse of Arthur Andersen) language that specifically barred accounting firms from serving as consultants while simultaneously performing an audit. Following public outcry and regulatory changes, the large accounting firms divested themselves of their consulting divisions, effectively ending the ascendancy of the

---

[9] Ibid.

[10] McKenna, *World's Newest Profession*.

multidisciplinary professional service firms. Much of the early 2000s was directed toward adherence to SOX and a recovery from the collapse in 2000.

After a brief recovery, business had an enormous downturn in 2008 and 2009, as multiple big banks faltered as a result of predatory lending practices and collapse of the real estate market. Declines in credit availability and damaged investor confidence had a negative impact on global stock markets and created a worldwide recession. This caused economies worldwide to slow down, with tightening credit and declining international trade. Fiscal stimulus packages, monetary policy changes, and institutional bailouts were put into place by the government to overcome this recession.[11]

The Glass–Steagall Act, which had increased consultancy after the Great Depression, was repealed in 1999. There was no longer a separation between investment banks and depository banks as there had been since the 1930s.[12] Credit-rating agencies and investors had done a poor job of pricing mortgage-related risks. To further complicate matters, government regulatory practices to protect consumers in the modern financial markets were not updated, which aggravated the problems that led to the Great Recession. Due to these and other factors (like growth of the Internet), consumers now more widely distrust big business. In turn, big businesses are starting to see the markets as saturated, and realize that they cannot win customers with half-truths and flashy advertisements.

While corporate spending on consulting decreased dramatically during the first decade of the twenty-first century, it has come back—just in different ways. Businesses for the most part have become smarter and have redirected their spending on consulting. The fluffy, no-tangible-outcome consulting, like strategy and corporate culture, is fading away. But consulting that leads to tangible outcomes, like IT implementation, is making a huge resurgence. Big consulting firms that sell themselves as one-stop shops are fading away, while smaller, more credible, specialized firms or individuals are taking their place. Given the vast inefficiencies that exist in all businesses, consulting will continue to grow.

Most managers are coming to the simple conclusion that what worked in the past will not work now. It is simply a different world. It is more competitive than ever, and most industries are considered "saturated" or "mature" or "hypercompetitive." New products and services come out faster than ever

---

[11] International Monetary Fund, *World Economic Outlook: Crisis and Recovery;* accessed 2009, www.imf.org/external/pubs/ft/weo/2009/01/pdf/text.pdf.

[12] Kevin Drum, "The Repeal of Glass-Steagall"; accessed 2009, http://motherjones.com/kevin-drum/2009/03/repeal-glass-steagall.

and change more frequently. In fact, thirty thousand new products are created every year, 95 percent of which fail.[13]

Customers today know more about price, quality, capability, reliability, and alternatives when they want to purchase something. They demand more information, more options, bigger discounts, and better service. On the business-to-business side, corporations have refined and structured their purchasing departments so as to turn the seller's product into a commodity and thereby get the absolute, rock-bottom price.

These facts have left all companies facing several questions.

- How do we differentiate ourselves and position our company as uniquely valuable?

- How do we manage information as working capital?

- How do we protect our value proposition against inroads from our competition?

- How do we establish credibility?

- How do we gain and maintain access to key people?

- How do we operate in the most efficient and effective manner?

- How do we manage our employees to limit turnover?

- How do we deal with ever-changing environmental issues, like technological and regulations?

- How do we employ and leverage computer technology to improve our processes and financial returns?

To answer these questions, many companies find themselves turning to consultants. These trends will definitely continue into the future. Figure 3-2 illustrates the growth of consulting in relationship to the number of managers in the United States.

---

[13] Carmen Nobel, "Clay Christensen's Milkshake Marketing," Harvard Business School; accessed 2011, http://hbswk.hbs.edu/item/6496.html.

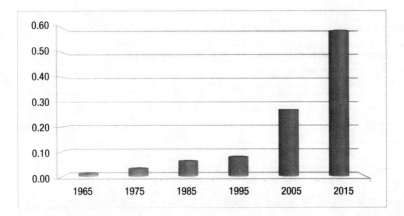

Figure 3-2. Consultants per salaried manager. Source: Christopher McKenna, *The World's Newest Profession: Management Consulting in the Twentieth Century* (New York: Cambridge University Press, 2006).

By looking at trends in this way, we can remove the potential bias of general business growth. As you can see, the consulting market shows no signs of slowing growth. But, as discussed in the previous chapter, that growth is being redirected toward different types of consulting and toward different areas. Companies are still in desperate need of keeping up with the ever-present change that characterizes our modern economy.

What It Takes to Become a Consultant

It is important for someone buying consulting services to understand how an individual becomes a consultant. Unfortunately, this section of the book is painfully shorter than it should be. Logic would suggest that, to become a consultant and be potentially able to charge a company hundreds of dollars per hour for consulting services, there would be rigorous qualification requirements.

In fact, there are no requirements beyond having the personality and techniques necessary to influence people effectively. And even these skills are not universal. Overall, the quality and skills associated with a consultant will largely depend on the due diligence that is performed prior to hiring and drawing up a contract—something discussed later in this book.

Certifications

One type of accreditation exists. The Certified Management Consultant (CMC) designation is awarded, upon application, to individual consultants by institutes in certain countries. However, most of the major global consulting firms do not mandate accreditation, and most people do not know to check for it. Likewise, given the relatively unknown nature of this accreditation, you cannot assume that it means much.

The process for becoming a CMC is shown in Figure 3-3. This certification process seems like a logical way to at least show some competence, and perhaps will help potential clients become a little more comfortable using a consultant with the CMC credential—but no assurances come with this certification. The process to become a project management professional (PMP) is much more involved; however, we have worked with PMPs who are less capable at project management than many people who are not certified. It is reasonable to assume that the CMC process, which is even less robust than the PMP process, will yield consultants of widely varying quality.

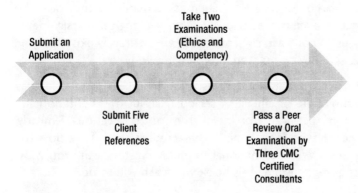

Figure 3-3. Certified Management Consultant process. SOURCE: Institute of Management Consultants USA. www.imcusa.org/?page=CERTHOW.

For example, most colleges and universities in the United States go through extremely rigorous accreditation procedures that involve verifying everything from teacher degrees, to business experience, library resources, research facilities, finances, and curricula. The demand for rigorous review reflects the demand for college degrees and the competition among programs.

The demand for accredited consultants is so limited, on the other hand, that the same rigor is not applied. In addition, given the wide variety of consultants, it is doubtful that any single accrediting body would cover the specific area of specialty. Instead, the accreditation seems to be more about ethics, contracts, and managing the client-consultant relationship.

Some professions require accreditations, such as in law, financial planning, accounting, and Six Sigma knowledge. Obviously, if you were to hire someone for legal advice, you would want someone with a law degree and some experience practicing the area of law in question. However, even in areas where some kind of qualification is required, there may be no established standards.

For instance, for Six Sigma, there is a body of knowledge that should be demonstrated, but no central certification group controls the quality of training. So, people can take online training and earn a "black belt" in Six Sigma expertise without having had to apply the skills or show a history of success. In more formal Six Sigma programs, a person takes all the necessary course work (roughly four weeks of full-time, forty-hour a week classes) and performs a project in an organization, taking it from development to implementation. Also, the project must show some considerable savings in efficiency and effectiveness. Only then does the person receive the "black belt" designation.

Programs offered in large corporations, such as General Electric, take the "black belt" designation even more seriously, requiring long-term assignments to improve processes. In contrast, rigorous requirements rarely exist in online programs. Most can be fully completed in less than two hours.

So, just as a prospective student would investigate the reputation and history of a university, so should he or she think seriously about the reputation and history of any program that grants online degrees or certifications. Similarly, before you hire a consultant, look at his or her credentials and see how the experience was gained. With no national or industry standards, you must perform due diligence—something this book will teach you to do.

These are just two examples of certificate programs that consultants use to gain credibility. There are many others that are available to anyone who wants to change careers and move into consulting. You can even get a Ph.D. without needing to meet some of the basic requirements of accredited university Ph.D. programs. For example, online programs do not typically expect the advanced statistics and research training that the reputable universities do.

Career Paths to Consulting

There are several different career paths people take that ultimately land them in consulting jobs. The big consulting firms take MBAs out of the Ivy League schools. This is their primary recruiting source. Realistically, though, an MBA from Harvard does not necessarily demonstrate an ability to be effective. Recent graduates rarely have on-the-job experience, and thorough education without demonstrated ability to execute is worthless, regardless of the education pedigree. The whole notion of a 24-year-old walking out the door of college with a degree in hand and no experience, and strolling into a major, multi-billion-dollar, multi-national consulting firm, is quite offensive to many. Yet, this is the business model for the large firms, and it works.

These firms send the new graduates into equally large, multi-national firms and tell them to perform basic MBA-level analyses, and then advise them on how to run a business. This entire process is described in a negative, cynical fashion by Martin Kihn in his book *House of Lies: How Management Consultants Steal Your Watch and Then Tell You the Time*.[14] While many critics doubt the accuracy of Kihn's tales of his time at McKinsey & Company, the book is accurate to the extent that most big-name consultants have only a college degree, rarely a PhD, and very little on-the-job experience.

However, normally there is a lack of actual skill associated with management consultants in the types of projects performed by the big-name consulting firms. Specifically, these folks are taught a formula that is used by the consulting company and then they implement it as part of their job as consultant. It is frequently something like a blank SWOT analysis and the subsequent strategic plan. (SWOT stands for Strengths, Weaknesses, Opportunities, and Threats.) This, along with many other tools used by these consultants, are MBA-level worksheets that can be filled out with very little prior knowledge or any deep level of strategic analysis.

In order to be hired as a consultant at a big firm right out of an MBA program, it is best to have a good network of people. In fact, the big firms will want to know in the interview process whom you know. The key is: can you bring in a million-dollar account to the firm?

This is an important criterion for independent consultants as well. In fact, as an independent, all a consultant needs is great networking skills, word-of-mouth endorsements, and a good reputation. Many consultants get their start by writing a book that is moderately successful and then selling their expertise to organizations based on this success. (This is not one of those books!) Some of these authors so far as to rate their own work on sites like Amazon and ask their friends also to rate the work online, showing the author as a valuable business leader.

Once a consultant has established a network and has a name, then he or she navigates the proposals, contracts, and working relationships to maintain an ongoing business pipeline. The barriers to entry are almost nonexistent. The only real risk is the potential lack of income if there is not enough business to keep the pipeline full. The independent consultant can take several other career paths, too. Some business executives become consultants when they

---

[14] Martin Kihn, *House of Lies: How Management Consultants Steal Your Watch and Then Tell You the Time* (New York, New York: Business Plus, 2005).

retire, get laid off, or quit a job. Similarly, business professors often consult during their educational career to supplement their income, or they retire from teaching and enter consulting. Believe it or not, none of these career paths is necessarily more likely to yield a great consultant than is the right-out-of-the-MBA program candidate.

While MBAs usually lack real-world experience, many retirees or career changers have entered the consulting world because they could not perform well in their past jobs. Great performers do not get early retirement packages or experience downsizing. If someone is performing well, the company will likely find some way to keep the person. Additionally, even if the consultant is a good employee or executive, his or her experience is usually limited to one or a few companies. That experience often does not translate to other companies.

The academic-to-consultant career comes with many dangers. Most people who received their Ph.D.s after roughly the year 2000 have the appropriate level of statistical training to conduct necessary research. Those from before 2000 often do not, meaning that they tend to use their guts more than their research skills to solve problems. However, especially in Ivy League situations, the academics quickly become so far removed from the business reality that their knowledge and applicability quickly grows out of date. These academic professionals may tend to produce publications and research with no real application in the business world, leading to admiration from colleagues, but no real benefit to business leaders.

Are you depressed at the thought of hiring either a 22-year-old or a washed-up retiree or academic? You do not have to be. Later in this book we talk about what to look for when hiring a consultant in order to have a successful relationship.

How Consultants Build Their Business

Unless a consultant is hired directly into a large firm, to get work a consultant needs to identify a market need and build a network. Clients are customers, and the process is no different from how a company invents a product and builds awareness and sales for that product. Other than having the necessary prerequisite skills, networking is of the utmost importance. Many people start by attending local events and seminars directed toward their line of expertise. They talk to the right people until they get a "sale" or two, which sometimes starts the chain of endless business deals through referrals. This is hard work and takes an exorbitant amount of time. Consultants also have to assume that most of the big opportunities with major companies have been taken by the large consultancies. Thus, they tend to aim at niches and market their unique talents and skills in those niches. However, if a consultant is really good and gets results, word should travel fast.

For management or business process-redesign consultants, there is a good reason to start that career by consulting at a large firm. By doing this, it is possible to get lucky and build relationships that will spin off a private consultancy—assuming a rock-solid, no-compete contract does not prevent this.

For any type of consulting, it is helpful to attach to an organization, such as a private equity firm, that frequently purchases companies with the potential to be great with the right guidance. By building this type of relationship, an entrepreneurial consultant can maintain a steady flow of business based on his or her ability to turn around any business performance.

What's a Manager in Need to Do?

Chapters 2 and 3 were meant to give you the necessary background to understand why this book was written and why you should be happy that you own it. The rest of this book is devoted to helping you navigate the process—of picking the right person or tool for the job.

As mentioned in Chapter 1, we have acted as consultants and have many friends and acquaintances who are skilled in consulting work. We have worked with consultants who deliver on promises, provide a real return on investment, and have credible resources that show this experience. Working with a consultant who does not deliver results is as much the fault of the manager hiring the consultant as it is the consultant who is hired. The rest of this book will help you avoid the common mistakes of hiring the wrong people.

Summary

This chapter has revealed how the field of consulting has grown into such a huge business phenomenon. More or less, as business cycles, fashions, and fads come and go, businesses in need of help look for people who can solve their problems. The need will always be great, and it will likely continue to grow exponentially, as businesses will always seek to catch up in this ever-changing world.

As rapidly as business changes, there are new people entering the consulting profession. Currently, there are no real certifications or qualifications necessary to become a consultant. Thus, this industry is one in which careful due diligence is required before entering a client-consultant relationship. This creates problems, the remedies to which are discussed throughout the book.

ROI

Calculating the Return on Investment of Consulting

Success is neither magical nor mysterious. Success is the natural consequence of consistently applying the basic fundamentals.

—Jim Rohn

Understandably, having a realistic return on investment (ROI) for monies spent on a project is a fundamental of business success. Unfortunately, this fundamental is often ignored. This is frequently the case with the decision of whether or not to hire a consultant. In fact, in the survey of firms done for this book, only 14.75 percent of firms actually performed an ROI analysis prior to entering the consulting relationship. Keep in mind that the survey was conducted with a multitude of organizations small and large, in many different industries around the world. These were not necessarily small consulting projects, either. What's more, even when an ROI analysis is conducted, the assumptions in the analysis often are not realistic. Given the costs, time, and commitment involved with consulting, not conducting an ROI analysis is a grave mistake.

Conducting the ROI analysis should be the very first decision associated with hiring a consultant. If you cannot forecast a gain, there is no reason to move forward. Therefore, it may sound blunt, but there is never a reason *not* to conduct an ROI analysis, even though 85.25 percent of the companies studied for this book did not.

Executives often think they cannot conduct an analysis because the topic is too vague or is not quantifiable. If this is the case, then why think of hiring a consultant at all? Presumably, you need a consultant to repair something wrong, to cut costs, or to take active steps to grow the business. There are, for example, many types of measurable savings possible, such as time, money, customer satisfaction, employee satisfaction, and productivity.

You might be wondering how, for example, you would quantify employee satisfaction. If you are considering hiring a consultant to fix employee satisfaction, you must think you have a problem with employee satisfaction. To begin, you need to ask yourself what results the negative satisfaction is causing. In most cases, negative employee satisfaction is probably causing a reduction in other factors, such as lower customer satisfaction, lower productivity, higher turnover, or an overall lower profitability. In fact, most studies have shown that happy employees lead to happy customers. Likewise, studies have also shown that happier employees lead to greater profitability.[1]

Pretend you know that your employees are miserable. How do you conduct an ROI? If you have never collected any data on business variables, you might need to do some educated guessing. Assume that you have low customer satisfaction. You could calculate this factor based on lost accounts due to customer complaints. Then, to project the results after the consultant's work, you could try to assess the company's profitability without those lost accounts.

This might produce a very rough ROI analysis, but it is better than nothing. In this particular case, it is crucial to start measuring current employee satisfaction, customer satisfaction, and other related variables. Then, you would continue to measure them after the consultant has left, usually at varying points like one month post, six months post, and twelve months post. Bottom line: If you cannot measure a positive ROI for a consulting job, in most cases you should not hire a consultant.

ROI Calculation

The ROI calculation is simple in theory:

$$ROI = \frac{Gain - Cost}{Cost}$$

When calculating a consulting ROI, however, errors are frequently made in terms of both costs and gains estimates. One common error, for example, is to overestimate the gains by making faulty assumptions. Another is to

---

[1] L. M. Orr, V. D. Bush, and D. W. Vorhies, "Leveraging Firm-level Marketing Capabilities with Marketing Employee Development," *Journal of Business Research* 64(2011): 1074–81.

underestimate the costs by not including internal resources in your assumptions.

The rest of this chapter is designed to help you identify these and other errors before committing to a consulting relationship.

Categories of Gains

The first step toward building an ROI analysis is learning to identify the opportunities for the return (gains). These opportunities come in six distinct categories: cost reduction, cost avoidance, risk reduction, revenue increase, capacity increase, and cash flow increase. These are shown in Table 4-1.

Table 4-1. Types of Gains

Gain Category	Explanation
Cost Reduction	Project eliminates problems or waste that result in lower costs
Cost Avoidance	Project results in avoiding unnecessary or wasteful planned expenditures
Risk Reduction	Project reduces specific risks and/or potential exposure
Revenue Increase	Project increases sales, customer loyalty, and/or reduces lost opportunities
Capacity Increase	Project creates or improves capacity to service more customers
Cash Flow Increase	Project reduces cash requirements and financing costs

Cost Reduction

The first of these categories is cost reduction. This is also the most common one used to justify hiring a consultant because it is often the easiest to quantify. It is also an easy one with which to prove success because the calculation is simple. Cost reduction, after all, is merely finding expenses currently incurred. Then you try to find a way to eliminate those expenses while maintaining the same level of activity, like sales revenues, in the organization.

Many organizations operate under the assumption that greater profitability can be achieved by lowering costs. Sometimes it can, but too many managers do not understand the extent to which some costs are necessary to ensure sustainability of the organization. This cost-cutting mindset has become all too common, especially among U.S. publically held companies. Shareholders are always looking for quick shareholder return and want to see an immediate gain. Yet, many initiatives worth doing generate large initial costs, thus reducing short-term gain while setting the foundation for significant, long-term gain. Many managers are loath to undertake such initiatives, knowing they have to please shareholders looking closely at quarterly results.

Other managers, fortunate enough to work in an organization with a history of taking the long-term view of the business, find it easier to launch projects without short-term gains. Managers who need to show short-term gains will have to do more work to sell a long-term project to shareholders. Some management consultants can offer advice on how to do this effectively. After all, it is in the consultant's best interest to convince shareholders to undertake the long-term project.

Cost Avoidance

The second category is cost avoidance. This is an underused method to save on costs. For example, it's useful to think in terms of cost avoidance when you are planning to invest in assets or people. Can you instead improve current operations to avoid the need for that expense? Humans commit psychologically to spending once they begin to use resources to research the expense and develop a justification for it. Rather than identifying the cost of this research and justification as a sunk cost, we can subconsciously become committed to the expense. This is a dangerous mindset to have.

Sometimes, therefore, it can make sense to bring in an outside perspective. A consultant can identify alternative methods or processes that eliminate the need to spend.

Risk Reduction

The third category is risk reduction. This is the most difficult gain to support because risks do not necessarily become real to upper management until some kind of failure has occurred. Until the point of failure, risk reduction can appear to others to be a weak argument in support of fresh spending. Other types of gains are easier to justify in an ROI calculation. Once a risk has caused expense to the organization, however, it becomes easier to justify additional expenses, usually through an old-fashioned formula for getting a decision maker's approval: sowing fear, uncertainty, and doubt. In some cases, a consultant can help you make a better case for risk avoidance. They likely have dealt with similar situations in other companies and know the real, quantifiable risks.

Revenue Increase

The fourth category is revenue increase. Although the concept of increasing revenue is attractive, especially since it is often based on using current resources more efficiently rather than on lowering operating costs drastically, it is often wishful thinking. All organizations run at a certain capacity level. This capacity level is often low, which makes it obvious to an intelligent leader (or an astute consultant) that there is an opportunity for growth. So why is revenue growth wishful thinking? Because most markets are currently saturated, which makes any revenue increase contingent on creating a new market or on stealing market share from a direct competitor. Both of these strategies are very difficult to implement. (However, see the next category, capacity increase, for an idea of when increasing capacity makes sense.)

To create a new market, vision—coupled with effective execution—is necessary to define a market need and convince prospective customers to adopt the new product or service to fill this need. This assumes your competitors will remain static—which they will not. Some companies, like Apple, are experts at this business model, but most businesses either are not experts or are not in an industry where this is possible.

In order to steal market share, a company needs to convince loyal customers of another organization to switch to their organization for the product or service. Unless the company has a significantly less expensive product (which is never a good long-term strategy), or the competitor has had poor-quality products or no differentiating advantage, this will be difficult to accomplish for the long term.

Every business executive should read the classic article by Michael Porter, "What Is Strategy?" In it, he discusses what he calls the "Growth Trap." In Porter's words, "Among all other influences, the desire to grow has perhaps the most perverse effect on strategy."[2] He goes on to describe how growth almost always causes the death of companies. Companies take on the desire to grow as a goal in itself—growth for the sake of growth—without any legitimate market advantage that might lead to growth. Walmart, currently, is a prime example of this. It originally grew because of a great distribution strategy, which led to a lowest-price strategy that eroded the markets of industry stalwarts like Sears and Kmart. Eventually, there was little room to grow domestically. So it grew by expanding internationally and expanding into new categories, such as groceries.

---

[2] Michael Porter, "What Is Strategy?" *Harvard Business Review* (November-December 1996): 61–75.

Now, however, Walmart has little room to grow. It may just be too big. It has lost any real advantage in the marketplace; people shop at Walmart only for low price. Given that, on most items, they do not truly have the lowest price, they have been left with a clientele that is not likely to grow or be willing to spend more for higher-priced items or services. It will soon be competing with Kmart for the bottom spot, as retailers in distinct categories with real competitive advantages take over—companies like Target, Whole Foods, and Walgreens.

Current stock prices of these companies demonstrate the increases. The Whole Foods stock price has increased 1,019 percent since the bottom of the recession in 2009! Walmart's has increased 55 percent. Similar, but not quite so dramatic, statistics can be found when comparing Walmart to Target. Target has had a 130.1 percent increase in their stock over the same time.

As can be seen, even in the case of low price, coming to market with a lower price is almost always a very dumb decision. Price is the easiest "strategy" to copy because it can immediately be seen by competitors. Prospective customers who switch easily to your organization will likely be short-term customers, which will not make your business sustainable for the future. Quickly, a price war is created, forcing everyone to lower price, thus reducing revenue. This strategy may be effective for a private equity group or an entrepreneur trying to boost sales in order to sell the company, but for almost any other organization, this is a recipe for lack of success.

On the opposing side of this argument, is a company implementing price increases to grow revenue. Many times in our consulting experience we have dealt with companies looking to do just this. Typically, companies are caught up in "the distribution trap,"[3] and think they need a low price to get their products sold in the marketplace. A good consultant can help companies understand how to sell on value and control distribution channels. This allows for price increases across the board, and is typically a much easier way to increase revenue than trying to increase unit sales.

Management consultants can sometimes help identify other legitimate areas where growth could happen—if they have intimate knowledge of your specific industry trends. On the other side, if a consultant attempts to drive growth areas without this knowledge, it could give the company a fatal blow. You seriously should question price-reduction strategies or growth strategies, which includes pursuing large customers that may eventually have too much leverage over your company or would lock it into a competitive war.

---

[3] Andrew R. Thomas and Timothy J. Wilkinson, *The Distribution Trap: Keeping Your Innovations from Becoming Commodities* (New York: Praeger, 2009).

Capacity Increase

The fifth category is capacity increase. For example, say a restaurant currently takes one hour to serve each table. You think this is too long, and you look into the issue. You discover a bottleneck in the kitchen, and you fix it. Now you serve customers within 45 minutes. Voilà! You have just increased capacity, which in turn significantly increases revenue.

This is a great category to pursue, but only if it is possible to use excess, available capacity to drive profitable growth by increasing the number of customers. For industries like healthcare, which is likely to grow as populations increase, capacity increase is a great way to avoid future capital expenses. On the other hand, capacity increase can be a weak ROI category because businesses will often increase capacity while not increasing the utilization of the capacity that is created (no increase in customers, as described above). When this happens, there not only is no real return on investment, but also ROI may become negative.

A consultant with knowledge of the specific business environment for the company may be able to give credible advice as to whether the capacity increase will yield a real opportunity for growth. A good internal financial team should question assumptions made by salespeople about growth due to capacity increase. This is the "If you build it, they will come" strategy. It may seem logical to salespeople, who tend to be overly optimistic, but a consultant can ground the company in reality by doing a real market study to show opportunities where revenue can be captured.

A good consultant could also pinpoint other areas of savings from capacity increase. Take the restaurant example. Perhaps there are no excess customers that the restaurant cannot currently serve. However, perhaps the excess capacity allows the restaurant to have more limited operating hours (go from being open 10:00 a.m.–12:00 a.m. to 11:00 a.m.–11:00 p.m.) while still servicing the same number of customers. This would permit the business owner to save 730 hours of operating expenses per year, which could translate to hundreds of thousands of dollars per year!

Cash Flow Increase

The sixth and final category is cash flow increase. This category is often used as a justification for implementing consignment supply-chain strategies. For example, a business can avoid the carrying cost associated with inventory by having inventory on consignment. Another way companies increase cash flow is by delaying payables. This strategy is popular in the manufacturing sector, where large users of manufactured components, like automotive or aerospace companies, use their size to push sixty- or ninety-day payment terms. By using this strategy, the organization can minimize the time from incurring an expense to generating revenue, and thereby maintain more cash on hand.

Yet another way companies improve cash flow is through real estate and asset sale deals. Companies that are in a mediocre cash situation may choose to pursue a sale-and-lease-back strategy for its assets. By selling facilities and equipment with a deal to lease those assets for a period of time, the company can have more cash on hand to pay for liabilities.

Management consultants who specialize in supply-chain management may be able to help identify opportunities for cash-flow increases from both the inventory-management and payment-term angles. For companies with unsophisticated purchasing and warehousing practices, a consultant can really help.

▥ **Note** By identifying the types of gains, you can focus on how you will measure your baseline and success. This also helps you avoid undertaking a project without a gain.

Understanding Types of Gains

Before you engage a consultant, you need to categorize and identify potential gains. Once the gain is categorized, you can better understand potential gain and identify the risks associated with the gain category.

For instance, if the projected gain is from capacity increase, then there must be a solid marketing plan or customer commitment to utilize that increase in order for the gain to be realized. You must have solid market research to demonstrate that an increase in customers will occur. In sales, these percentages are referred to as "hit rates" and are easy to calculate if you have been gathering sales data. Significant increases in hit rates must be projected to claim that capacity increases will provide a return on investment.

Two examples of ROI calculations are presented in the following cases. One demonstrates gains based on increasing revenue, and the other shows gains made through capacity increase. Although a lot of data are necessary to make such calculations, no executive should be making business decisions without understanding how to perform them. If you do not have the required data, your first order of business should be to start collecting and using data on a regular basis.

Calculating Gains from Sales Training

Say you decide you would like to increase sales. You pinpoint sales training as a means to do that. You are thinking of hiring a sales trainer to help your salespeople sell more. Does it make financial sense?

Table 4-2 shows potential measures to support gains from sales consulting. Each of these measures has been categorized by gain type for analysis. When you look closely, it becomes clear that the greatest gain associated with sales training is an increase in sales—as you would expect. For many organizations, this is a realistic goal; therefore, the training may be beneficial. However, there is, of course, a risk that the training will not result in better performance.

Table 4-2. Sales Training Measures of Success

Measure	Category of Gain
Marketing costs	Cost Reduction
Sales costs	Cost Reduction
Gross margin by product line, customer group, order size	Cost Reduction
Direct selling expenses	Cost Reduction
Number of canceled orders	Risk Reduction
Number of lost accounts	Risk Reduction
Accuracy of forecasts	Risk Reduction
Total sales volume	Revenue Increase
Sales by territories	Revenue Increase
Sales by products	Revenue Increase
Sales by customer classifications	Revenue Increase
Number of orders	Revenue Increase
Average size ($) of order	Revenue Increase
Number of new accounts	Revenue Increase
Batting average (orders / calls)	Capacity Increase
Percentage of accounts sold	Capacity Increase
Percentage of time spent on nonselling activities	Capacity Increase
Breakeven calculations for sales force size	Capacity Increase
Percentage of our sales force meeting their quota	Capacity Increase

In this case, the sales manager or general manager should be asking how the training will yield an increase in sales. Questions might include:

- Is the market big enough to get more sales with the current territories in place?

- Are salespeople so ineffective that current customers are not buying what they should be from the organization?

- How can you be sure that additional sales will be profitable?

- Will the training ensure that customers remain happy or become happier, leading to higher sales in the long term?

Other areas affected by sales training are cost and risk reductions. How will the manager ensure that, when the training is completed, the tactics are institutionalized and thus lead to long-term cost reduction and the reduction of risks associated with the sales?

These questions are crucial for the outcome of the investment in sales training. The consultant must meet concrete objectives throughout the training; otherwise he or she will not be effective. If the training is not effective, the company will likely not be much better off after the training than they were before the training.

Whatever the case, the sales manager should be tracking all of the variables listed in Table 4-2 for each sales rep. He or she should then be able to estimate the potential increase or decrease in each area based on other sources of data. Finally, the actual increase or decrease should be measured at 3-month, 6-month, 9-month, and 12-month intervals post training.

Calculating Potential for Revenue Increase

We have worked with companies on consulting projects that were able to develop hit rates and forecasts to a very precise detail. This allows them to calculate near-perfect ROIs. We provide this case as an example so that you can see that, with enough data, precise forecasts can be created.

Case Example: Bruno Builders

With modest beginnings in 1937, as a small construction family business run from the dining room table of Alfonzo and Christina Bruno, Bruno Builders has grown to be among the top 100 largest general contractors in the United States, building everything from our nation's most elite hospitals, to esteemed universities, to top-secret government buildings. Bruno Builders is an award-winning "turnkey" construction company performing a wide range of services from small jobs, service and emergency work, to full base-building renovation and shell construction. Bruno offers resources to support any and all general construction needs. They pride themselves on their solid financial strength, 24/7 service department, fully equipped warehouse and millwork shop, large field force, self-performed trades, and in-house painting. Their dedication to doing business "The Bruno Way," maintaining integrity while delivering high quality and timely construction and service projects, has earned them a positive reputation in the construction industry. Customers see this integrity and want a very close, personal connection with Bruno.

Ned Caldwell is the current director of business development for Bruno. He is a unique and intelligent individual. In his initial career, he was an architect. After achieving much success in that area of his life, he gained a good reputation and was recruited by Bruno to assist with their sales goals. Ned makes an excellent director. He has the people skills to sell, the architectural background to understand almost any building project, and the analytical insights required for any sales manager today.

He has worked hard to develop an extremely accurate sales-forecasting method that will enable him to know with 99 percent accuracy how likely he is to gain a new customer or understand how much he will be able to increase sales.

A "sale" in the construction industry is very complex. Ned makes all initial contacts with buyers. This is because most buyers are at extremely high levels of decision making and do not want to be bothered by lower-leveled sales reps. Clients include governors, mayors, presidents of universities, and CEOs of hospitals. After the initial contact, there is a long bidding and negotiation process. Ned has a large staff that works under him and helps him with proposal writing, checking legal requirements, analytics, and other tasks. The moment the sale is final (or the bid is accepted), the contract gets handed off to one of many project managers, who handle the entire construction process and follow-up after that.

As mentioned, Ned created a very elaborate forecasting tool to determine which accounts were the best to pursue. After looking at large amounts of data, Ned realized that his "hit rate," or likelihood of getting a particular sale, was determined by three factors: (1) relationship, (2) ability, and (3) perceived value. The formula for calculation is described in the following.

- Relationship (potential 50 points)
  - 50 points if it is a past client

- 33.4 points if it is an introduction from a past client to a new client

- 16.7 points if it's a referral

- 0 points if it is a cold call

- Ability (potential 25 points)

  - 25 points if Bruno has had five very similar project experiences (same size in dollar amount and in area square footage)

  - 16.7 points if Bruno has had three very similar project experiences

  - 8.4 points if Bruno has had one or two very similar project experiences

  - 0 points if Bruno has not had any similar experience

- Perceived value (potential 25 points)

  - 25 points if Bruno has had have five similar projects in the same geographic region

  - 16.7 points if Bruno has had three similar projects in the same geographic region

  - 8.4 points if Bruno has had one or two similar projects in the same geographic region

  - 0 points if Bruno has not had any similar projects in the same geographic region

To calculate the hit rate:

- Total the Relationship + Ability + Perceived value

- Divide the number by the number of organizations bidding on the project

- Divide by 100 to turn that number into a percentage

This formula was created by examining every sale that the company received. Then, Ned looked back retrospectively and ran analyses to see what made clients buy in the past and why. In other words, this formula was a result of how every customer in the past behaved.

The following is presented as an example of a possible project. See Table 4-3 for results.

Potential Client (Prospect)

- Healthcare project = $50 million in size

- Geauga County

- Learned about it in the BX (The Builders Exchange is a commercial construction trade association); additionally, the owner was told what a trusting, reliable company Bruno is by his brother

- Qualifications based selection

In this case, Bruno would likely not consider this a potential customer. However, more importantly, if Bruno was able to perform this calculation for all potential accounts, and then were able to build a cumulative total for all potential customers, he would be able to know a fairly accurate sales forecast for the time period in question. In fact, this company was able to use each hit rate to build a sales forecast for the company that was 99.7 percent accurate. Imagine if you had the ability to forecast like that! Imagine how perfect your ROI calculations would be!

However, note that it is only after doing an analysis with this level of detail that a decision maker can calculate potential customer gains to fill a potential increase in capacity. As mentioned, you must thoroughly investigate each area of potential gain and arrive at a real, quantitative numbers to calculate gain before embarking on a consulting relationship.

Consulting Costs

Once all the assumptions associated with the ROI gains categories have been challenged and validated, you must break down the anticipated costs from the consulting relationship. You may start this process by first identifying direct costs, both fixed and variable. Next, you will want to identify hidden costs.

Table 4-3. Example Hit Rate Analysis

Section	Question to ask	Answer	Points
Ability	Do we have 3 to 5 projects of similar size and type in our resume?	Yes, 3	16.7
Perceived value	What other projects have we done in Geauga County? Are we perceived as price competitive in that geographical region?	None	0
Relationship	How did we hear about the job?	BX/ referral	16.7
Competitors	How many organizations will likely qualify, get short-listed and be able to compete?		3 including us
Chance of winning			11.13%

Direct Costs

The most obvious, direct costs are the consulting fees. These may be hourly costs or a project fee for a long-term project. Figure 4-1 shows some typical consulting rates for consulting fees with larger firms. In this scenario, a senior consulting partner will often sell the job and then have a more junior consultant do much of the work. Although this will save money for the company, it may not produce the best results. Most of the smaller firms or independent consultants will also charge an hourly rate based upon the length of the relationship with the client and the complexity of the job. These rates can vary between $100 an hour to as much as $500 an hour.

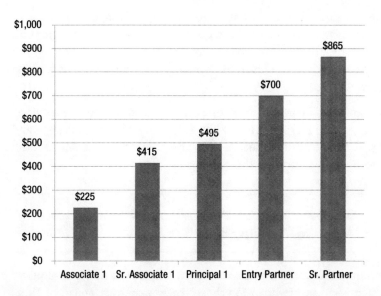

Figure 4-1. Consulting hourly rates. Source: Martin Kihn, *House of Lies: How Management Consultants Steal Your Watch and Then Tell You the Time* (New York, New York: Business Plus, 2005).

A good benchmark for hourly rates for an independent consultant or consultant from a small firm is three times a person's annual salary if the individual does the work full time. For example, a full-time market research analyst might make $100,000 a year, which equates to $50 an hour. So, this market research analyst would charge $150 an hour to do independent consulting work. The same consultant might charge different rates for different projects based on complexity. For example, the consultant might charge $150 an hour for basic market research, but charge $200 an hour for advanced statistical analyses. This is justifiable because few people possess the ability to perform these types of analyses.

In regard to length of relationship, a consultant may charge a higher hourly rate for short-term projects (hours to a few days), because the peripheral work that needs to be done upfront cannot be spread across the hours of the work. This is also a reason that, when looking at very large projects that take months, consultants sometimes charge a flat fee so that all hours do not need to be tracked all the time. The advantages and disadvantages of flat and variable consulting rates are discussed later in the book.

Along with these costs, though, are expenses many people overlook. The consultant will be drawing on your resources—telephone, cell phone, computing power, office space, and so on. Even if these infrastructure costs are already part of your company's budget, include them in the ROI calculation.

You should also include variable costs such as paper and office supplies. Consultants will almost never incur these costs out of their own budget, but, rather, expect the organization to cover these expenses. The variable costs may also include resources to be used by company personnel, such as training manuals, CDs, or DVDs.

Often the consultant will travel to the company location to provide services. You will need to pick up travel expenses like airfare, hotel costs, mileage, and meal expenses. A smart business leader will have these expenses negotiated contractually to be able to predict the expense.

■ **Note** Negotiate travel expenses and include them in your contract. That way, you can safely predict the expense over the course of the assignment.

There may also be travel expenses for your own employees that are required by the consulting relationship. Plan for these travel expenses ahead of time. Although the detail of these expenses may not be apparent in the beginning, there needs to be a plan.

In the course of the consulting engagement, there will likely be a combination of meetings and conferences. These carry their own expenses, such as catering and fees associated with webinars. There may also be continuing education for employees after the consultant leaves, which should be considered part of the consulting expense.

The final group of direct expenses is related to services. These may be legal services, insurance services, or some other service need that cannot be provided by the consultant, but are necessary.

By taking the time to work with the consultant to create a solid budget for the direct expenses, there will be some predictability to the overall cost of the consulting engagement. For almost all of the costs noted, except direct salary costs, we strongly recommend that you buy materials and other necessities yourself rather than have the consulting firm bill you for such items. This way, you have control over the quality and quantity of goods purchased. Frequently, a consultant is required to charge a mark-up on goods. For example, the consultant may cost out a training manual at $25 per person. The consultant will then add another $5 or more to the materials price to be sure they have covered all their costs. All consulting firms, no matter the size or location, will do this. They will not incur continual small losses on materials and equipment. Thus, even though there will be some personnel time required to purchase materials, catering, travel, and other expenses, it is likely always in your interest to do so.

After these costs are identified and quantified, you can focus on some of the less obvious consulting costs. The important thing is to be able to identify direct costs and ensure that they are all quantified prior to moving forward.

Hidden Costs

After all direct costs have been identified, it is time to anticipate potential hidden costs. Hidden costs are often overlooked, but there are three you must take into account.

The first of these is the *internal project management cost*. In order to be successful, the company must place the success of the consulting relationship in the hands of a full-time employee. This full-time employee will probably be 100 percent occupied by the consultant in a large consulting project, so the entire cost associated with that employee should be considered.

In smaller companies, the business owner or a management team may share this responsibility. In no way should a small-business owner consider hiring a full-time employee just to manage a consultant. However, you do have to calculate the time internal employees will spend on the job. In situations where a team of people will be dedicating a portion of their time to the project, this time should be included in the ROI. Make sure you consider both salary and benefits. It is normally safe to assume the total cost is around 130 percent of the person's salary.

In addition to this key human resource, there will be other people who are necessary for the project to succeed. The consultants should be required to help develop a budget for these internal human resources because the consultant may know from experience what kind of internal help he will need. Do not forget that if people are managing or otherwise aiding the consulting project, they are not doing their regular jobs. That, too, is an additional expense that should be planned for and quantified. An example is IT staff. While they may not be put entirely on a project, they may have to spend 80 percent of their time for days, weeks, or months performing various tasks. These costs mount up very quickly when considering the amount of payroll required.

■ **Note** Internal personnel hours are not free. Don't forget to include them in the ROI.

The second major type of hidden costs is *capital expenses*. Depending on the type of consultant you hire, and the purpose of the assignment, a potential outcome is a recommendation that you invest in hard assets of some kind to ensure the success of project goals. For example, a factory might hire an efficiency expert to help improve the factory's productivity. Then, when the consultant begins their analyses, they realize that the factory needs all new equipment. Another example: a company might hire IT consultants to help set up and implement a customer relationship management (CRM) system. Once the consultants begin work, they realize that additional software is necessary to integrate the CRM system with other, existing systems.

You should always identify and budget for capital costs prior to the start of the project. Where will you get the money? Identify the source and make sure funds will be available when you need them. You do not want an inability to obtain the necessary capital to become an excuse for project failure.

Contingency costs are the final group of hidden costs that should be included in the ROI calculation. These can be caused by numerous factors, including project timeline degradation leading to increases in direct costs that not anticipated on the planned timeline. As the consultants work on the project, internal and external resource needs may arise that were not anticipated. Moreover, consultants may make mistakes. These mistakes can be caused by multiple factors, some of which are out of their control.

For example, as part of the project, the consultant may mess up data collection on the project and spend time collecting data only to realize later that the data collection needs to be restarted. In the growing sector of IT consulting, a consultant may make mistakes with interfaces or configuration of a system, leading to delays having to redo the work. In IT conversion projects, consultants often have internal company employees perform data entry, which can contain errors. Likewise, the internal employees might not have the computer skills to perform the data entry. Such mistakes cost the company time on the project and resources used to collect the data.

Here, is another common mistake. Consultants are often used to drive change. Yet even a seasoned consultant may fail to build consensus on a change prior to implementation. This failure could lead to slow adoption of the change or even having to reverse the change. In either case, the change is less effective and more costly.

These mistakes are just a few examples. We have seen these mistakes made by good-quality consultants. As part of the ROI, therefore, there should be a plan to address an acceptable level of mistakes, increased costs, and timeline degradation.

Note Consultants are people. People make mistakes. Plan some time and money to address honest mistakes.

Payment Structures for Costs

When doing an ROI calculation, identify the payment structures. There are two typical payment structures: hourly rates and fixed fees. These may be further supplemented by some level of risk sharing. (There are other pay structures that are not as popular, including the per-unit method and share-based payments. We discuss those later in the chapter.)

Which is better? From your perspective, hourly rates make it easy to add or remove resources as needed. However, they make it difficult to anticipate overall project costs. To offset the risks, you need to manage scope, change orders, and minimize hours needed. That is why having one of your own employees manage the project is critical.

On the other hand, you may like the idea of a fixed fee structure because of the certainty of expense. A potential risk associated with this structure is that it incentivizes the consultant to push change orders. The consultancy will likely fill the allotted time for the project regardless of what is actually necessary to complete the work because that is a way to justify the expense. Moreover, there is no visibility into the rates, which may mean that the consultant is getting paid a premium. With a fixed fee, there is also less control over which people are assigned. Consultants working on a fixed fee may also be inflexible and unreasonably pedantic about what is within their scope. They are looking out for their interests.

Regardless of the structure you choose, ensure that there is shared risk in the project. That improves the chances the consultant will be well aligned with your business objectives and it will improve the potential for project success.

From the consultant's perspective, there are positives and negatives to each payment structure as well. The hourly rate is very safe. As long as the client does not challenge the capability of a single consultant, there is no risk. The downside to an hourly rate is that the consultant cannot charge for excessive or expensive resources.

A fixed-fee structure allows the consultant to manage expenses tightly and maximize overall profit. However, if managed poorly, there may be cost overruns, leading to a loss on the overall project. Sharing risk can be a positive for the consultant, but it gives more power to the client about whether or not the consultant will be paid. (Sharing risk often means that consulting fees are partially tied to the actual project benefit. This could be as little as 10 percent of the overall fees or as much as 75 percent.)

▓ **Note** Sharing risk by having the consultant fees be contingent on outcomes helps ensure success if properly managed.

There are other considerations when choosing a payment method. Hourly rate models are great when the scope is unstable or hard to define. You, the client, end up being the primary project manager in this model. The model can be improved by placing a cap on the overall cost of the job and including expenses such as office supplies as part of the hourly rate. Fixed-fee models allow the client and consultant to have a common understanding of the scope. The situation can be improved by putting a time-based run rate associated with the fee and excluding expenses as part of the fee. The run rate helps identify how much time is expected on the project to see if the level of work is commensurate with the fee. By excluding expenses in the fee, you can keep tighter control of this part of the project. If tangible or immediate business benefits are necessary, risk sharing is a great idea. It can be improved by setting penalties or bonuses based on deadlines defined along the overall project timeline.

▓ **Note** One effective way to share in the risk that you'll ultimately get what you pay for with a consulting engagement is to include both penalties and bonus payments in the contract.

Putting It All Together: The ROI Spreadsheet

Once all of the associated benefits and expenses are quantified, they should be placed into a ROI spreadsheet. This spreadsheet should follow the SMART acronym for goals. That is, each element should be specific, measureable, attainable, relevant, and time bound. The spreadsheet should also take into account the time value of money and any interest expenses or application fees associated with borrowing money to pay for the project.

Once set up properly, this spreadsheet will be the "point of truth" as to whether or not the consultant should be hired. Therefore, take great care in designing and validating the tool. Figure 4-2 shows an example of an ROI spreadsheet. Adapt it for your own use. The format of the spreadsheet is not important, and you should customize it to meet your specific needs. The important thing is that it is easy to understand and that it provides the ability to quantify all costs and benefits.

ABC Services, Consulting Agreement Return on Investment, December 31, 2012					
Contract Overview					
Project Name	*Big Savings Project*				
Project Manager	*Davis Cromwell*				
Date of Analysis	*1/10/2012*				
Consulting Company Name	*J&T*				
General description of benefits:	This project includes increasing revenue and reducing costs to turn around company				

Cash flow and ROI statement					
BENEFIT DRIVERS	Quarter				
	0	1	2	3	4
Revenue Increase					$375,000
Capacity Increase					
Cash Flow Increase					
Cost Avoidance Capital Expense					
Fines/Fees					
Cost Reduction					
Labor Costs					
Material Costs					
Reduced time spent handling customer complaints					
Total Quarterly Benefits		*$0*	*$0*	*$0*	*$375,000*
Implementation filter		85%	90%	95%	95%
Total benefits realized		*$0*	*$0*	*$0*	*$356,250*
Costs	0	Quarter 1	Quarter 2	Quarter 3	Quarter 4
Total	$0	$387,950	$387,950	$605,625	$475,625
Benefits	0	Quarter 1	Quarter 2	Quarter 3	Quarter 4
Quarterly benefit flow	*$0*	*($387,950)*	*($387,950)*	*($605,625)*	*($119,375)*
Cumulative benefit flow	*0*	*(387,950)*	*(775,900)*	*(1,381,525)*	*(1,500,900)*
Discounted benefit flow	0	Quarter 1	Quarter 2	Quarter 3	Quarter 4
Discounted costs	$0	$373,928	$360,412	$542,300	$410,499
Discounted benefits	0	0	0	0	307,470
Total discounted benefit flow	0	*(373,928)*	*(360,412)*	*(542,300)*	*(103,029)*
Total cumulative discounted benefit flow	0	*(373,928)*	*(734,340)*	*(1,276,640)*	*(1,379,669)*
Costs	Year 0	Quarter 1	Quarter 2	Quarter 3	Quarter 4
Consulting Fees		$232,050	$232,050	$271,375	$271,375
Travel Expenses		$39,000	$39,000	$65,000	$65,000
Personnel Costs		81,900	81,900	104,250	104,250
Project Management Costs		30,000	30,000	30,000	30,000
Capital Expenses				130,000	
Supplies		5,000	5,000	5,000	5,000
Total costs	$0	$387,950	$387,950	$605,625	$475,625
ROI measures					
Discount Rate	3.75%				
Net present value	*($1,379,669)*				
Return on investment		*0%*	*0%*	*0%*	*18%*

Figure 4-2. Sample ROI form (for only one year).

After you set this up and all of the inputs and assumptions are properly vetted, your decision on whether to hire a consultant becomes black and white. If there is no positive ROI at any point in the future, do not hire a consultant. If there is a positive ROI, then address the qualitative issues. These issues are presented in the next two chapters.

In the example in Figure 4-2, note that the net present value is negative. This may be the case for a short-term project that turns positive when the return is evaluated on a longer term. Depending upon the specific business needs, the required ROI may be three to five years. An ROI that turns positive in 12 months or less is typically a "no brainer" and should be pursued.

※ **Note**   ROI assumptions are a key to a good analysis. Spend the time necessary to get good cost estimates and projections on the return.

Calculating the Return on Investment: An Example

The following story shows how you can use a ROI analysis to make the ultimate decision on whether or not to hire one of three consultants. This is a fictional case about a business executive, John Saunders, who has already decided that he will hire a consultant to reduce labor cost and provide some revenue-increase opportunities. However, he is not sure which one will be the best deal based on the commitments made by each consultant. As in the real world, not all consultant payment structures are the same. In addition, the promises on gains and investments needed to get those gains are not consistent across all of the choices.

Also, note that in this fictitious scenario, projected gains are "promised," something consultants often do in real life. Even when the consultant is promising a certain gain, these should never be taken at face value. You should always perform due diligence and calculate actual forecasted gains, perhaps as shown in the earlier Bruno Builders case.

John has been interviewing consultants for the past three months. During each interview, he allowed the consultants to perform a review of the company situation in order to get a good business proposal from his top companies. He has reduced his list down to three consultants. All references have been checked, and each organization has the experience that John needs to help his company. John needs to develop an ROI analysis for each organization, based upon their proposals, and decide on his best solution.

Proposal # 1

The first company that John is considering is Jameson and Tiottuete Consulting, Inc (J&T). They have assured John that only full-time employees would be used during the engagement and that each person would have a minimum of fifteen years' industry experience. John reviews the resumes of each of the proposed consultants and is happy with the qualifications and other qualitative specifics of the consultants.

Based upon J&T's situation analysis, Kip Owens from J&T proposed that six consultants work on a three-year project with varying engagement time. The first six months would have a team of three people. The lead consultant would get $175 per hour, with the two others getting $125 per hour, plus expenses. Weekly hours for each consultant would average 42. The third through sixth quarters of the project would use four consultants at $125 per hour, with an average of 40 hours per week and with five hours per week of the lead consultant's time. The following two quarters would be two consultants working an average of 30 hours per week at $125 per hour, with the lead consultant working three hours per week. The contract includes supply expenses of $5,000 per quarter and capital expenses of $133,000 in quarter 3, $94,000 in quarter 5, and $131,000 in quarter 6.

J&T promised $375,000 per quarter in revenue increase starting in quarter 4. The budget shows a major capital expense—$1.5 million—planned in quarter 6. J&T has promised to improve the efficiency of operations enough to avoid this cost. The plan also shows labor cost decreases of $65,000 per quarter starting in quarter 5. Due to quality improvements, J&T plans that by quarter 7, John will be able to downsize an employee with a salary of $60,000 due to a decrease in customer complaints.

Proposal # 2

Slavin Management Improvements is the second company that John is considering. Slavin is a small company of only five consultants. The firm's owner, Doug Slavin, is dedicated to business development and spends only about five hours per week on projects. Doug proposes that he bring two of his consultants with him for the first quarter of the project full time. Then, after that, he would have four consultants work for five quarters. He would put two consultants on the final quarter of the project to work on wrap up and auditing. This would be the only quarter in which Doug would not be involved in the project. Doug's fees are $195 per hour for himself and $115 per consultant for his employees.

Slavin did not identify any specific capital needs, but told John to budget $45,000 per month for capital just in case. He also suggested John pencil in a supply fee of $3,700 per quarter.

Doug promised to deliver a labor savings in quarter 3 of $50,000 per quarter. He also forecasts a $3,800-per-month miscellaneous reduction in costs starting in month 7. Doug also believes that he can deliver a quarterly $250,000 increase in revenues, which would increase 15 percent per quarter, starting in quarter 2.

Proposal #3

John's final candidate is a large consulting firm. John was concerned with getting junior consultants on his project, so Jonas Quinn from Baileys International said he would dedicate three senior consultants to the project at $215 per hour for 36 months. Because of this promise, Jonas said that the consultants would work four-day weeks at nine hours per day. The supply fee would be $6,000 per quarter. Jonas has promised a head count reduction of 20 employees by the beginning of the third year of the engagement, and a revenue increase of $175,000 in quarter 4, growing by 22 percent per quarter thereafter.

Other Information for All Options

John plans on using his employee, Davis Cromwell, as the internal project manager. Davis makes $80,000 per year. John also estimates that he will spend $10,000 per quarter for the project from his own time and the time of other executive staff members. His experience is that he will need to plan for two employee hours for every consultant hour during the project. He plans to spend that money for internal personnel with a minimum of two employees for 40 hours each during any given week. An average employee in John's company makes $25 per hour. John also assumes $1,000 per week per consultant for travel and expenses. He plans to have whatever consultant company he goes with to agree to this fee. One of the key points that John also required all consultants to promise was a reduction in material costs of $82,000 per quarter starting in quarter 5.

The Best Choice

This example is not meant to be a math test, but rather, a realistic view of what the decision-making process could be for someone when the decision is solely based on the finances of the contract. In the real world, you cannot always compare apples to apples. Keep in mind that no decision would ever be made solely on ROI. However, for illustrative purposes, it is important to understand how revenue numbers that may seem better on the surface look drastically different over time and when compared to costs.

Since a spreadsheet like Figure 4-2, set up over 12 quarters, is impossible to present in a book, Table 4-4 shows the discounted benefit flow for all 12 quarters, split into three sections for Proposal #1. The net present value of this proposal is $1,444,555. The proposal becomes profitable after eight quarters. These will be the two key data points when evaluating each proposal against the others.

In order to evaluate the other options, Table 4-5 shows the discounted benefit flow for Proposal #2. In this proposal, the net present value is $1,861,821, but it takes until the tenth quarter for the project to become profitable.

Table 4-6 shows the discounted benefit flow for Proposal #3. In this proposal, the net present value is $1,503,984, and the project becomes profitable in the 11th quarter.

By looking at the net present value of the cash flows and when the project becomes profitable, you can make a decision based on facts. For instance, Jameson and Tiottuete Consulting, Inc. yielded the quickest results because it produced positive results by the end of the second year. If John's focus was to get the quickest payback, he would be inclined to hire this firm. Slavin Management Improvements yields the most value by the end of the third year. If John can afford to wait a few more months to have a profitable project, he may decide to choose Slavin and maximize his future potential profit. Baileys is out of the running; John's gut tells him it is not the right crew for the job.

There are, of course, risks associated with each of the consulting firms. Size of the firm and the varying experience levels of personnel within those firms may increase or decrease the risks of the consultant promises. John also needs to make sure that there are some guarantees regarding the promises made about the return on investment, such as setting up the contract on a risk-sharing model.

John should choose to interview each of the members from Slavin's team to develop comfort levels with each of them. Since Slavin has promised the largest amount, if he is happy with their skills, then he may want to consider hiring that group. If the interviews with Slavin's team do not go well, he should evaluate using J&T instead, even though they promised the least amount of return. The experience of the personnel may give John a sense of comfort around the project. There is less perceived risk with this group.

Table 4-4. Discounted Benefit Flow for Option 1: Jameson and Tiottuete

	Q 1	Q 2	Q 3	Q 4
Discounted costs	$373,928	$360,412	$542,300	$410,499
Discounted benefits	$0	$0	$0	$307,470
Total discounted benefit flow	(373,928)	(360,412)	(542,300)	(103,029)
Total cumulative discounted benefit flow	(373,928)	(734,340)	(1,276,640)	(1,379,669)
	Q 5	**Q 6**	**Q 7**	**Q 8**
Discounted costs	$473,858	$486,398	$168,071	$161,996
Discounted benefits	$412,528	$1,540,196	$394,259	$380,008
Total discounted benefit flow	(61,330)	$1,053,799	$226,188	$218,012
Total cumulative discounted benefit flow	(1,440,999)	(387,201)	(161,013)	$56,999
	Q 9	**Q 10**	**Q 11**	**Q12**
Discounted costs	$0	$0	$0	$0
Discounted benefits	$366,273	$353,034	$340,274	$327,975
Total discounted benefit flow	$366,273	$353,034	$340,274	$327,975
Total cumulative discounted benefit flow	$423,272	$776,306	$1,116,580	$1,444,555

Table 4-5. Discounted Benefit Flow for Option 2: Slavin Management Improvements

	Q 1	Q 2	Q 3	Q 4
Discounted costs	$488,386	$550,745	$530,838	$511,651
Discounted benefits	$0	$209,029	$299,690	$324,217
Total discounted benefit flow	(488,386)	(341,716)	(231,148)	(187,435)
Total cumulative discounted benefit flow	(488,386)	(830,101)	(1,061,250)	(1,248,684)
	Q 5	**Q 6**	**Q 7**	**Q 8**
Discounted costs	$493,158	$475,333	$283,087	$0
Discounted benefits	$416,494	$444,883	$476,957	$513,093
Total discounted benefit flow	(76,664)	(30,450)	$193,870	$513,093
Total cumulative discounted benefit flow	(1,325,348)	(1,355,797)	(1,161,928)	(648,835)
	Q 9	**Q 10**	**Q 11**	**Q 12**
Discounted costs	$0	$0	$0	$0
Discounted benefits	$553,710	$599,274	$650,303	$707,369
Total discounted benefit flow	553,710	599,274	650,303	707,369
Total cumulative discounted benefit flow	(95,125)	504,149	1,154,452	1,861,821

Table 4-6. Discounted Benefit Flow for Option 3: Baileys International

	Q 1	Q 2	Q 3	Q 4
Discounted costs	$438,419	$422,573	$407,299	$392,577
Discounted benefits	0	0	0	$143,486
Total discounted benefit flow	(438,419)	(422,573)	(407,299)	(249,092)
Total cumulative discounted benefit flow	(438,419)	(860,992)	(1,268,291)	(1,517,383)
	Q 5	**Q 6**	**Q 7**	**Q 8**
Discounted costs	$378,388	$364,711	$351,529	$338,823
Discounted benefits	$233,529	$260,866	$293,509	$332,372
Total discounted benefit flow	(144,859)	(103,845)	(58,020)	(6,451)
Total cumulative discounted benefit flow	(1,662,242)	(1,766,087)	(1,824,107)	(1,830,558)
	Q 9	**Q 10**	**Q 11**	**Q12**
Discounted costs	$326,576	$314,772	$303,395	$292,429
Discounted benefits	$1,087,888	$1,116,974	$1,157,042	$1,209,811
Total discounted benefit flow	$761,312	$802,202	$853,647	$917,382
Total cumulative discounted benefit flow	(1,069,247)	(267,045)	$586,602	$1,503,984

As can be seen from this case study, quantifying the costs and benefits associated with a consulting contract can significantly help in deciding whom to use. In addition, we can learn from this situation that just having the best return on investment does not necessarily mean that it is the best consulting company. There are risks and potential rewards to every consulting contract. The key to evaluating these contracts is getting an acceptable reward by minimizing the risk to your organization. Many organizations get greedy when evaluating consultants and end up working with a consulting group that has overpromised to get the contract, but in the end underdelivers on tangible results. Well-intended contracts designed to ensure performance might yield unintended consequences by giving the consultant incentives that may lead to dishonesty.

For example, we have seen a consulting contract that was well written with an "at risk" portion of the overall payment. The one weakness in the contract was that the data used to calculate the baseline performance and the method used to estimate the gain were not vetted between the consultant and company prior to the project start. In this case, there was frequent arguing over whether or not gains were achieved. This, ultimately, was one of many factors that led the consulting company to split into two companies in the middle of the project. The unethical half went one way and the ethical half went the other way. Luckily, in this instance, the brunt of the negative consequences fell on the consulting firm. However, it very well could have been disastrous for the company. Therefore, all figures should be accounted for, checked, and double-checked in the ROI calculations before, during, and after consulting engagements.

Paying for the Consultant

Once the return on investment for the consulting project has been validated, it is time to ensure that the company can afford the consultant. Since companies often hire consultants to bridge a performance gap, this can be a real concern for the organization. There are a variety of payment options, favored by the various consulting companies. Some of the most common options are lump sums, daily or hourly rates, the per-unit approach, or share-based payments.

Payment Options

When hiring a consultant based on a lump sum, or flat fee, it is critical to make sure that everyone knows exactly what is required for the project. On the plus side, if your brief is comprehensive, there will not be any hidden surprises. On the downside, any additional items that crop up along the way are likely to be the subject of heated negotiation.

The second option is a daily or hourly rate. Everyone knows exactly how the billing will work. Each party can add up the days, or hours, and keep track of costs, and the consultant can easily add extra services to the contract without worrying about payment. The only real downside to this is that the company will be charged for every hour or day. If the consultant works slower than expected, that can add up over time. Historically, consultants do tend to take longer than promised; rarely do they take a shorter amount of time.

The per-unit method is an approach where payment is based upon completion of goals. By limiting payment to units completed, companies can ensure that the consultant they hire works as hard as possible on the project. Results-based payments are similar to the per unit basis, but on a grander scale. In this method, the consultant typically waives a portion of the fee that will later be made contingent on a specific result. For example, the portion will only be paid to a consultant if a particular metric increases by 25 percent.

Share-based payment is initiated by the client, who is normally a startup lacking sufficient cash flow. When hiring a consultant to pay for services rendered, this type of arrangement involves the company's offering the consultant a share in the business in return for the work. Other options are available beyond these, but these are the most common. Each has its own cash- flow implication that may require financing options.

Financing Options

If a large payment or a series of large payments during the consulting contract are part of the final payment method used, then you need to look at how these payments will be made. If the business keeps enough cash on hand and has enough income to afford the consulting fees, then this is of little concern. On the other hand, if the business is a startup or a struggling business, then you must consider other alternatives for payment.

As noted earlier, you may be able to negotiate a share-based payment plan if accurate business models show the consultant that shares in the business is worth the investment of resources. There is a fine line between when this payment model makes sense for the client or consultant and when it does not make sense. If the company truly has a bright future, the shared-based option may end up over rewarding the consultant.

If a shared-based model does not work, companies may consider a lump-sum payment option tied to results. If the consultant agrees, it's a good way to encourage the consultant to get results. In this model, the majority of the payment would be made after results are verified and the company does indeed see nice revenue gains. Many consultants will not agree to this method because of the risk associated. In addition, this method may lead to confrontation with the consultant and client over how results are measured. A solid contract with contingencies that protect the consultant from providing free or discounted services is required with this method.

Yet another option is obtaining financing from a third party to pay for the consultant. Depending on the financial health of your company and your assets, this may be easy or difficult to obtain. It is difficult enough to make a consultant-financing industry necessary. Most likely, your current bank or another bank that has a positive relationship with your company will provide the best deal for financing. You would still need to have enough collateral or financial strength to get the loans. If your company is strong enough to get a loan for this purpose, it is likely that you could afford to pay the consultants using cash reserves.

If a traditional bank does not offer a loan that will cover the expenses on decent terms, then the final option is the consulting-financing company. These are third-party financing firms that have no affiliation to consulting firms. This is likely only an option for smaller companies and is limited to small amounts of cash to pay for a consultant.

Regardless of the situation, paying for a consultant can be a challenge. The funding source needs to be secured prior to signing the contract and committing to the relationship. The good news is that if you can construct a solid ROI analysis, then it is easier to get money to pay for the consultant. This is yet another reason to calculate an ROI. Especially in cases where one is going to be taking on additional interest charges, the ROI absolutely has to be positive, even after interest.

Summary

Obtaining a return on any investment is a fundamental of business success. Often, businesses claim success of a consulting relationship based on qualitative impressions over a quantitative return on investment. The return on investment must be built with fair assumptions. The best-case scenario is when the calculation works out to be a positive ROI even under the worst possible assumptions about costs and benefits.

Under no circumstance should you embark on a consulting relationship where no return can be found. Furthermore, the step of building the consulting relationship must support ensuring the achievement of the promised return. If data are not available to calculate the ROI, then it is likely your company has greater problems, which must be addressed first.

Mistakes
When Not to Hire a Consultant

Consultants have credibility because they are not dumb enough to work at your company.

—Dilbert

Previous chapters have described the consulting industry and how to conduct a complete ROI analysis to determine, from a strictly quantitative standpoint, if a consultant should be utilized. This chapter details those specific situations when consultants should *not* be used.

The crux of this and the ROI chapter are, perhaps, what inspired this book. Here is what we mean: Both of us have spent our careers watching businesses make stupid decisions, then follow even dumber consulting advice to remedy the situation. As mentioned already, this did not lead to the decision to write a negative, "This is how bad consultants are" book. In fact, we know that many times consultants can be of great value.

However, this chapter is of utmost importance because the examples presented here show situations when consultants should definitely not be used. These situations can lead to lost money—in the short term because of the consultant's fees and your internal costs, and in the long term because of the domino effect of bad business decisions.

▨ **Note**   There are many reasons not to hire a consultant. Most of them, if used as a justification to hire a consultant, ultimately will make your business weaker.

The Decision Rules

Many consultants sometimes give very bad advice. More importantly, many times they are simply not needed. You decide not to hire a consultant based on several decision rules, which are presented in the flowchart that follows (Figure 5-1).

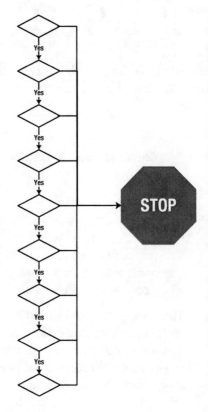

Do I need to have this skill in my company to survive?

Am I looking for training for a skill that cannot be trained?

Am I trying to validate an initiative that I plan to do anyway?

Am I looking for a quick fix?

Do I fail to come up with a return on investment that is realistic?

Do I lack internal resources to manage the consulting relationship?

Am I unable to articulate my problem?

Do I plan to end the relationship without further follow up once the project has ended?

Do I fail to have the time or ability to control and manage the consultants?

Figure 5-1. Decision map: when not to hire a consultant

In these situations, it almost *never* makes strategic or financial sense to hire a consultant. For example, when the problem area is too vague or ambiguous, like "leadership" or "strategy," consultants should not be used. While leadership training might be used as a motivator, data show that a consultant cannot really train a leader. In this chapter, we use personality theory to explain why this is so. The remaining decision rules are also explained in terms of a series of "bad reasons" for hiring a consultant.

Bad Reason #1: To Replace, Repair, or Enhance a Survival Skill

All managers and executives face business problems whose solutions seem to fall outside of the experience of their staff. Managers frequently follow the typical logic: "I need a consultant to help me with this skill, which I do not possess in my company."

This situation sometimes occurs when human resources or senior management refuses to hire someone with the right skills or training. As will be discussed in the next chapter, sometimes this situation does require a consultant to remedy the problem. However, you would go this route only when: (1) you need a specific skill set that is not required on an ongoing basis, (2) it involves specific skills that a consultant can teach or provide to allow the company to use independently in the future, or (3) the company is too small to have a separate employee perform the task. If these conditions do not exist, a consultant is not needed.

The first condition to consider is whether or not the skill set is needed on an ongoing basis. Some skills, like marketing, strategy, leadership, public relations, human resources, and process improvement, should absolutely never be hired out to a consultant. Figure 5-2 lists these "survival skills." The list might surprise you; after all, these skills are those that consultants are constantly selling. However, if the skill is a survival skill for the business, it should not be handled by an outsider.

Figure 5-2. Survival skills a company cannot live without

Think about it. If you hire consultants to do these things, it is like paying someone to cook all your meals and pay all your bills, and you are never learning to do these things for yourself. While those at the highest income levels may indeed hire out these tasks, 99 percent of humans would not go through life not knowing how to prepare a meal or pay a bill. Most people, most of the time, need to know how to take care of themselves—and so does your business.

As mentioned, these business survival skills are some of the most popular categories of consulting. Table 5-1 shows the number of consultants, based on area of specialty. (Note that the data were gathered without an "Other" category, so smaller segments are not considered in the total percentage.) It soon becomes obvious why you should never hire a consultant to advise in these areas. They are just too important for the health of the business.

Table 5-1. Management Consultants by Category

Type of Consulting	Percentage of Market Share
IT consulting	27 percent
Program/project management	20 percent
Operations	12 percent
Outsourcing advice	9 percent
Financial	8 percent
Strategy	8 percent
Business process re-engineering	7 percent
Human resources	7 percent
Change management	3 percent

Source: Datamonitor. Global Management and Marketing Consultancy, October 2008.

For example, take the survival skill, marketing. Consultants are making money in this category these days, as every business seems to think it needs help with social media marketing or Web impressions. We recently heard about a consultant selling consulting advice based on the premise that the business owner needed help with these new emerging social media outlets. All it took was one quick analysis of the firm's website to find out that social media help was the last thing this client needed. In fact, the business, which was an Italian Restaurant, that had a menu with offerings right out of the 1980s, complete with roughly seven veal dishes and numerous very heavy pasta dishes covered in heavy red sauces—all displayed on a canvas of black and burgundy. It was no great mystery that they were seeking consulting services to try to figure out how to reach a "younger crowd." Because, while successful, their main clientele was over age 60. The inherent problem was not with marketing, but instead with the core strategy. A company cannot live without marketing and strategy capabilities, both of which are survival skills and are critical to the success of the firm.

In this case, the restaurant owner was all too happy to buy into the fads and fashions of the day, adopt the marketing buzzwords, and seek out help in "social media marketing" (but, not in terms of his menu). If he understood strategy and marketing at the core, this issue would not have arisen. Now, while the future is yet to be determined, if this business owner gets recognition via social media, it will nonetheless be with the wrong menu, thus securing illusory gains that might drive even more business away from the restaurant.

Note   Avoid hiring a consultant to supply a survival skill unless your business is too small to hire a full-time person.

The Typical Excuses

Any firm, selling any product or service, needs to market itself effectively to its potential consumers. If a company does not have marketing skills, it cannot identify its possible customers and their needs; it cannot make the right products or offer services to meet those needs; and it will not understand the industry's pricing, distribution, or promotion. These marketing decisions are absolutely *not* common sense. All of these decisions must be made by someone with the education and experience to make them effective and efficient. But, and this is a big but, if a company does not have these skills internally, it will not survive. No business can survive for any period of time without a solid marketing department. A company can survive in the short term only if it has a clearly superior product, but this cannot go on in the long term.

Let's look at several "buts" that managers often offer when faced with a skills shortage.

But, Survival Skill Mistakes Are Too Costly . . .

There are many reasons you might consider going to an outsider to secure a survival skill like marketing. First, there is nothing as costly as a marketing mistake. This is very true. When a company plans to take its message to its customers, as in the Italian restaurant example, it wants to use the right approach that is customer focused. However, not only might the business owner choose the wrong approach, but by the time it is identified it may be too late to turn back due to budget constraints.

Marketing decisions are not one-time events. They are made on a daily basis, then evaluated and reevaluated. With roughly 30,000 new consumer products introduced every year,[1] no firm in any industry can afford to let its marketing strategy stagnate. So, if you hire a marketing consultant to help with your marketing strategy, you might get great results. But, how does this help you in the long run? If your senior marketing staff does not have the skills to develop, implement, measure, assess, and correct those marketing strategies, you have the wrong marketing staff. This may be a painful realization, but it is, unfortunately, true. For advice on hiring right, refer to Chapter 9.

But, Objectivity Is Needed . . .

Another common reason to hire a consultant for marketing or strategy is for the objectivity of an outside view. Leaders may lose objectivity about by be too heavily immersed in day-to-day operations and lose sight of the big picture; they focus on the forest and ignore the trees. It is not the job of a consultant to provide a clear, unbiased opinion. Any well-functioning unit of a firm should have processes in place. Process-improvement techniques such as Lean Six Sigma are means for obtaining unbiased opinions within an organization.

The Six Sigma concept of "Define, Measure, Analyze, Improve, and Control," commonly known as DMAIC, is often used to quantify and validate the opinions of an internal cross-functional team. This is an example of a set of tools and a process that can be used to come up with an objective evaluation of a problem with internal resources. Nearly 2,000 books have been written on the Six Sigma problem-solving methods, with 1,000 combining Lean methods from the Toyota Production System with Six Sigma from Motorola. The reason DMAIC, from Six Sigma, has become so popular is that the methods can be applied almost anywhere—from marketing and sales to production. Since Motorola developed the Six Sigma process, it has been used in hundreds of manufacturing and service organizations to drive improvements in efficiency and effectiveness.

For developing new processes or products, the Six Sigma practitioners developed DMADV, or "Define, Measure, Analyze, Design, and Verify." This is a modified version of DMAIC, using other tools to come up with good process

---

[1] Gerard L. Manning, Michael L. Ahearne, and Barry L. Reece, *Selling Today*, 12th ed. (Englewood Cliffs, NJ: Prentice Hall, 2011).

designs. How does Lean or Six Sigma help you gain objectivity and eliminate the need for outside consultants? Good question. At the heart of these processes lies the opinions of experts, and these "experts" are the people actually doing the work—the front-line employees. These employees are closer to the problems and can identify the root causes easier.

As mentioned, there are thousands of books on the subject, but here is a brief overview. In the *Define* phase of Six Sigma, you form a team to work on a project that has been clearly defined in a project charter document. The team gets information from the customers of the process, which may be another person or another department in the company, or may be external customers. With the information gained, what the customer wants is identified. This is the first step toward objectivity because the focus turns away from what business leaders want to what customers want.

In the *Measure* phase of Six Sigma, you collect the opinions of those experts on the front line. Where physical processes are available to observe, the team observes and documents those processes. You create a data collection plan to figure out the baseline performance of the process versus the *customer* expectations. You also validate the opinions with the data defined in the data collection plan during the analyze phase. A series of tools is applied to take all of the possible root causes of the problem that is defined in the charter and sort them down to the most critical causes. This process of reducing to the critical few root causes is the second step to objectivity because it is difficult for the team to be steered towards an individual's personal agenda.

In the *Analyze* phase of Six Sigma, you validate the process maps and expert opinions that were created in the measure phase by the data you collected. In this phase, the objectivity is enhanced by taking opinions and either refuting or supporting them through the data.

In the *Improve* phase of Six Sigma, you use a set of tools to identify all of the possible solutions the team can come up with and reduce them again to a key few. These solutions are then piloted one at a time to see the effect of the solution on the problem. You collect data during the pilot and use some hypothesis tests to show if a real statistical difference is achieved. The use of data to validate the effectiveness of the solutions is the third step of objectivity using Six Sigma.

The final phase, *Control*, involves putting the actions into place, thereby standardizing the new process to ensure long-term sustainability. Although control does not contribute objectivity to the project, it avoids having to repeat the DMAIC process to solve the same problem again.

Now let's look at how the Six Sigma process can help you develop something new, using DMADV to create a strategic plan. We will go back to the Italian restaurant example. The first step in DMADV is to *define* the project. This is where the owner of the process, which in this case would be the head of the marketing area or the company owner, defines the problem to be solved. In this case, it may be that a strategy needs to be developed.

The next phase, *measure*, is where you assemble a cross-functional team, and then collect their opinions. As part of the measure phase, the team works on a plan to collect data to support their opinions or refute them. This portion of DMADV is about developing hypotheses. Why are sales slumping? Why are all our clientele over 60? Hypotheses around these ideas need to be formulated.

The *analyze* phase is where the team collects applicable data and scrutinizes it to come to conclusions about the validity of the team opinions. This is really where "objective" opinions are discovered automatically. A business owner cannot perform a complete marketing strategy plan without objective decisions from the outside via appropriate measurement techniques. In this situation, data used to validate the opinions of the team are collected from the outside. Ideally, if the owner of the Italian restaurant wanted to increase his business to the younger crowd, he would survey the younger crowd and ask them why they do not frequent the restaurant. Hopefully, these reasons, such as outdated menu options, would be identified and understood.

The next stage is *design*, where the lessons learned are applied to the process. In the case of marketing strategy development, the new strategy is based on the valid opinions of the team. A new menu is developed and integrated with the overall theme of the restaurant.

The final stage of DMADV is *verification*, whereby the business owner makes sure that the new design can be successful. If the product is a new marketing strategy, as in this case, then it is tested on a limited scale to make sure that it works prior to doing a full marketing campaign. For example, the new menu items could be test marketed as specials, or as a small part of the menu and advertised directly to young individuals. Sales of those items could be tracked through coded coupons sent out in advance. The business owner can know exactly who redeemed the coupons. This would help the restaurant owner continue his plan for future success with objectivity. An outside consultant would have likely performed these same types of analyses, but would not have any knowledge of the internal dynamics of the company. Therefore, in this case, it is better to set up the processes internally. As can be seen with marketing skills, you can develop the process design and improvement skills of internal employees, which becomes a good alternative to hiring from outside, especially when funds to do so are unavailable.

▓ **Note**   Quality improvement processes, such as Lean and Six Sigma, can help you use internal resources to solve problems objectively.

But, There Is Not Enough Time . . .

A common excuse to hire a consultant for help with marketing or any other survival skill is a shortage of time. Business owners often assume that, if they take on the added tasks of marketing, their attention is diverted from other projects and responsibilities. Inescapably, differing focus and competing demands are bound to push and pull any executive. So hiring a consultant— someone dedicated to one and only one issue—is attractive. But, we will be blunt: if marketing, strategy, or any other crucial aspect of your firm is not your top priority, you need to reassess those priorities and begin developing those survival skills internally.

Let's consider an example. A privately owned manufacturer needed to generate more profitable growth due to a declining customer base. There was no sales force or business strategy. Rather than hiring an external sales rep or a sales consulting organization, the president chose to develop the capability within the organization. He took someone who had strong technical skills and provided training and incentives to sell the company's products. By combining strong engineering skills with sales skills, the president was able to increase sales in addition to customer satisfaction. This also made it possible to analyze the needs of current customers and eliminate those whose business could not be profitable for the company.

The decision to build necessary capability within the company led to an almost immediate improvement in profitability, as well as provided a longer-term sales pipeline that would generate profitable growth for years to come. Although a seasoned sales consultant should have been able to produce these quick results as well, the knowledge gap about the industry and technical aspects of the products would have produced slower results than teaching the skills necessary within the organization. Likewise, once the consultant left, the company would be back to the beginning and not possess the internal skills to continue to move forward.

But, Consultants Are Flexible . . .

Another typical excuse for hiring consultants is that they are ready at a drop of a hat. Hiring a full-time employee seems to be a complex process in which there are human-resource rules to follow and a potentially lengthy selection process to get the perfect candidate. However, although it is rarely done, similar due diligence should be taken when hiring a consultant.

Roles demanding any of the survival skills are not short term. The company will be faced with the same decisions multiple times as it grows. Any successful organization has to have these resources in place on an ongoing basis; one-shot marketing plans should never happen. This same argument works for the commitment-phobic. Although, yes, consultants do not require a long-term commitment, not to mention all the benefit costs that go along with full-time employment, their survival-skill decisions leave when they do. These skills are ongoing business needs and require dedicated human resources.

Other Survival Skills That Consultants Cannot Supply

The arguments so far against using a consultant are true for topical categories mentioned as survival skills (marketing and PR, strategy and leadership, human resources, process implementation or improvement, operations, IT, and finance). In short, if the skill is necessary for the survival of the firm, the company cannot go to a consultant. The company has to find an employee with the necessary skills to perform the tasks on an ongoing basis or train a current employee to perform those tasks.

In some rare situations, such as extremely small firms, a consultant is needed for these areas. In the next chapter, we talk more about this situation. But, if a firm needs the skill on an ongoing basis, they have to hire. If the company is too small to hire someone with the skill, it also probably cannot afford to have a consultant perform this function. In these cases, the solution is to develop the skill with current personnel and have employees who "wear many hats."

Bad Reason #2: To Provide or Repair a Skill or Knowledge that Cannot Be Trained

Pretty much any skill that is vague and is an innate aspect of human behavior cannot be trained, so it is ridiculous to expect a consultant to be able to do so. Some of these "innate human skills" that consultants say they can improve are leadership development, change management, culture development, and employee engagement. Let's consider these fields.

Leadership: An Untrainable Skill

Can you train someone to be a leader? No, you cannot. This statement is probably very offensive to enormous numbers of leadership consultants in the industry and the authors of the staggering 73,079 leadership books that appear on Amazon. One of us, Linda, has taught leadership in universities and has read dozens upon dozens of leadership books. When we say leadership cannot be trained, this is not to say that leadership is not a skill needed for a successful firm. It absolutely is. Unless a firm has a product or service that is so unbelievably distinct from everything else in the market that cannot be copied by competitors, ever, an organization has to have a good manager truly "leading" the firm.

Take a look at Figure 5-3, the leadership effectiveness model. There are outside factors that may hinder or help a leader's ability, like time constraints, the nature of the task, and the history of the specific situation. There are also some basic skill sets that can be trained, which include basic verbal and nonverbal communication, understanding your own personality, understanding how to hold an efficient and effective meeting, and knowing how to make a decision using an analytical problem-solving methodology. (Some key points about these topics are presented in Chapter 9.) However, nearly every other aspect of the leadership effectiveness model comes down to the personality and EQ (Emotional Intelligence Quotient) of the leader and the employees.

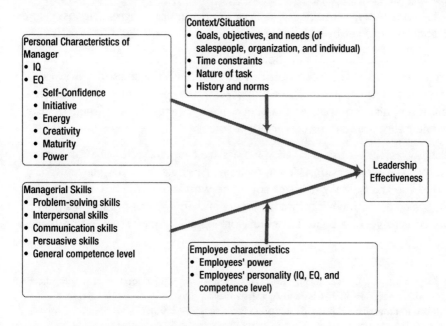

Figure 5-3. Leadership effectiveness model

Personality Theory

To explain how consulting cannot be seen as a remedy for leadership issues, we need to take a look at personality theory. As can be surmised from general experience, there are two different types of leaders. There are leaders who are real "leaders"—people you trust to lead the way into the unknown—and there are leaders who are merely managers or supervisors. Most true leaders have legitimate authority, (i.e., they were granted the position and power of "manager"), though this is not always required. However, being a true leader goes way beyond being an actual manager. It also requires what we normally call charisma, or the ability to inspire loyalty. Charisma makes a person more powerful and, therefore, makes subordinates likely to listen to that leader, and do what the leader asks. Successful change management, for example, cannot occur without a powerful leader at the helm.

Most people would agree with these statements. The problem with consulting in this area is that no one can train someone to have "leadership charisma." Most psychologists agree that human personality is set by age 5. Multiple studies have followed children for many years, examining childhood, adolescent, and adult behaviors. One study that tracked children over 19 years found that the personality tendencies and behaviors, such as shyness and aggressiveness, evident in childhood as early as age 3, are carried through to adulthood.[2]

According to contemporary psychological theory, the "big five" personality factors—openness, conscientiousness, extraversion, agreeableness, and neuroticism—are set by at least age 5.[3]

Discipline, organization, and being achievement oriented are traits of conscientiousness. The conscientious employee is the person who almost always follows through on tasks and always shows up on time. Emotional stability, impulse control, and anxiety are characteristics of neuroticism. Extreme neurotics tend to be very high-strung.

Sociability, assertiveness, and talkativeness are characteristics of extraversion. Many mistake extraversion as loving to be with people and being very outgoing. While these are typically traits of someone who is extroverted, extraversion has more to do with what brings happiness and energy to a person. If a person is the type to go to a banquet or networking event and return home feeling

---

[2] J. J. A. Dennissen, J. B. Asendorpf, and M. A. G. van Aken, "Childhood Personality Predicts Long-term Trajectories of Shyness and Aggressiveness in the Context of Demographic Transitions in Emerging Adulthood," *Journal of Personality* 76 (2008): 67–99.

[3] P. T. Costa, Jr., and R. R. McCrae, *Revised NEO Personality Inventory (NEO-FFI) Manual* (Odessa, FL: Psychological Assessment Resources, 1992).

emotionally drained, he or she is probably an introvert. On the other hand, if the person feels emotionally stimulated, he or she is probably an extravert.

Intellectual curiosity and liking novelty and variety are characteristics of openness. Open people tend to be tolerant of different beliefs and ideals. Helpfulness, cooperativeness, and sympathy are characteristics on the agreeableness scale. This trait does not necessarily refer to someone who is a pushover but, rather, someone who likes to cooperate when possible.

For all traits except neuroticism, the higher on the scale one is, the more likely he or she is to have successes in life. In other words, a good leader is probably very open (tolerant of employees' needs and goals), extroverted (they like people), agreeable (to a point—not a pushover), conscientious (gets things done), and very low on neuroticism (easy going, low stress level—this trait does not help anyone at its higher levels.)

Psychologists say that roughly 50 percent of our personality is linked to heredity, and roughly 50 percent is a product of our environment and upbringing. This means that, at most, only 50 percent of a person's personality can be changed, or affected after birth, then even if someone does not believe the "set by age five" theory, there is even less and less of a percentage that can be affected after birth and then in each successive year. Thus, the notion that a consultant or coach can teach these positive traits is nearly impossible.

Emotional Intelligence Theory

Emotional intelligence (EQ) is the ability to analyze and control one's emotions and behaviors, with the consequent ability to achieve more positive interpersonal outcomes at home and work. EQ is not necessarily a component of personality, but it is strongly related. Cognitive intelligence (IQ) accounts for up to 25 percent of the variance in a person's professional success and job performance. Personality and EQ account for the other 75 percent.

Emotional intelligence is made up of five components, according to Daniel Goleman:[4]

1. Intrapersonal: assertiveness, self-regard, self-actualization, independence, and emotional self-awareness

2. Interpersonal: interpersonal relationships, social responsibility, and empathy

3. Adaptability: problem solving, reality testing, and flexibility

4. Stress management: impulse control and stress tolerance

---

[4] Daniel Goleman, *Emotional Intelligence* (New York: Bantam, 1995).

5. General mood: happiness and optimism

EQ is measured in the same manner as is IQ, with 140+ representing genius, 120 to 140 indicating very superior intelligence, 110 to 119 showing superior intelligence, 90 to 109 being normal or average intelligence (100 is the exact center), 80 to 89 indicating dull, 70 to 79 representing borderline deficiency, and under 70 being indicative of definite feeblemindedness.

According to some psychologists, approximately 95 percent of the world is emotionally illiterate. Since EQ is so critical to leadership and to success in life, interventions designed to improve EQ have expanded greatly. Yet, many so-called leadership-training modules do not acknowledge the psychological theory behind their practices. And those that do, and that promise to increase EQ, generally have no results.[5]

The Faulty Mechanics of Leadership Training

The reasons these leadership training programs do not work are numerous. First, they lack theoretical and methodological rationale and they employ a mix of dubious techniques. Second, they cover only some EQ dimensions— for example, they target emotion identification, but not emotion management—and they add a number of skills that are not considered part of EQ, such as problem resolution, team building, and diversity skills. Third, where evaluations of these programs exist, they are often limited to subjective impressions gathered right after training. There has been no evaluation of long-term effects, and almost none of the studies have included a control group to test for the placebo effect.[6]

If you look again at the leadership effectiveness model (Figure 5-3), you will see that the majority of leadership aspects are controlled by personality and EQ. Other factors include situation, which is just that—situation specific. The only remaining box in the model is management skills. These are problem-solving skills, interpersonal skills, communication skills, persuasive skills, and skills relating to general competence level (i.e., job/company-specific knowledge). These skills can be taught if the training is conducted by someone with specific knowledge of these areas (Ph.D. in psychology or similar field).

In sum, you cannot change people's personalities. You might be able to improve their EQ. However, it is highly doubtful that you could find a consultant who would have an impact on your group's EQ. For employees to grow and change as a result of a skills-training program, they have to be able to identify their

---

[5] G. Matthews, M. Zeider, and R. D. Roberts, *Emotional Intelligence: Science and Myth* (Cambridge, MA: MIT Press, 2002).

[6] Ibid.

faulty behaviors, and that requires a high EQ. Now, we are back to square one and a circular argument.

One of our favorite sarcastic "demotivational poster" from www.despair.com is, "Dysfunction: The only consistent feature of all your unsatisfying relationships is you." This quote is sarcastic, but if people do not have the necessary ability to see faults in themselves and to repair those problems, training is neither practical nor effective. Furthermore, it is highly doubtful that a general consultant has the Ph.D.–level training required to impact these issues. Most of the individuals, who can have an impact, are not consultants, but instead are practicing psychologists.

Other Untrainable Skills

Leadership is just one of the innate skills that cannot be trained. As for the other skills mentioned earlier (change management, culture development, and employee engagement), the point is the same: if a company is seeking training for an innate skill, which is dependent upon personality change in the participants, it cannot work. You will waste your company's money. A consultant can train tactics to handle these types of activities, but without the EQ and personality traits present to manage change, develop culture, or engage employees, a consultant will show little measurable improvement.

Change management, for example, is a skill for which managers often hire consultants. Harvard professor John Kotter has made a good career out of selling books and training associated with his eight steps for effective change management. Other organizations have developed similar models for changing human behavior, with varying degrees of effectiveness. As mentioned earlier, a degree of charisma and command and control are necessary in order to fully implement change. Some of the softer skills in these training models can be effective in augmenting managers' natural leadership abilities, but they cannot initiate it.

Cultural development is nearly a comical concept to train in an organization. The culture of the organization is a complex interaction of many factors, including the named and unnamed values of the organization. CEOs and human resource leaders are infamous for creating missions, values, and goals meant to communicate the company's focus and also to motivate employees. Although such statements are necessary, they are of little value if they do not reflect the actions of the organization and its day-to-day decisions. Upper management can most affect culture through its actions, but culture in itself cannot be changed through a one-shot consulting or training endeavor. Only through a long-term program can upper management control the organizational culture.

Employee engagement is also an area in which a consultant cannot train effectively. Employee engagement is mostly affected by employee perceptions of the ethics and motivations of a company's leaders, as well as the faith that those employees have in the strategy those leaders have shown the employees. HR people spend large sums of money surveying their employees and enacting programs designed to improve employee engagement. In reality, the only factor that can influence employee engagement is a sound strategy that is clearly communicated to employees and implemented in an ethical and sincere manner. Provided there are no problems of ineffective management or management bullies, the employee engagement should come naturally.

Most studies show that employees are more engaged when leadership is effective. In other words, bad leaders = non-engaged employees.

Executives who have been party to the types of "soft skills" training discussed here will often swear to their success. But, that is often due to a funny little psychological principle called "commitment and consistency."[7] This principle says that once people commit to something, they will attempt to rationalize their decision and become even more committed to it. This principle is so strong, that they will then rationalize any sales increase (or whatever similar metric) to their decision to hire a consultant. In other words, once an executive has decided to pay for consulting, he or she will then almost assuredly see an improved outcome from that consulting. So, if a consultant ever tries to sell you on a "fluffy" topic, run away. Long-term, ingrained, innate behaviors of both people and company culture cannot be coached away in a few brief training sessions. They simply cannot.

▓ **Note**   Skills training is a great way to develop employees' abilities, but some skills require personality traits that cannot be trained.

Bad Reason #3: To Validate an Initiative that a Company Already Plans on Doing

Commonly, companies will use a consultant to validate a decision its executives have already made. This type of ruse reflects an unwillingness to be transparent. The 1999 movie *Office Space* poked fun at this bad excuse for hiring a consultant. In the movie, the firm Initech hires two consultants to "downsize" the company. Even though the movie is an over-the-top joke, this is a very real

---

[7] Robert B. Cialdini, Influence: The Psychology of Persuasion. New York, Morrow (1993).

scenario and serves as a barrier to mutually beneficial employee and employer relationships.

Consultants as the Bad Guys

Using the consultants as the bad guys who suggest and implement unpopular initiatives erodes the trust that an organization has in its leaders because most employees realize the consultants are brought in by the leaders for specific purposes. Even those who do not come to that conclusion on their own will hear it enough times from others within the organization that they choose to believe it themselves. Word travels fast—especially bad news. Since employees know that the consultants interviewed employees with a clear purpose in mind, any actions taken by those consultants and supported by management are perceived as part of the plan all along. As a result, employees may begin to lose trust or faith in their leadership.

When employees lose faith in their leadership and see through the manipulative techniques the leaders use when they bring in a temporary, external consultant, there can be unintended consequences. The high performers in the organization may understand why the leaders have made choices and help with the change. But, more likely, they will feel a sort of betrayal that then leads to looking for employment elsewhere, sensing that there is not a long-term future for them in the organization. This is a pivotal point in the change process, because these employees can often steer the behavior of others in positive or negative ways. The unofficial leaders within the organization are normally a mix of both these high performers and those other mid- and low-level performers who have a long tenure within the organization. If the executive staff fails to address potential mistrust issues, the high performers with the most marketable skills may choose to leave. If it becomes obvious to others in the organization that an exodus is happening, the high performers are likely to lower their level of engagement with both the changes brought on by the leadership and in their regular roles. They may also choose to look for other employment options. Although it may take longer for most of the employees to find employment, it is likely that once those people have chosen to leave, they will continue to look for employment until they find it. Even later improvements in employee morale will have little effect on the decision to jump ship, as those employees have already fallen victim to an internal lack of commitment.

Additionally, low-performing employees may undermine any change efforts through silent actions. Bad managers rarely realize the power that lurks in employees when they all join together in a disdain for management. This slowly seeps into every part of the organization. Fear mongering increases the power of low-performing individuals and undermines the goals of the company.

This situation nearly guarantees an unsuccessful engagement with consultants. If the high performers are astute enough to see through the actions of the executive team and still support those actions, however, the engagement has a chance of succeeding. In fact, executives can help minimize the negative effects of consultant-sponsored change by meeting with the most valued employees and ensuring them that their position within the company is good and that the company wishes to have a long-term relationship. Executives also have the ability to seek input from high performers at all times.

This leads to an important question: Why wouldn't the executive team just work with those high performers and implement the good idea without wasting scarce resources on hiring a consultant? Even if the high performers support the changes suggested by the consultants, they will likely lose faith in the executive team because it resorted to finding an outsider to do the dirty work. Additionally, using an outsider to carry through a change will make it more difficult to initiate effective change internally in the future.

A better strategy is to work with the high performers to identify potential training and personnel resource gaps that could be filled within the organization. This can lead to a more sustainable change that is supported within the organization by those who managed the change. It would also be an effective way to develop future leaders and build trust in the executive team's ability to execute its vision. This means more work for the executives to manage the change process, but in both the short and long run, it will yield better results.

In essence, bringing in a consultant to execute an unpopular change shows a lack of true leadership. True leaders can make and enforce decisions and strategies even when they are negative ones. If the desire to downsize or implement an unpopular strategy is a sound business strategy that will lead to long-term viability of the business, then the executives should be able to explain why that action is necessary.

This explanation, in hand, sets the stage for change within the organization. Although many employees may not be happy with the decision, they will respect the leaders after the strategy is implemented for their honesty and transparency. Even more, if the new strategy yields the planned results, then the executives will have earned the employees' trust. Figure 5-4 depicts the hiring of a consultant to validate a bad idea.

Figure 5-4. Consequences of hiring a consultant to be the bad guy

Consultants as the Good Guys

There is also significant risk in hiring a consultant to validate a good idea. For example, suppose the management of a company decides to launch a new product. They bring in consultants to sell this idea to the workforce as if it were the consultant's idea. Management might be doing this, so that if the product fails, it was not management's fault.

When Executives Hire the Consultant

Although consultants may be hired to perform specific tasks with clear criteria, as will be discussed in Chapter 6, many times they are not familiar enough with the organization to implement the ideas as well as an entrenched leadership team would. People bring their own biases to their roles in the business world. In the case of consultants, this bias may bring some assumptions. For example, the consultants may assume that your particular organization is similar to others where they have worked. These assumptions naturally lead consultants to implement changes that they have seen work successfully in the past. This "packaged deal" approach is sold by nearly every large consulting firm, and reflects the natural inclination to repeat what has worked before. But, prepackaged solutions are not necessarily the right solutions.

For this new product example, the company might find a consultant from a large firm specializing in new-product launches. They likely have a standard template for product launches. (If you do a Google search for "product launch consultants," you will find hundreds of these prepackaged templates.) There may be value in hiring one of these consultancies if you have never done a new product launch. However, these templates are so standardized that they do not consider a company's individual needs. For example, most of these templates include trade show appearances as a step prior to launch, yet trade shows do not apply to every industry.

The point is that very little consulting is truly customized and bias free. Consultants spend all their time going from company to company, and in the process they establish biases about how companies work. And the more companies they deal with, the quicker these biases form. One would surmise that consulting experience is good, but in reality, the more one has performed consulting, the more standardized one's "package" becomes. This is not necessarily a bad thing, but in this case, it is.

The flaw behind this approach is that every company is different. Each comprises a variety of skills, cultural norms, market pressures, and core competencies. Real change should come within the firm, because the organization's leaders best understand the interactions of the various processes. A good idea from executives might not be fully understood by the consultants, with the end result being something that the executive team did not intend. An improperly implemented change will require further work within the organization to fix or, even worse, the hiring of new consultants to do the job correctly.

The pattern of hiring one consultant to fix the problems caused by another is expensive, considering not only the cost of these consultants, but also the overall cost to the business. Frequent and repetitive engagements with consultants drain the organization's resources, keeping that money from being spent on primary business functions. The alternative to this is overworking employees, which leads to more mistakes and burn out. When multiple consulting engagements are made due to errors from other consultants, it is likely the mistakes made in the first engagement will be repeated in the replacement consulting relationship.

Executives of the organization are familiar with the culture and unofficial leadership of the employees, so they are more equipped to deal with resistance to change. Internal resources are less likely to misinterpret the leadership vision and goals of the organization leading to a more successful improvement. Typically, the official and unofficial leaders of the organization are more likely to go along with a change that is led by someone who has something to gain from the long-term success of the organization than a consultant who will leave after the assignment is done.

This also leads to improvements with the engagement level of the employees, which could lead to the long-term sustainability of the change. Even with the best control measures put in place and thorough organizational training, if employees do not see the value in the idea, it has a low probability of success. Figure 5-5 depicts the hiring of a consultant to validate a good idea.

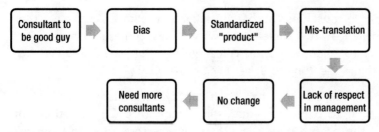

Figure 5-5. Consequences of hiring a consultant to be the good guy

When Middle Management Hires the Consultant

Not all consultants are hired by upper management. Sometimes a consultant may be hired by middle management to support its ideas and help with managing senior executives. If a manager has to hire a consultant to get commitment from an executive to support actions that the manager would like to take, the chances are that the manager lacks courage and leadership ability. The same lack of leadership applies to the upper-level management initiatives discussed previously as well.

When middle management employees look to hire a consultant to validate an idea, they should instead think of how to get the idea approved without wasting company resources. While consultants can at times add great value to a company, they should never be brought in with the sole intention of validating and enforcing a predetermined strategy or initiative. This only erodes trust in management and, ultimately, the organization's culture and performance. Consultants are a short-term help, not police.

▓ **Note**   Consultants are short-term help, not police.

Bad Reason #4: When a Company Is Looking for a Quick Fix

It seems that everyone, everywhere, wants a quick fix to everything. Even in our personal lives, we want a pill for rapid weight loss, or a scheme to get rich quick. In business, the quick fix is commonly driven by investors who want to see fast financial results.

However, there are no quick fixes in business. It's a cliché, but relevant here: anything worth doing is worth doing well. If executives are chasing the latest fix because they want to move the company forward, they are setting themselves up for serious disappointment.

Businesses bring in consultants as that quick fix; they expect them to use their industry knowledge to implement what the "Joneses" have done (benchmarking) to improve performance quickly. But, there are no good results when things are done to drive quick growth.

For example, a small firm that had been run by its founder and CEO for decades was sold to a private equity firm upon that CEO's retirement. Unfortunately, the private equity firm had its investors to satisfy and had bought the firm with a "pump and dump" mentality. (Very rarely do private equity firms come in with the intention of building real equity; instead, they look to build "paper equity" that can be resold in a couple of years.)

In this case, the private equity firm saw a company with a really great product; the company had been run like a family business for decades. They thought that, if they came in and transformed the management and marketing, they could rapidly expand the company. In other words, the private equity firm thought that the only thing holding the company back was its "mom and pop mentality." They thought that, with "world class" ideals, they could rapidly turn a profit on the small business.

The first line of business, after the buyout, was to hire consultants. These consultants quickly analyzed the company and made recommendations. With the help of these consultants and their recommendations, the company eliminated old product lines, invested millions in developing new product lines, fired and replaced almost all of management, started buying up similar companies, and formed joint ventures with foreign companies to manufacture more of the products abroad. After all, "innovation," and "international expansion" seemed to be the buzzwords that were easily sold to management. Without going through the idiocy of each decision, suffice it to say that, within five years of the buyout, the firm was several million dollars in the hole, having carried a multimillion dollar loss for a couple years.

Every one of the decisions the new owners made were ones that should have taken a lot of time, money, and research to produce. To try to implement all those changes in roughly two to three years, with no backup research, was not a good idea and so they failed. There simply are no quick fixes for businesses.

Benchmarking and Best Practices as Quick Fixes

Companies can occasionally be innovative and implement a rapid improvement, but more often, improvements are successfully implemented through consistent follow through and long-term thinking. This is why benchmarking within the same industry can often be ineffective. Benchmarking within the industry is good for tracking a company's performance against similar companies—if the company is a follower in the industry.

But, once a company has overcome a gap in performance, benchmarking will yield only mediocrity. The firm will, at a maximum, always be number two. In addition, the company will be following strategies that were successful in the past, not now or into the future. Having a consultant bring industry information to an executive because of their experience in the industry can be as ineffective as benchmarking.

For instance, suppose an executive at Chrysler wants a consultant familiar with the methods of Honda or Toyota. This is because the Chrysler executives may be able to adapt those methods to make their company more successful. In contrast, an executive from Honda probably does not want to gain industry knowledge from an expert in the General Motors way of doing business.

This type of comparison works in any industry. The appropriateness of using a consultant to bring industry knowledge to an organization largely depends on that company's position in that industry and the company's ambition to improve itself. If a company aspires to be an industry leader, it needs to understand its competition. However, it should be aiming to pass the competition and to build a continuous-learning culture so that future innovation comes from the inside.

Similarly, trying to implement a "best practice" approach without first performing a comprehensive needs analysis will only yield a new process within the company that likely will not add value. Similarly, being second to market with a concept will only yield a diminished return. Consultants will not help a company leap-frog to a leader position via benchmarking or best practices—it is impossible.

Quick Fixes Do Not Offer Long-term Differentiation

What makes a company profitable and sustainable is its ability to offer a high-quality good or service that is in demand at a price that the market will bear. This product or service should have a distinctive competitive advantage or real value proposition. As part of this consistent and proven formula for success, good management methods include cost control and intelligent resource use. None of these components for a successful organization can be quickly fixed or copied from successful organizations. The entire premise of a differentiating advantage is just that—it is different! A company will not be different if it copies the leader.

Rather, an organization needs to define its niche and determine its formula for success based on its core capabilities and the talents of its people. A consultant's value to an organization may be an ability to introduce concepts foreign to the organization. New ideas or concepts, even when they may help the company, can never be implemented quickly and effectively because they need to be adapted to the needs of the organization. Likewise, a concept not grown within the ranks of the organization will likely be rejected by the culture, without input from the unofficial leaders within the organization. There is a significant time investment that is needed to assimilate the concept into the organizational culture.

Quick Fixes Do not Allow for Sufficient Research

When a business decides to bring in ideas from the outside via a consultant, it is naïve to believe that those ideas will be implemented immediately. There is a significant time investment needed for an organization to assimilate new ideas. It takes time for consultants to acquire the fact-finding validation for their consulting engagement. Anything less than this is a canned solution. If a consultant offers a canned solution that is "proven," and "easy the implement," RUN AWAY. Any solution to a problem should be fully integrated within a company's strategy and vision, which should involve long-range goals. For example, a consultant cannot come in and focus merely on "margin" and "cutting" when quality is what sets the company apart. If the solution does not fit within this "slash and burn" process, a manager will not allocate the appropriate resources and the implementation will be terribly under supported and ineffective. If a core value of the organization is to provide industry-leading quality products, but a proposed solution to reduce high internal scrap rates could potentially undermine this core value by increasing the chance of poor quality, then the company should not approve this approach.

A better use of resources than to purchase consulting services for a quick fix would be to implement processes that support the company's vision and will ingrain a culture of improvement. It can take much more time to do this well, but it will yield long-term results that do not rely on a charismatic leader or an audit process to be sustainable.

If the problem is a lack of fresh ideas or the need to understand how others have overcome similar challenges, then send some key personnel or contacts to gain additional experience. For example, many of the most successful organizations in the United States learned from the Toyota Production System by sending visitors to Japanese factories and studying how they performed the work. When those people returned, they did not copy what Toyota did but, rather, adapted the concepts to their own organization. This is a sustainable model for improvement because it allows the business to keep ownership of its own process while promoting internal learning. It also reinforces the idea that no organization can be expert in everything. Figure 5-6 is a model for sustainable business improvement.

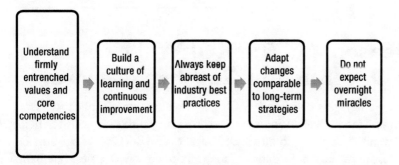

Figure 5-6. Sustainable model for business improvement

A Quick Cover-up for Poor Performance

Here is another quick-fix danger: painting over something ugly to make it look pretty to investors, stakeholders, or customers. If these are your reasons for hiring a consultant, do not spend the money. Unfortunately, pressures from stockholders do encourage quick-fix schemes, but you should know in advance that they will not stick. Besides, schemes like this are much more transparent than you would think. It is reckless to waste company resources on such attempts. News stories of the 1990s and 2000s support the idea that painting a pretty picture of a failing organization will end up catching up to the management of that organization and yield a much worse result for those individuals. Being honest with all stakeholders about actual performance, and having a solid improvement plan that may or may not include the use of consultants to improve performance, is a better approach for an executive team to take. It would be more responsible to save the money and be transparent about the company's poor performance with a solid improvement plan to be delivered at the same time as the admission of failure. If you are considering bringing someone on board to work through a few minor problems, make sure the consultant is aligned with the company's vision and values, and that the initiative is an integral part of the company's strategy. Make sure also that the consultant spends ample time conducting a needs analysis and doing the internal and external market research. If, in fact, the proposed actions are supported by long-term planning activities, then they will be easy to explain to stakeholders and should be supported by shareholders and employees alike.

■ **Note** Be honest with all stakeholders about actual performance and present a solid improvement plan.

Bad Reason #5: The ROI Will Never Work Out, But You Go Ahead Anyway

Doing an ROI analysis is discussed in Chapter 4, but it needs quick mention here. When you face a challenging situation, it is natural to reach out for help. This could result in deciding to hire a consultant. The decision to go outside one's own resources can be a difficult one, but once this decision has been made, it is equally difficult to reverse course.

Often, once the idea to get a consultant's help has been communicated to the entire executive management team and obtained preliminary approval, it becomes difficult to save face and decide against the engagement if the return on the investment shows it is not worth the effort. By the time the company realizes there is not going to be a positive return on its investment, it is likely that multiple consultants have been interviewed and numerous proposals submitted. This process may have included leaders outside of executive management as well. Folks from multiple disciplines may have become involved, including finance, marketing, sales, legal, and operations. Having these team members included has shown an organizational commitment to move forward with hiring a consultant.

Of course, it is right to bring those folks into the decision-making process so that a better decision can be made, and some key employees can be engaged in the consulting project. Although this is a good idea, it also means that this inherent commitment to bring in an outside resource has been made. Also, it is more than likely that there is some information leaked to a larger population of employees, leading to a further emotional need to be consistent with the decision.

All of these influences may lead to an unspoken commitment to make the contract work so that the executive team can appear to be consistent. Nonetheless, the final decision to move forward with a consulting contract *must* be based on a realistic return on investment. This means that all assumptions in the proposal that lead to a conclusion of adequate return on investment must be properly vetted by subject-matter experts in the organization. Without this step, you may be tempted to believe the assumptions made by the consulting "experts" and their own ROI analysis.

Often, consultant contracts have an "escape" clause stipulating that the assumptions must be validated and that the management team must support the consultant's recommendations for the return to be achieved. It is paramount for the business owner to eliminate any potential escape clause that frees the consultant from commitment to a certain return on investment.

Also, the consultants' proposals often neglect to mention internal resources needed to support the work. These resources may include capital, expenses, and human resources. As mentioned in the last chapter, when reviewing the proposals, you need to ensure that accurate estimates of internal costs are included in the ROI analysis. Ideally, the contract will come with a guarantee of return whereby the consultant will reimburse the company if the return is not realized.

Part of the project process must include a transition stage, with required internal resources suitably identified. Although this process is a standard for consulting engagements, it should also include bringing back the consultants a few times to reinforce what was done and make any necessary modifications. Companies often neglect to include these later costs in the ROI justification. By doing so, it is more difficult to justify the follow-up visits.

If, after all the consultants have been interviewed and all the proposals have been evaluated, a solid ROI cannot be identified, then the company needs to revisit the decision to hire the consulting services and find other options to correct the problem.

Bad Reasons #6–9: The Company Does Not Have Time, Resources, or Abilities to Effectively Form and Manage the Relationship

Items 6 through 9 on the decision map (Figure 5-1) deal with forming and managing the consulting relationship. These topics are discussed at length in Chapter 7, but they need mention here. If you cannot do the necessary tasks required before hiring a consultant, and, once the decision has been made to hire a consultant, commit resources to manage and support the consultant, you should not hire one.

Think about what is involved when you bring a consultant on board. For the consultant to get up to speed with the company, you will use the time of internal resources to "show him or her the ropes." This is much like training and developing a new employee, and it may take weeks. Meanwhile, the consultant has to show some benefit from the rising cost of the engagement, so internal resources must be used to ensure that any "quick wins" are controlled and are not counterproductive. This also means that the people working with the consultant will guide him or her through the data and policies of the organization, as well as slow down any improvements that may not be in line with organizational culture or strategy.

■ **Note** If you're not prepared to provide resources to bring a consultant up to speed and manage the assignment, do not hire one.

The Internal Resources Needed Are Too Great

Normally it takes more than one or two people in the organization to represent all of the company's interests. Thus, it is likely that you will need a team of employees engaged in the consulting relationship. You must be prepared to dedicate these resources for the entire period. Some employees will be busy with the consultant for the entire time; others will be necessary for particular projects. Additionally, a thorough approach requires regular, multidisciplinary meetings. In Chapter 8, about managing the consultancy relationship, we talk more about the purpose and scope of these meetings. All that you need to understand here is that there is a level of commitment that the leaders of your company need to have prior to hiring a consultant. If you cannot commit to assigning people and responsibility at this level, do not hire a consultant.

The Deliverables Are Unclear

Before starting a project, there should be very expectations about both deliverables and the resources necessary to achieve those deliverables. The consultant may request that money for capital or human resources be spent to meet the project's deliverables. The resource needs should be identified and justified upfront by management. Any changes to these resource requirements should be handled as a change to the contract, triggering a re-evaluation of the consulting relationship. By setting this expectation early on in the consulting relationship, you ensure that the proposal is as complete and accurate as possible. This expectation also alerts you to have the resources available for actually committing to the contract.

It is also important to remember the concept of sunk costs. If during a consulting relationship, it becomes clear that the apparent ROI has disappeared, perhaps because of changing deliverables or increasing resource needs, the contract should be cancelled. If you cannot commit to any of these principles, do not hire a consultant.

Define the Problem—As Best You Can

Some consultants believe that a company should articulate its problem before hiring a consultant. In reality, if most organizations could define their problems, they would also be in a good position to develop an internal solution. One of the benefits of using a consultant is to obtain a diversity of experience.

Expect, therefore, significant variation in the proposals you receive from consultants unless you have scoped the project tightly. This is a good thing. If the proposal request is too specific, then consultants are likely to solve a symptom rather than perform a root-cause analysis. Ideally, there is a balance to be achieved: the company articulates the problem in general terms to get good proposals, and consultants use their varied experience to propose a process for finding a long-term solution.

The evaluation phase lets you judge the capabilities of the consultants. It is natural to expect them to play to their strengths when engaging a client or take very good notes during initial interviews and, thus, become good at rearticulating the problem from the perspective of the company. Thorough analyses of the organization by an adequate number of consultants who are all carefully crafting proposals should generate a couple of solutions. These solutions should reveal similar conclusions as to what the problem is, which should guide you in your decision. Even if there is no clear, predominant root cause, having multiple perspectives will help.

Executive Time Commitments

You need to be prepared to make yourself available, regularly, to any consultants working in your organization. If you cannot make this commitment, do not hire a consultant.

This is mostly because you need to ensure that the consultants stick to the plan. Also, you have to make quick and effective decisions to avoid wasting consulting and internal resources. If you and your colleagues make yourselves available for scheduled weekly meetings only, it slows things down.

By removing yourself from the project and not being fully aware of all activities, you will require debriefing prior to any decision. These debriefings can also slow down the project. Additionally, by counting on external debriefing, you allow the consultant to frame the decision instead of basing it on your own observation.

Only by being willing to make the time commitment will you ensure that a consultant engagement generates a real return on investment. Only then, will you build a relationship with the consultant that opens the lines of communication and makes future work easier. Bottom line: If you cannot commit the time to working closely with a consultant, do not hire one.

Summary

This chapter discusses those situations when consultants should absolutely *not* be hired to solve business problems. The goal was not to criticize the use of consultants or put the industry on trial. Rather, its purpose was to show how a potentially helpful industry can be used *ineffectively*. As history has shown, consultants are used to hide bad management decisions, unethical behavior, and incorrect assumptions. They have also caused unethical behavior through their advice. The decision rules discussed here are red flags for managers considering whether to engage consultants to solve their problems. Make sure that you consider the motives behind your decisions and ensure that you hire consultants only when they will provide real value.

6

Good Decisions

When You Should Hire a Consultant and Why Consultants Can Be Effective

We simply assume that the way we see things is the way they really are or the way they should be. And our attitudes and behaviors grow out of these assumptions.

—Stephen R. Covey

Business leaders tend to make assumptions every day, based on their own experiences. They often assume that they have the skills and insight to deal with the situations at hand, even when they are ill-equipped to do so. No one has the ability to view all situations from all perspectives at once. Likewise, no one has all the necessary skills to make every decision every time.

There are two basic types of books on the market about consulting. Most books about consulting tell the average person how to become a consultant, while the remainder focus on telling the world how evil consultants are and why business leaders should never use them. The reality is that there are good reasons for using a consultant. When the conditions described in this chapter are present, you should consider using a consultant.

The consulting industry is often seen to be evil because (a) consultants are often hired for the wrong reasons, resulting in poor outcomes; and (b) there is so much money to be made in consulting that it leads consultants to promise more than they can deliver.

There are ten main reasons to hire a consultant:

1. The business is too small for a full-time hire

2. You need a skill for which an employee can be trained

3. You are conducting a search for a full-time employee

4. Your employees and existing methods fail to find the root cause of the problem

5. Your need is temporary

6. You need a breakthrough change that can be sustained internally

7. Your company is in need of creativity, innovation, R&D, ideas, or cross-industry fertilization

8. You need someone with a highly specialized skill who is difficult to find (or resource, lab, etc.)

9. You need an objective or anonymous opinion

10. You require professional expertise, such as compliance or auditing

Too Small for a Full-Time Hire

Companies vary greatly in size and capability. According to the 2008 U.S. Census, over 98 percent of companies employ fewer than 100 people.[1] Nearly 90 percent of these "small companies" employ fewer than 20 people. Figure 6-1 shows the breakdown for the most prevalent company sizes. As can be seen here, the majority of companies are very small.

Companies using consultants will typically fall into a couple buckets. The habitual users are likely to be the larger organizations that tend to avoid building the survival skills described in Chapter 5. Instead, they add an unnecessary expense by hiring consultants to do what internal employees should do. Unfortunately, large companies can do this because there is so much money sloshing around in them that it is easy to miss a few thousand here and a few thousand there. Some companies habitually hire consultants and even get to the point where they know the consultant on a personal level from working together for years. Likewise, some companies sometimes go to a consultant as the first course of action when faced with a challenge. These, along with those discussed in Chapter 5, are not OK reasons to hire a consultant. However, there are legitimate reasons for a large company to hire consultants, which we discuss throughout this chapter.

---

[1] U.S. Census, 2008; http://www.census.gov/econ/smallbus.html.

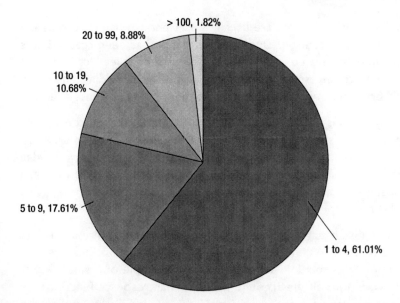

Figure 6-1. Number of employees per U.S. company

Another category is comprised of the group that has more than twenty employees but less than one hundred. This is the group that is most likely in need of consulting help. For these organizations, the lack of resources to employ full-time employees for certain skills, can be a problem that consultants can help solve. In small companies like these, it is impossible to have all of the necessary skills for all business situations.

Companies with fewer than twenty employees may also hire consultants for good reasons. Such companies are, however, less desirable customers for a consultant because they may not have deep-enough pockets to pay for a consultant over the long term. These companies may be more price sensitive because of the pure economics of their business. Since consultants tend to focus on the other groups when looking for work, we will focus on them when talking about consultants. But, the tools and techniques discussed in this book can be applied regardless of your company size if you decide that you need to explore hiring a consultant.

One of the keys to business success is identifying when your company has needs outside of its own capabilities. Since companies with between 20 and 100 employees are typically built by sole proprietors or partners, these owners tend to be confident in their capabilities. After all, to start a successful company, the owner has had to learn multiple skills and put in the long hours and hard work necessary to succeed. To admit to a weakness or a lack of skill within the organization may be difficult for the business owner who "did it all himself."

However, small business owners are usually smart enough to see, eventually, that a problem needs attention. Once this realization has been reached, it is time to come up with a plan to solve the problem. Business leaders then have to choose either to invest in current employees by providing additional training or to bring in temporary resources to meet those business needs.

There are many reasons why consultants are hired. In most cases, consultants are assisting with the "survival skills" mentioned in Chapter 5—IT, marketing, strategy, and the like. In that chapter, we stressed that it is never a good idea to hire a consultant to supply a survival skill. However, the reality is that, in a smaller company, it is often less expensive to hire a consultant than to have a dedicated full-time employee.

If the missing skill is an ongoing need, you absolutely need to hire a full-time employee or develop a current employee. This is why in small businesses, one person often performs multiple survival tasks. An example of this is a front-office person who does all the accounting and human resource functions for the organization. Even in larger companies, the owner likely handles the strategy, marketing, and sales functions.

One such organization is in Ravenna, Ohio. The owner is a technically skilled person who can operate a blow molding machine to make good-quality hollow plastic components. He started the business by getting some necessary equipment and selling his services to a company with whom he had a prior relationship. Initially, the owner held every position in the company, including engineering, plant management, accounting, human resources, purchasing, and sales.

This is typical. However, as the company grew, the owner found it necessary not only to hire low-wage employees to trim the plastic components, but also to invest in other skills. For example, he hired a setup technician and bought office equipment to help manage the other functions. Even though he and his technician are highly skilled, and the company has a few years of success behind it, the owner will probably need to bring in consulting help to improve his business. Later, he may need help with inventory management, sales strategy, or predictive maintenance. Since the company has only a few employees, in order to move forward, a consultant or a new hire will likely be necessary.

To repeat: consultants should not be brought in for the long haul. If they are, then they begin to replace survival skills. Instead, they should be hired occasionally for short-term projects—to get the company over the "humps" of growth. Once revenues increase, you should hire employees with the survival skills your business needs.

▓ **Tip** Businesses on the upswing can make good use of consultants to set up systems that will accommodate future growth.

Example: Companies Too Small for Full-Time Trainers

Some very specialized skills, like sales training, are hard to maintain in most organizations. All companies rely on their salespeople to drive business volume, and it is imperative that even seasoned sales professionals regularly get training in the latest, proven sales techniques. As a result, even seasoned sales people need to get continuing education. Though they may have impressive experience, they can become ineffective due to antiquated skills and false assumptions about what customers need. Also, what is perceived as acceptable sales ethics and techniques changes over the years.

On average, the top 20 percent of any sales force generates 62 percent of a company's revenue. What is more, Accenture estimated that, in 2009, 51 percent of salespeople failed to meet their quotas.2 Thus, sales training must be given to both incoming and seasoned sales reps. Table 6-1 shows that, for a company to break even when hiring a full-time sales trainer, the sales force needs to total more than forty-two people. (This assumes average training costs and salaries.) Typically, to have a sales force as large as forty-two, the company would have more than a few hundred employees. According to the 2008 census, only about 0.15 percent of companies are this large.

This analysis assumes that the sales trainer performs only sales training, yet this is the case only in very large companies. In medium-size companies, the sales trainer would perform multiple roles, such as sales supervision, evaluation, support, and even possibly some sales duties. However, if the sales trainer is hired to perform multiple jobs, then this staffer could train fewer salespeople. Therefore, most companies are better served using a qualified consultant to perform sales training. (The exception is a company that only performs sales activities or primarily performs only sales activities.)

Even larger companies may find it difficult to hire a full-time person to perform sales training. Moreover, if you hire a full-time employee, there is the risk that the training will not yield the desired results. It is much easier to find another consultant than to hire a new employee.

---

[2] Accenture, "Sales Competency, Behavior and Personality: An Integrated Approach to Improving Sales Force Performance," 2009; http://www.accenture.com/SiteCollectionDocum ents/PDF/Accenture_Sales_Competency_Behavior_and_Personality.pdf.

Many trainers have come out of the human resources fields and will, therefore, have virtually no university-level sales training and possibly little sales experience. Thus, full-time sales trainers tend not to be abreast of the latest sales theories. Once again, this shows the need to recruit a consultant, even though this advice goes against our principle of not using a consultant when a full-time employee can do the job. There are times when the applicant pool does not include qualified candidates; in these cases, it is okay to hire a consultant, preferably in the short term, to ensure that you get the right person to do the job.

Table 6-1. Yearly Sales Training Costs

Sales Force Size	Cost of Fully Loaded Sales Trainer	Cost of Sales Consulting	Cost Difference
20	$83,200	$40,000	($43,200)
40	$83,200	$80,000	($3,200)
60	$83,200	$120,000	$36,800
80	$83,200	$160,000	$76,800
100	$83,200	$200,000	$116,800
120	$83,200	$240,000	$156,800
140	$83,200	$280,000	$196,800
160	$83,200	$320,000	$236,800
180	$83,200	$360,000	$276,800
200	$83,200	$400,000	$316,800
220	$83,200	$440,000	$356,800
240	$166,400	$480,000	$313,600
260	$166,400	$520,000	$353,600
280	$166,400	$560,000	$393,600
300	$166,400	$600,000	$433,600

We used sales training as an example, but this phenomenon is common across all company functions in all industries. Certain professionals, such as those in healthcare, quality control, and project management, require continuing education from approved training sources to maintain their credentials. Many other professions could benefit from such continuing education rules, as well.

When companies identify their critical needs, a cost/benefit analysis similar to the one for sales training can be performed. Smaller companies should not forgo training just because they cannot afford a permanent resource. In such situations, it is appropriate for these companies to include an annual consulting budget for professional education.

Example: Market Research

Another common need for companies is market research. It is a common skill used to effectively develop new products and services that will sell well. And if a company does not understand its customers, it is nearly impossible to develop the right strategies.

The costs of hiring a firm to conduct market research surveys versus hiring a full-time employee are shown in Table 6-2. This is another example of when quantitative analysis can be used to decide whether to hire a consultant or a full-time employee. Less sophisticated companies may perform market research using local focus groups or by talking to loyal customers via social media or online surveys. This is ineffective, however, because it ignores people who are currently not customers. Instead, the company should utilize methodologies to find out why the non-consumers do not buy the company's products and services. Because market research is a difficult skill to get right, even though it is a survival skill, companies may choose to hire a consultant rather than get a full-time employee.

▓ **Tip** If you cannot afford a full-time employee or have a hard time finding someone with the right skills, hire a consultant.

Table 6-2. Market Research Survey Breakeven

Company Size	Cost of Fully Loaded Market Research Employee	Consulting Costs	Cost Difference
20	$65,000	$25,000	($40,000)
40	$65,000	$50,000	($15,000)
60	$65,000	$75,000	$10,000
80	$65,000	$100,000	$35,000
100	$130,000	$125,000	($5,000)
120	$130,000	$150,000	$20,000
140	$130,000	$175,000	$45,000
160	$130,000	$200,000	$70,000
180	$195,000	$225,000	$30,000
200	$195,000	$250,000	$55,000
220	$195,000	$275,000	$80,000
240	$195,000	$300,000	$105,000
260	$260,000	$325,000	$65,000
280	$260,000	$350,000	$90,000
300	$260,000	$375,000	$115,000

To Fill a Skill Gap for Which an Employee Can Be Trained

Companies often hire consultants to build capability in their organizations that will change how they operate. The sales training example just described could be used here, as well. Previously, we discussed the cost/benefit trade-offs relating to company size. Here, we show the benefit of using a consultant to transfer knowledge to the company, and then leave so the company can prosper on its own. The math may not work out in the short term, but it does in the long term because the company gains requisite skills to prosper without further consulting help.

As noted, *sales training* is an important need for companies, but the majority of companies cannot afford to hire a full-time, qualified trainer. However, competency in sales can be improved through sales training, making the choice to hire a consultant a wise one. The consultant comes in and passes skills along to the employees that, ideally, then transfer those skills to the company for the long term. Then, perhaps a special incentive could be offered to a senior sales person who had been through the training, to perform the sales training own their own.

Similarly, many consultants offer training in *specialized business skills*. The Lean Six Sigma training and consulting markets alone are estimated to be between $200 and $300 million per year. Lean Six Sigma is a specialized skill set that is serviced by a relatively small network of professionals. When you include specialized training in Lean or Six Sigma tools, this market would likely be closer to $500–$600 million. These numbers reflect a reality: organizations have identified skill gaps in important areas within their operations and have turned to consultants to fill them for the short term.

Another example is *forecasting*. Many software vendors offer forecasting modules to assist companies in developing models to develop budgets and staffing needs. Most organizations, for example, build forecasts by relying on past performance figures, to which they add arbitrary increases of a few percentage points in certain categories. Others use more sophisticated algorithms to generate their forecasts. Conversely, they may base their revenue forecasts on the sales force's instincts. Using these methods, more often than not the companies fail to meet their projections.

This is unfortunate, because ineffective forecasting leads to inaccurate budgeting. Inaccurate budgeting leads to drastic measures, such as layoffs or price changes, or ultimately to the end of the business. Even though most business leaders understand this fact, it is astonishing that many do no more than hope or pray that they will reach their forecasted sales goals.

Good forecasting requires high-level skills in statistics—knowledge that most business people do not have. For small to medium companies, these survival skills can be trained by an external person until an employee shows adequate competence. Smart business people eventually realize they need to reach outside of the organization for help in developing their forecasts. This is one of those skill-building services for which consultants provide good value.

A good forecast, of course, requires more than solid statistical analysis; you also need specialized industry skills. For instance, a consumer products company may need to look at industry trends, promotions, and product placements in order to build and revise sales forecasts. A custom-manufacturing organization may build forecasts based on the forecasts of loyal customers, plus a reasonable estimate of new business gained through the sales efforts. Service organizations may build forecasts based upon the populations they serve and changing economic conditions. Understanding the intricacies of each industry takes a great deal of experience. Even though forecasting is normally a science, this is where science meets art. Even if forecasters are trained in statistical analysis, they will not be truly effective until they gain enough experience to grasp the instinctual part of the job.

Many organizations lack the skills required to make effective forecasts, so hiring a consultant a good choice here. The consultant works on the statistical aspects of the forecast, while the employee focuses on gaining the experience to improve the accuracy. By investing in consulting to take care of the first half of the equation, you can set your forecaster up for success and continuous improvement.

Supply chain management is yet another example of a skill for which a company can look outside its borders for short-term assistance. Supply chain management means many things to many different organizations, but in most cases it encompasses purchasing, vendor management, warehouse organization, warehouse management, logistics, and inventory management. Consultants can help train workers in each area.

Warehouses, for example, are often managed by people who started as warehouse workers. Through their hard, loyal work, they were promoted into positions of management; however, they may not be aware of warehouse management best practices or how to utilize tools that can improve efficiencies and reduce inventory loss. Then, there are managers who are willing to employ new technologies, but who may overpay for an ineffective solution. For this reason, a supply chain consultant can help build competence internally. This competence can help identify a supply chain vision and develop a strategy, build implementation plans, and establish continuous-improvement efforts. The consultant can then leave and let the business be successful on its own.

Software training is another skill area that can benefit from a consultant's contribution. There is a mix of providers in this area. Some consultants are hired for software setup or user training; often they are simply employees of the software company. They help companies implement the software because the software may require an expert to configure and debug the installation. This is a great profit center for these companies. These consultants may be necessary because they promote user best practices and offer expertise in the software capability. They also show users techniques on how to utilize the software. When the trainer leaves, the employees understand how to get the most from the software and are in a position to show new users in the future. (Of course, the strength of any advice is a function of the competence and experience of the consultant, rather than a function of the software itself.

This is why you need to structure the relationship to ensure qualified resources—something we cover in later chapters.)

Another segment of the software training market is the independent market. These consultants may be implementation partners for software providers that do not implement their own software, such as SAP or Oracle ERP. They train organizations that have identified a market need for skills. Often these independent consulting organizations are often founded by former employees of the software company who use their familiarity with the software company to find clients. Some organizations train employees on how to use design software such as Pro Engineer, Catia, or Solidworks because the software is expensive and difficult to use. The amount of consulting business done by these software consultants is significant. They may also offer more general training, such as in Microsoft applications, and offer certificates for the training.

Other potential skills that can be trained by consultants include negotiation skills, environmental regulations, and government regulations. The point is that, if your business has a skill need that can be trained, then start looking for a consultant to infuse the necessary skill into your organization. The consultant's role is short term; he or she stays only until your employees gain the ability to do the work themselves.

Tip   Consultants are a great way to transfer skills into an organization and build employee capabilities.

The alternative to hiring a consultant to train certain skills is to develop people within the business to fill that role. An example of this is sending an employee for training at a college or obtaining a professional certification. However, if you take the consultant route, you need to ensure that you use a high-quality consultant. That way you do not waste money on training poor skills. The more popular a consulting need is, chances are the more consultants will be in the market. It is not possible that all these consultants have all the required credentials to perform well. Just as it is rare to find a full-time employee with a statistics degree, so it is rare to find a consultant with one. However, consultants readily proclaim that they know how to perform forecasting.

In sum, if there is a skill your business needs that is so specific it does not exist in any company, it will likewise be hard to find it in a consultant. Backgrounds and qualifications must be checked, as always. We will cover this and more in coming chapters to ensure you find the skills and abilities you need in consultants.

While Conducting a Search for a Full-Time Employee

You may decide that you have an immediate skill gap that will extend well into the future. However, you also know that it will not be easy to find a full-time employee quickly. This is often the case when a great deal of experience is needed. There are many consultants who will perform various functions for three to twelve months, while you look for a permanent employee.

For example, you may need someone to fill a financial position, such as a controller or chief financial officer. In fact, there are temp services with people who can provide many executive positions on a short-term basis while you locate candidates for a permanent position.

A longer-term, senior-level temp can also be useful for companies in transition, when the professional required to help transform the business is different from the type required to maintain the company.

A consultant can be a lifesaver when a key employee departs suddenly. A good example is what happened in 2009 after the stock market crashed. Large financial banks looked for people to blame; naturally, high-level financial positions were in the line of fire. Many people were fired quickly, often with no succession plans in place. But, a Fortune 500 bank cannot go without a CFO for long. That is why the consultant-as-temp option became a good idea.

Although many companies find this type of consultant necessary, it may not always be the best idea. As discussed in Chapter 2, interim managers have skills and experience. However, unless there is a plan to bring the consultant on full time or to use her to develop an employee, there will be no improvements during the interim. With a lack of permanency also comes a lack of accountability and a lack of commitment to the organization.

The upside to this method, nevertheless, is that the temporary employee sometimes becomes a permanent one. This trial period gives the company the opportunity to evaluate competence before committing to a full-time position. If the consultant does not work out, it is easy to get rid of the person at the end of the contract.

■ **Tip** When hiring a consultant to serve as an interim manager, look for someone who may be interested in the permanent position so the interim job can be an on-the-job interview.

When Your Employees and Existing Methods Fail to Find the Root Cause of the Problem

Businesses have limited resources, skills, and experiences. This is especially true in small to mid-size organizations. Sometimes, organizations run into a new problem that has not been faced by the current workforce and the root cause is not clear. Although people are problem solvers by nature, it can be difficult for those without exposure to different kinds of failure to identify the causes when failure occurs. Consultants offer the benefit of diverse experience through dealing with multiple companies, so they can help with root-cause analysis.

This legitimate reason to hire a consultant may also be a poor reason to do so, however. The difference between a good decision and a bad decision here depends on the problem. Every company should have at least one person skilled in root-cause analysis. If the consultant is hired because you do not have such a person, then it is a failure of management and not a good reason to hire the consultant. Even if the company is so small that a full-time professional is not necessary, arm a key person in the organization with the necessary skills.

If, however, the reason you lack a root-cause analysis of your business problem is a lack of experience with similar problems, then it is appropriate to hire a consultant. In other words, if your company is experiencing a unique problem it has never faced before, and there are consultants who have handled the same problem in the same area, then hiring a consultant is a wise idea. Remember, though, that outside help cannot replace the solid abilities of those in the company to diagnose the situation. Use the consulting engagement as a learning experience for people in your firm.

▓ **Note** If people in your company have analysis skills, use a consultant for root-cause analysis only when the problem is unique.

When Your Need Is Temporary

Companies in need of drastic change often bring in a consultant to implement the changes, realizing that the consultant need is not permanent. For example, organizations realize this need when they decide to implement a quality-management system. Quality managers are good at executing the requirements and specifications that have been clearly defined for them, but typically they are not good at thinking creatively and efficiently. This is one of the reasons Six Sigma is regarded as a quality tool while Lean is a management tool. In this situation, hiring a consultant on a six- to twelve-month contract helps in the implementation of a quality management system that is compliant with the desired standard. The risk here is that the consultant might not keep the implementation simple enough for the organization to be able to maintain compliance. This sometimes happens when the consultant lacks company knowledge or applies a preconceived notion of what a quality-management system should be rather than adhering to your specific requirements.

Another example of when a consultant is helpful on a short-term basis is the need for help with information technology. For good reason, information technology consulting is a large and growing segment of the consulting industry. And there are many niches within this segment. One such niche is the data security world. It is highly unlikely that an employee in any, but the largest of organizations would have the necessary experience to make an organization PCI or HIPAA compliant.

In information technology, there is also a need for consultants familiar with software that has recently been purchased. This could include customer relationship management (CRM), enterprise resource planning (ERP), electronic health record systems (EHR), and other enterprise-wide systems. As discussed earlier in this chapter, commonly these software systems include in the purchase price a consulting plan for implementation and employee training on the software. This is definitely a valid and necessary reason to hire a consultant.

Since information technology consulting is a growing segment and an expected part of a new software implementation, it is easy to get trapped in some non-value-added consulting. This is consulting designed purely to increase billable hours. As with any other type of consulting, you need to tie all consulting expenses to clear deliverables. Rather than make consultants account for time spent on the project, have them relate their time to set expectations or budgets for completing each action. When consultants are skilled in implementation, this is not an unreasonable expectation. They should have enough history on the time it takes to perform workflow analysis, for instance; the budget then shows that time allowance, but not in excess of the budget.

Another temporary need that consultants may provide includes focusing on improving operational efficiencies, safety practices, and human resource processes. The consultants who enjoy setting up these processes often get bored when it comes to maintaining the systems. Therefore, the initial setup is a perfect role for a consultant, who can provide great value to organizations in need of transition. In addition, since these transitions are typically culture changing, the consultant is more likely than the company's employees to have the skills to implement the initiatives. At the same time, the consultant can train those employees in the skills needed for making the improvements permanent.

Hiring consultants who specialize in change activities such as these are more expensive than accomplishing the change with traditional employees. Nevertheless, it is good value for companies to hire these change agents for a short period of time, rather than try to hire them for a permanent position that requires more mundane maintenance skills. One exception to this rule is when a large organization needs constant change to keep up with market changes. When a large organization is in this situation, it most likely makes sense not only to have one change agent fully employed in the company, but a whole team of these folks to drive improvements.

Be careful to use the "temporary" excuse only when your need for a consultant is truly temporary, and not when it fits one of the negative reasons explained in Chapter 5. For example, a company's executives could very easily say that they need to downsize. This will happen only once, so it *is* a temporary situation. However, there is nothing a consultant can tell a manager about downsizing that the manager does not (or should not) already know.

The consultant does not know the company or its people well enough to make sound recommendations. Anyone can come in, look at benchmarking reports, and tell you what the average number of employees per department is in a similar company. However, this speaks nothing to the actual needs, strengths, and weaknesses of the company. Then, when the consultant performs the firing, he is put into the role of bad guy, which is never wise. In short, temporary needs have to be some random skills that are not tied to the internal workings of the company and that you probably will not need again soon.

■ **Tip** Hire consultants for temporary needs, not when ongoing skills are needed.

When You Need a Breakthrough Change, or Creativity, Innovation, R&D, or Cross-Industry Fertilization

Consultants will sometimes be brought in to present fresh ideas. This is different from the "bad" example, presented in Chapter 5, of hiring someone to get objectivity. Here, the idea is to use a consultant to go way beyond objectivity and to generate tremendous breakthroughs.

An example of this service is HPI, Inc. HPI is a consulting company that serves hospitals to drive innovation in ways that employees think about safety, operations, and root-cause analysis. This organization is an innovator in the healthcare industry because it bases its methods on other industries. HPI's roots are in the nuclear power and airline industries, and it employs some of their best practices to achieve high reliability. For example, its consultants focus on preventing human errors by fixing system weaknesses that cause human errors. It says about itself, "HPI provides knowledge and a framework for improving and sustaining a culture of reliability that optimizes results in safety and performance."[3] This is both creative and innovative because it shows the application of proven methods in certain industries (nuclear power and airlines) into an industry drastically in need of change (healthcare).

Research-and-development companies and marketing companies also bring in consultants to help spawn fresh ideas, whether for new products or for different marketing campaigns. Since we know from the beginning of this chapter that most companies are small—fewer than 100 employees—having a pool of creative thinkers in the organization is cost-prohibitive. A consultant can, however, "specialize" in creativity, thereby adding value to a company that lacks this talent.

In the manufacturing industry, for example, there are many companies that specialize in this skill. Because companies that are driven by new product development on a rapid product life cycle rely on innovative ideas, it is often necessary to employ external design firms frequently to develop new ideas. This type of consulting is necessary because even the most creative employees become stale over time. By maintaining a relationship with a few creative consulting firms, the company gains an infusion of new ideas periodically, which can lead to more creativity within the full-time staff.

Exercise great caution, however, with this approach, for two reasons. First, when consultants come in to contribute fresh ideas, it is easy to have conflicts

---

[3] "ABOUT HPI: Healthcare Performance Improvement Making"; accessed November 2012, http://hpiresults.com/index.php/intro/who-we-are.

over who owns the ideas. Your contracts need to ensure that the company owns all the ideas generated. Second, creative consultants are just that: creative. They do not understand the company's strategy, customers, competitors, or even the industry. They can suggest great ideas, but you must vet those ideas. No one should ever be innovative simply for the sake of being innovative. If you have a great product and loyal customers, there is likely no reason to change, even if your competition is changing. Consider all innovations within the greater scope of your strategic goals for the company.

When You Need Someone with a Highly Specialized Skill

Many times, the skills or tangible resources your business lacks are so specialized that it does not make sense to hire someone to gain those skills. For example, if you are creating a product that carries a ten-year warranty for the customer, you need to make sure the product will last that long. This may mean testing a variety of factors to ensure reliability. For instance, if you need accelerated weathering conditions to test the product's durability would be when exposed to the outdoor conditions, a consultant may be the best option. A company that produces hundreds of millions or billions of dollars of merchandise that needs such testing might invest in the technology. For the other 98 percent of companies, it makes sense to hire a consultant to perform this service.

A decent quality weathering machine typically costs between $10,000 and $50,000. Then, once it is purchased, there is a long calibration process involved. First, the actual product must be set outside in normal conditions to assess how much weathering occurs naturally over the course of twelve months. Then, the equipment must run several samples, which simulate the weathering of twelve months outdoors. Then, these samples are compared to make sure the equipment is working properly to calibrate performance versus real environmental factors. Since weather that is experienced through natural exposure takes longer to affect products than accelerated weathering, validating the use of the equipment to ensure results would take years.

In addition to the capital cost for the equipment, there is a significant cost in learning how to use it. A company that produces hundreds of millions or billions of dollars of merchandise that needs testing such as accelerated weathering may invest in the technology. For the other 98 percent of companies, it makes sense to hire a consulting company that owns the equipment to perform this service.

Another example of a specific skill is related to parts of information technology. Certain niche businesses will not have a large enough employee pool to contain individuals capable of handling particular information-technology matters. Or, the volume of work may require only 24 hours of work per week, versus 40, so a full-time employee would be underused. For example, managing an RFID inventory system might well be a part-time job. Although this technology is not new, it has not grown to the point where companies will typically keep full-time people internally to maintain RFID. Thus, hiring a consultant to perform this specific service makes sense.

Environmental factors in business might also call for the work of consultants. Typically, there are no employees with the experience necessary to drive regulatory compliance and/or save money through improved resource utilization. Companies sometimes hire auditors, consultants, or attorneys experienced with environmental matters to do a gap analysis and to develop action plans to reach minimum performance standards. This might include things like ISO 14001 compliance, where just a few companies specialize. These consultants help develop necessary processes to maintain a minimum level of performance and enable your company to be audited to the standard successfully. In addition to environmental compliance, there are regulations that must be met, such as storm water compliance, proper disposal of chemicals, or compliance with air-quality regulations. Maintaining regulatory compliance may be a moving target as standards change, and it often is better to have an ongoing relationship with consultants who specialize in this skill than to try to maintain the skill internally.

There are many situations involving these difficult-to-find skills for which consulting is a positive option. As discussed in Chapter 5, the trick to finding out whether it is an appropriate decision to hire a consultant or a better decision to maintain an internal resource is deciding whether the skill is a long-term "survival skill." If you will need someone with that skill over the long term, a consultant is not the right choice unless your intent is to convert the consultant to a full-time employee. As always, you must assess the ROI. Typically, with the types of specialized consultants discussed here, there are large barriers to entry, such as expensive equipment or extensive training, so having the skill or equipment in house is not possible.

▓ **Tip**   When hiring a consultant to gain a specialized skill, ensure that the person can prove that he or she actually has the skill.

When You Need an Objective or Anonymous Opinion

Many times, consultants are brought in because a company needs an objective or anonymous opinion. This legitimate reason to hire a consultant is also one of the most abused reasons. Business leaders who are unsure of which direction to take may reach out to a consultant for fresh ideas. For companies stuck in a rut, this is an acceptable strategy to initiate effective change—if the right consultant is picked. The consultant is free of internal politics, which leads to a more impartial opinion.

One purpose for bringing in such consultants is to analyze the current operation and interview employees, helping define what changes are necessary. They may also be asked to validate what the business leaders have been thinking, usually in a "Does this make sense?" way. But, this is where the opportunity for abuse exists. We discussed this in Chapter 5, but basically, when the need for validation is real, there is a good reason for bringing in help. However, when the manager or leader is too scared of the employees to implement unpopular change without an excuse of blaming a consultant, then hiring the consultant is a bad idea. Instead, the business should replace the manager or leader.

There is sometimes a need for anonymity or confidentiality, such as in new-product development. By the nature of this type of consulting business, these consultants are sworn to keep the confidence of the client. Other times, the company is conducting an executive search or pursuing an acquisition, and this requires secrecy. For instance, private equity firms and holding companies are famous for using consultants to validate their executive hiring choices. They may bring in consultants from multiple disciplines to do a full evaluation and recommend the best candidates.

We were once brought into a large company to perform a complete assessment of the sales force. We looked at factors such as ethics, deviance, conflicts with managers, communications, and feelings about the managers, company, and job. It would have been virtually impossible for management to interview every employee and solicit both positive and negative feedback. However, knowing that the results were going back to the management in aggregate, anonymous form, we found the employees to be surprisingly open.

Consultants are sometimes asked to validate an opinion regarding an acquisition. As with executive hiring, private equity and holding companies will almost certainly utilize a consultant network to evaluate potential acquisitions. They look for hidden value within the prospective company and want to avoid major risks in the acquisition. Consultants in this case will probably include disciplines such as human resources to evaluate company culture and personnel issues. Consultants are also hired in this case to ensure property to be acquired hold no environmental hazards or violations. An accounting consultant may be used to validate the financial profile of the acquisition. For a manufacturing organization, there may be a need for an operations consultant to look for errors in the current processes to identify opportunities for creating value through improvement.

In a typical acquisitions situation, multiple consultants are necessary. Using consultants to validate the business decision is, therefore, often legitimate. All of these reasons for an objective opinion are valid and necessary to ensure good decisions are made. In most cases, confidentiality is extremely important, and it can be easier to keep something secret if it is managed outside the company. When these good reasons are replaced with using the consultant to make the business case for the management or be a fall guy for an unpopular choice, company resources are wasted, and suboptimal results are obtained.

You Require Professional Expertise Like Compliance or Auditing

All industries have their own requirements to meet, such as regulations and statutory standards. In the manufacturing sector, these may include the ISO 9000 family of standards, used to design quality-management systems that ensure customer needs are met. The standards, in this case, are published by the International Organization for Standardization.

Third-party certification bodies confirm that organizations meet the requirements of ISO 9001 in order for a company to claim ISO 9001 certification. Over a million organizations worldwide have been independently certified. This simple standard also sets the framework for other certification standards that are industry specific. Thus, ISO 9001 has been applied to many types of organizations and is not limited to manufacturing organizations. Due to its design, it can be used universally to improve operations in nearly any industry.

One industry that developed its own standard based upon the ISO 9000 series is the automotive industry. The automotive standard, TS 16949, provides more specific requirements governing process control, design, service, and supply chain management. A separate group of consulting organizations serves as third-party certification bodies for TS16949. These firms probably will also certify to ISO 9001, but the reverse is not necessarily true. Other industry-specific examples are AS 9100, which was designed for the aerospace industry, and ISO 14001, which is for environmental management systems.

The healthcare industry has two main types of accreditation. The first, based on the ISO 9001 standard, is the NIAHO. This has been used to accredit acute-care and critical-access hospitals and was approved by the U.S. Centers for Medicare and Medicaid Services (CMS). Prior to this decision, the Joint Commission was the only approved source for accreditation. Both sets of standards require audits for compliance, although the NIAHO standard is geared more toward the process, like an ISO standard, than is the Joint Commission, which has more prescriptive requirements.

In these industries, it is often necessary to draw upon experts to help guide you towards compliance. In most cases, the companies that offer these certification services are not permitted to perform consulting services for those companies that they certify. This is due to a perceived and likely conflict of interest. For this reason, there is a large network of consultants that assist companies in complying with these standards. These services may be as simple as offering training or as involved as independent auditing in preparation for the certification audit.

These consultants sometimes develop the company's policy manual and the associated controls, too. However, companies should create their own policies and procedures that are representative of the company's practices. Often, when a consultant is brought in to develop a system, the result is a copy of a previously successful system with just a company name change. In fact, this is the major risk in using consultants for this type of service. To get full value of these standards, and not just a stamp of approval, the document processes should be tailored to your company's specific operating methods so that employees can find it easy to comply with policy.

Summary

Although consultants are often brought in for entirely wrong reasons, there are legitimate reasons to hire a consultant. These reasons are listed at the beginning of this chapter, and each has been discussed here, with examples. There are of course other potential reasons that business leaders must consider. If faced with a reason for a consultant outside of the list above, consider the reasons not to hire a consultant from Chapter 5. If the reason is similar to any reason in that chapter, consider other options.

CHAPTER

7

Selection
Finding the Right Consultant

Most consulting relationships have an inherent conflict of interest. . . . On one hand, consultants strive to solve their clients' problems. On the other, they hope to extend the relationship as long as possible, so they come up with solutions just fast enough to keep the client happy, but no faster.

—Patrick Schwerdtfeger

With so many consultants available in the market to solve a multitude of problems, there are likely both high-quality and low-quality suppliers. The quote from Schwerdtfeger represents the latter type. Unfortunately, with little industry-wide quality control in place, there is no reliable way to tell the difference. Managers often have less experience in developing the relationships with consultants than the consultants do. So, in the request for proposal, interview, and contract stages, the consultant most definitely has the advantage.

Even though the consulting industry has grown over the past few decades, many people have developed mistrust when it comes to consultants. An empirical study conducted by Ed Delany shows that 59 percent of chief executive officers said that the consultant they hired made no difference.[1] In contrast, only 2 percent of the chief executive officers said the consultant had a major influence.

With these results, it makes us wonder why anyone would ever hire a consultant. In reality, as we discussed in Chapter 6, there are many times when hiring a consultant is a good idea. Some of the poor results can be

[1] Ed Delany, "Strategy Consultants—Do They Add Value?" *Long Range Planning* 28, no. 6 (1995): 99–106.

attributed to the fact that the consultant should not have been hired, but the rest reflect poor hiring and poor management practices.

Likewise, some consultants are good at showing results that do not actually exist; this leads to the illusion of success that creates a happy customer blissfully ignorant of the real return on investment.

Our qualitative study of industry leaders who have dealt with consultants showed that over half of those surveyed were happy with the results. Yet only 15 percent of respondents had actually conducted an ROI analysis of the project.

We believe this to be representative of how many businesses structure the consulting relationship, from their selection of consultant to completion of the project; they simply do not watch the results closely. Without first agreeing on how success will be measured and establishing a baseline, the consultant finds it easy to claim great success when the result has actually been failure. In other words, if you tell a consultant to do X, Y, and Z, and X, Y, and Z get done, it is easy to feel satisfied. The X, Y, and Z may have been vague, unnecessary goals, but that does not determine satisfaction in this case.

Satisfaction should be based on real financial gain, as well as a host of other quantitative and qualitative measures. If achievement of these are not measured, you cannot assess the achievement. Therefore, it is important to establish specific guidelines and metrics ahead of time.

When you are hiring a consultant, there are many methods you can use to pick a specific consultant. By understanding these methods, you will be better prepared to select the right consultant. We begin this chapter by showing what is actually done inside companies when they hire consultants. We finish by showing what *should* be done and the advantages and disadvantages of such decisions. The chapter also discusses what you should do to hire a consultant who will generate a real ROI improvement that benefits your firm financially.

Processes to Select Consultants

The study we conducted for this book (described in Chapter 1) sheds interesting light on some of the issues involved in the selection of consultants. The first question we asked was an open-ended one about the process itself and the reasons a certain consultant was selected. Surprisingly, even though the question was completely open ended, only three themes emerged. Table 7-1 shows the main processes used for consultant selection.

The first of these processes is based on specific metrics associated with a lengthy request-for-proposal (RFP) process. This is the way consultants *should* be selected. However, only 34.43 percent of the firms surveyed utilized the metrics and RFPs. The firms that did use a series of metrics and RFPs were primarily those looking for consultants in information technology, business process reengineering, and project management. When companies take on these tasks, it is pretty common to follow the RFP process. This is because these functions tend to be more analytical, and there is a history of using analytical means of hiring in these sectors. However, all firms need to establish metrics and calculate ROI prior to hiring. This process is described later in this chapter.

Table 7-1. Consultant Selection Process

Process to Select Consultant	Percent using method/ factor
1. Selection was based on certain metrics and a lengthy RFP process	34.43%
2. Upper management made the decision to choose a consultant (random selection, or management selected and interviewed)	29.51%
3. No selection process	36.06%

■ **Tip** Always, always, always establish goals and measures that will allow you to objectively assess consultants' work.

The second major process was for upper management to make a seemingly random selection of potential consultants based on interviews. In fact, 29.51 percent of firms used this arbitrary method. This partly explains the success of dysfunctional consultants. As our study showed, if a consultant was arbitrarily selected by management, there was an 11.1 percent chance that the firm would be satisfied with the consultant. More important, though, 88.9 percent of respondents were *not* satisfied. If the data are entered into a regression analysis, there is a negative, and significant, relationship between management selection and satisfaction. This means that management selection without quantitative process equals poor results. Figure 7-1 maps out the poor decisions involved when you arbitrarily hire a consultant.

The lack of structure for both the selection of consultants to be considered and the methods to evaluate them leads to unnecessary variation in potential results. Upper management likely selects the pool from a few sources, including their own business networks, including past coworkers and acquaintances from other companies.

Another potential source is random searching for the consultant. When a specific need is defined, such as a quality-system implementation, upper management may not have the required network relationships for such leads, so a Google search may be the primary tool for finding consultants. The third major source of the consulting pool may be the advice of other consultants. For example, consultants brought in to fill a specific need will often identify other opportunities for improvement that make hiring a second consultant necessary. The original consultant may "know someone who can do this" and bring in a friend for the company to hire to handle the second problem.

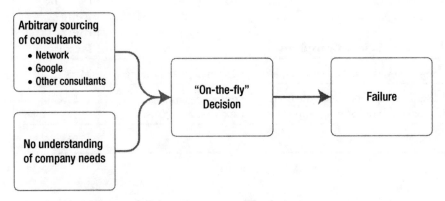

Figure 7-1. Arbitrary sourcing of consultants.

Even if the pool of potential consultants is good, management might not understand their company's needs. Without a thorough understanding of these needs, an appropriate selection metrics cannot be set. As is discussed later in this chapter, any good RFP process begins by surveying everyone involved in the project to assess needs. A step like this rarely occurs when decisions are arbitrary.

As for the third process for finding and choosing a consultant—that being no method whatsoever—we found that companies were rarely happy with the results. In this case, they got exactly what they deserve.

Criteria to Select Consultants

In our study, we asked the companies that did use a process to tell us the criteria they employed to select the consultant. We discovered that these companies used an average of three criteria to select the consultant—with word of mouth, cost, and consultant experience in the area being the top three factors. Using a linear regression analysis, we found that none of the factors, as shown in Table 7-2, had a significant impact on satisfaction results, except for selection based on management decision. (As mentioned earlier, selection based on management decision had a significant negative correlation.)

This means that no one factor affected the consultant results, with the exception of management decision. This is not surprising, since often it is lower-level company workers who directly interact with the consultant. Having senior executives, who may not work daily with the consultant, decide on hiring a specific consultant makes little sense. If a more detailed, criteria–based decision is made, it is likely the consultant will meet the needs of the workers.

The criteria-based process should include input from workers, so that selection is based on factors that workers believe will lead them to success. Also, including the workers in the selection process may ultimately help with their willingness to change. By providing initial input into the selection, these folks are psychologically bound to the consultant's success. Workers are more likely not to fight change introduced by the consultant and also will share ideas with the consultant that might yield success on the project.

Tip When devising the selection criteria, always include input from the workers who are affected by the consultant's recommendations.

Not including the input of affected workers likely leads to ineffective selection criteria. Since only 34 percent of firms used any selection process, only a maximum of 34 percent could have surveyed their workers and followed correct RFP development procedures. Nevertheless, our study, and some other larger studies discussed later, found that some of the selection criteria many companies use are not entirely reliable. If only 34 percent used any process at all, and some of this group used faulty criteria, then maybe only about 20 percent of companies actually selected consultants based on reliable criteria. Even when companies try to do the right thing, what actually happens when they select consultants is likely very different from what should have been done.

Table 7-2. Consultant Selection Factors

Factors used in the selection	Percent using method/ factor
Selected based on word of mouth or comments from colleagues	49.18%
Selection based on cost/competitive bidding	47.54%
Consultant level of experience in specific area needing consulting	44.26%
Consultant level of experience in total years	37.70%
Consultant level of experience in same industry	31.15%
Selection based on prior relationship (used the same consultant before)	27.87%
Consultant's education or accreditation	19.67%
Consultant's availability	9.84%

Word of Mouth

Due to the lack of quality control within the consulting industry, word of mouth is likely the most effective selection factor. There are really no viable options, no sources of consultant reviews. There are no "Angie's List" or *Consumer Reports* for the consulting industry.

Likewise, despite the enormous size of the consulting industry, there are no large, independent groups that rate and evaluate consultants. This means that the consultant's reputation for a skill in a specific functional area, which is typically passed along by word of mouth, is what drives clients to select certain consultants. Word of mouth is a huge driver of business for technical consulting companies that have a good reputation in that industry.

In the plastics injection-molding industry, for example, this is the reason Andy Routsis or William Tobin do not lack for work. They have a solid reputation, so when someone wants training or consulting, their names top the list of people that companies want to interview.

The reputation of a consultant in a specific functional area works great when the skill is specific, but for more general consulting skills, such as business process reengineering, there are not many famous professionals to call upon. Thus, in terms of word of mouth, if a consultant is truly effective and has high satisfaction rates with customers, then this method will likely lead to success—

assuming you have done your homework and provided specific, measurable goals. However, if the consultant is skilled in spinning the outcome of projects to make them look more successful than they are, then the word-of-mouth method can lead to hiring an ineffective consultant.

Using word of mouth as your selection tool is somewhat scary, considering the results of our research. Remember that, in our qualitative study, over half of those companies surveyed were happy with the results of their consulting experiences, while only 15 percent had conducted an ROI analysis. Therefore, one of your trusted colleagues could tell you that she had an extremely satisfying consulting experience when, in reality, that experience was based on no real improvement. Therefore, if a colleague recommends a consultant, your questions should include:

- "Why were you satisfied?"
- "What was that satisfaction based upon?"
- "Was an ROI conducted?"
- "How?"

Even when a consultant comes with recommendations from others or from your industry as a whole, you should evaluate that consultant carefully. Evaluate them on a few factors selected from an accurate and extensive needs analysis, then compare the proposals from each of the consultants you are considering to ensure consistency in their analyses of your situation.

In short, word of mouth can be a reliable process when the recommendation comes from someone who has used well-defined criteria to evaluate that consultant's work, such as an ROI analysis verified with standard accounting methods. The analysis should also have looked at how well the consultant worked in the organization, including a 360° evaluation of the consultant by those who worked on the project team. Only by having used structured evaluation methods, after completion of the project, will that client be able to verify consultant success.

■ **Tip** Do a consulting engagement "postmortem" to verify that the consultant succeeded in reaching goals and also worked well with your employees.

One of us had an illuminating experience. A company created a project team to evaluate potential software vendors for a large project. The team received proposals from various vendors and interviewed the references provided by each of them. This part of the process was designed to validate the information provided by those who submitted proposals. One of the references we questioned was a loyal and happy customer of both the software vendor and its preferred implementation consultant company.

We asked structured questions to determine why this was a happy customer. For example, we asked whether the project ended on budget. Another question we asked was whether the project was completed on time. The answers were negative in both cases. Our potential vendor knew it had been over budget and timeline, but still decided to use the reference. Likewise, the customer (reference) spoke highly of the consulting firm even though it had not met the agreed-upon results. Why would a company recommend a vendor who ran over budget and did not complete the project on time? Why would a supplier use that company as a reference? Did it have that few happy customers? Why did the reference feel that the consultant was superior even given the lack of success?

The only logical answers to such questions are that few consultants are held accountable to the standards discussed in the proposal stage. Even worse, sometimes no standards are set. Obviously, it is easy to be satisfied when you do not have anything to base that satisfaction upon. As shocking as it may seem that a potential supplier would provide such a poor reference, it is even more shocking to know that the project team voted to choose that supplier. The result? The company's project did not get completed on time. When projects run beyond the original timeline, they also run over budget, as did ours.

Business leaders are often led astray by the advice of people they trust. Plus, it is difficult to see reality when decisions have already been made. Word-of-mouth many times creates a halo effect and leads decision makers to make a bad decision. Nonetheless, word of mouth is a necessity in the consulting industry since there are no real independent third-party reviewers. That makes it all the more important to verify consultants' results with references. But, even then, use third-party references as only a small bit of evidence in the process of hiring a consultant.

Cost

Of course, most businesses base consultant selection partly on the total cost of the project. This makes troubling the finding that only 15 percent of those surveyed actually had calculated a return on investment.

When an ROI analysis was conducted in advance, managers assessed the typical metrics, such as cost reduction or revenue increase. This finding makes much of the satisfaction data in our study, or in any other study on consulting questionable. If you have not calculated an ROI, how do you know if you have increased gains or reduced costs? We found, in contrast, that when an ROI analysis was conducted, executives were significantly more likely to be satisfied with the results.

What would move an executive to use lowest cost as the selection criterion and *not* conduct an ROI analysis? Perhaps the decision maker assumes that the return will be achieved through qualitative methods such as employee satisfaction or quantitative methods that do not include finances, such as adherence to timeline or completion of agreed-upon tasks.

In our study, selection based on cost or competitive bidding meant that the company typically used the consultant that provided the lowest cost. When the cost is too high, it is difficult to create a positive return on investment. Also, there is no correlation between cost and quality of the consultant. For example, large firms tend to be pricier; that does not mean that they are better or worse than smaller firms.

In the case of market research, for example, a low-cost provider can come in and administer some surveys, and create some analyses composed of mostly frequencies and averages, without even having a statistics degree. Therefore, a person deficient in statistical abilities could offer services at a low cost, but would not provide any real information to the firm. A firm is likely to pay much more for someone with graduate-level marketing and statistics training. Yet even in this case, costs may vary—university professors with such skills often do these projects for much less than would a typical consulting firm. Professors, after all, do not have the large overhead for running their own businesses, and they typically do only two or three consulting projects a year. They consider it extra income and a way to stay in touch with the community, likely charging fairly reasonable rates.

This does not imply that all professors would make good consultants, however. Some are horrible, some are great, and some are everything in between. The point is that cost alone is a horrible criterion for deciding which consultant a firm should hire. Once an ROI analysis is conducted and is found to be positive, cost should not be considered further. That is, of course, unless two potential consultants are equal in everything *except* cost.

Experience

The consultant's experience level in a specific area is the third most prevalent of the selection criteria that companies use. Experience can be an indicator of quality, but not necessarily. Many of us have worked with people who have decades of experience, but they produce little results. Why should consultants be much different? Experience can be a hindrance, for example, when methods such as technology improvements have changed the way tasks are performed. It is often the less experienced, but highly skilled consultants, managed by seasoned professionals, who obtain the best results.

An example of how experience can lead to poor results is found in plastics manufacturing. The plastics injection-molding industry has been around for decades. The initial process included using mechanical gauges for pressure and temperature for control. In this environment, the worker with the best instincts often yielded the best results. Instincts are normally developed through experience, so experience was a key criterion when hiring a consultant to develop process control.

As the industry grew, however, machine controls became more automated and engineers developed in-depth knowledge of material behavior. Material suppliers developed higher-performing materials that led to more consistent results. The idea of scientific molding was created. This allowed for the development of mold designs that produced very little material waste. Computer programmers took this knowledge and created models to predict process behavior in product design and material selection variations. As technology levels continued to increase, industry gurus developed pressure and temperature sensors that could be used to control the machine without operator intervention. As these innovations progressed, the path by which a worker started as an entry-level laborer and progressed to a process expert disappeared.

Now the industry is led by engineers who often have less than twenty years' experience, but have training in the scientific techniques. Some of the more experienced workers have received continuing education to get up to speed on the latest technology. Instead of the most experienced worker being the most skilled, there is now a balance between experience and recent training that leads to career success. Workers with ten to twenty years of experience, combined with relevant training, are often the most valuable. Those who do not employ scientific techniques, but who have extensive experience, may be able to make a reasonably accurate guess when trying to solve a process problem. However, those who have both experience and trained skills can ensure results that are more accurate.

Therefore, when you go looking for a consultant with experience, be very careful to investigate that experience. Find out how much the industry has changed during the consultant's tenure, in terms of methods, processes, technology, tools, statistics, and general advancement. Many of the marketing and advertising campaigns around today, for example, are based on outdated models of advertising. It has been only a little over a decade since the emergence of the Internet, eight years since Facebook began, and five years since the first iPhone. These are just a few examples of radical change. It is impossible that any seasoned executive in any advertising firm would have grown up with the technologies that the market is currently using.

Experience can also cause consultants to become set in their ways. The longer someone has done something, the more likely the person will think he or she is doing it the "right" way. The person has been successful using these methods and continues to give believe habitual decisions and actions are appropriate.

Familiarity also breeds mindlessness. The more often we do something, the more likely we are to do the same thing on autopilot. Someone with much less experience is going to be more likely to examine things further and deeper, and not let preconceived notions affect his or her judgment. So, on one hand, experience is good; but in many other ways, experience can be a problem. When you hire a consultant, always consider your needs carefully and judge potential candidates based on these criteria. Experience may or may not be relevant.

Prior Relationship

The next selection criterion that is used to hire a consultant, as shown in our survey, is the existence of a prior relationship with the consultant. More than one-fourth of those surveyed picked a consultant they had used previously. This is similar is to using word of mouth as your selection criterion, only there may be a slightly greater risk. If the consultant is being brought back to work on the same process or project after the initial results could not be sustained, you may want to evaluate the effectiveness of that consultant. Otherwise, if the results previously obtained were successful and sustainable, then your selection based on a prior relationship could be an effective criterion. But beware: Some consultants are skilled in developing solutions that last long enough to keep the client happy, only to work with the client again after the original solution fails to sustain itself for the long term.

This mindset is similar to the planned obsolesce built into some manufacturing. America car manufacturers have become famous for constantly reengineering their products, sometimes with very minor changes, so that consumers need to trade in old vehicles to have the newest advances. Apple does this with the iPhone, too. There are not huge technological advancements with each successive model, but they are nonetheless able to get customers to line up overnight for the latest version. Similarly, some consultants get companies to produce just enough change so that the company almost becomes addicted to their services and needs to keep coming back for minor, incremental improvements.

You should not need to go back to a consultant to solve the same problem. To avoid this, have a plan as part of the overall consulting project to sustain changes that are implemented. The decision to rehire a consultant should then be contingent on the sustainability of the original solution.

Most of us have heard the expression that insanity is repeating the same behavior and expecting a different result. Equally, business insanity is hiring a consultant who failed to perform well in the first project and expecting a different result the second time around.

You may have a long-term relationship with a specific consultant or consulting firm. This is especially true for leaders who have developed a wide network over the years. As mentioned earlier, this is a great way to select a consultant because, prior to starting the project, you have a history and an understanding of how each other works. With this understanding, it is easier to structure the relationship for success. Even in this situation, though, you should follow a formal process of evaluation before proceeding. Even a known entity may not be the best consultant for every job. Consider your consultant acquaintances along with new ones; that ensures you get the best candidate for the job.

Education and Accreditation

Over 19 percent of the executives we surveyed used education or accreditation as a selection factor when hiring a consultant. The issue of education is an important one, but it is an uncertain criterion by which to evaluate a consultant's ability. On one hand, managers should always try to find the most educated consultant, in hopes that this education has transferred well to the consultant's abilities. On the other hand, a Harvard graduate with a master's degree in business administration is just as capable of making bad decisions as a community college graduate with an associate's degree in history. Even certifications in accounting, or other fields where certification is backed by quality criteria, cannot guarantee the competence of an individual. You have seen this yourself: employees with the same basic credentials often yield varying results. Why would consultants behave differently? Most consultants are people who were once employees similar to those you now manage.

Even greater risks are present when the education or certification is not regulated. For instance, the various Six Sigma certifications on the market have different levels of value. A black belt certification that is supposed to represent competence in process improvement, Six Sigma tools, and statistics for problem solving can be earned online by reviewing some materials and taking a test administered by certain universities. The total time required to obtain these online certifications can be as little as two hours. A legitimate, university-backed Six Sigma program takes four, forty-hour weeks and includes a project in which students make actual financial gains in a real company. Some organizations, such as the American Society for Quality, have made attempts to develop a certification program to ensure consistency and rigor across programs, but many people today have online black belts and have gained very little knowledge.

Regardless of the certification, or even the source of the certification, the quality of a consultant is directly tied to his or her past performance and experience, more than to qualifications. A Six Sigma professional's success is often affected by a few factors that need to be in place for success. These factors include quality training, whereby the consultant has shown competence in applying tools to achieve a quantifiable result to obtain certification. Additionally, there is an instinctual element to being a successful Six Sigma professional. Then there are many soft skills, such as a high emotional intelligence and skill in developing mutually beneficial relationships. In reality, in an area like Six Sigma, where the credentials are hard to verify, the best choice is based on references and proven project successes.

This issue extends well beyond Six Sigma programs. The Internet has a multitude of companies offering sales certifications, for example. Just as with Six Sigma, it is hard to imagine certifying someone in sales without having observed that person demonstrating sales skills, either in role-playing scenarios or in real-world coaching. Most of these certifications are awarded based on passing online, multiple-choice exams. Even worse, the programs frequently teach outdated, unethical subject matter such as the "assumptive close," the "puppy dog close," and the "continuous yes" close. These closing techniques emerged in the 1990s, and while they do work, they use psychological manipulation to get the sale. Someone professing to have the latest "sales techniques" has likely been trained in these outdated methodologies.

We believe that, as the consulting industry grows, more people will jump ship, leaving corporate America to become consultants, and they will use these online degrees to lend credibility. This is a huge threat to the industry. Online universities have flooded the market in recent years and have ramped up their advertising in an effort to attract students to their programs. Enrollment in these online courses increased 17 percent in the fall of 2008[2] with 25 percent of all students taking at least one online course. Some of these online programs never require a student to attend class. They offer a degree for a fee and

[2] Mark Parry, Mark, "Colleges See 17 Percent Increase in Online Enrollment," *Chronicle of Higher Education;* accessed 2010, http://chronicle.com/blogs/wiredcampus/colleges-see-17-percent-increase-in-online-enrollment/20820.

minimal work. Some even give their graduates an 800 number that the "student" can give to potential employers. When this 800 number is called, there are real people on the other end discussing the so-called rigors of the program, even though a student never went to class. These programs are extremely common in the MBA sector.

Even for the online programs and courses that are real, the legitimate accrediting body for the discipline does not generally accredit them. Even worse, some programs are accredited by questionable accrediting bodies that are popping up all over the world in an effort to make money from this online boom. It is very difficult for anyone outside of higher education to understand who the accrediting bodies are in each subject area.

For business degrees, for example, a program should be accredited by the Association to Advance Schools of Business (AACSB). In sales, the program should be a part of the University Sales Center Alliance (USCA). Accrediting agencies such as these ensure the rigors of the programs, the facilities and labs that the program has, the ethical nature of the subject matter, the subjects covered and methodologies used, and the academic standing and real-world work history of the faculty.

Anyone considering hiring a consultant should look, not just at the education, but also at the accrediting body backing the degree. A quick Internet search can likely lead to identifying the appropriate accrediting body for a particular discipline. Likewise, a phone call to a professor in the discipline at a prestigious university can likely yield information as well.

In addition, it is imperative to do thorough reference checks on the consultant's credentials—whether regulated or not. Consider the statistics presented in Table 7-3. These statistics are regularly tracked and summarized by the hiring advisory hireright.com. The data come from prestigious sources such as the Society of Human Resource Managers and the *Wall Street Journal*. When you consider that over half of the resumes you see are probably inaccurate, it is clear that you must validate all claims made on a resume and during an interview.

Table 7-3. Daunting Resume Statistics

Faulty Resume Area	Percent of Faulty Resumes
Resumes with inaccurate information	53%
Job applicants caught fabricating some part of his/her resume	49%
Applications containing lies about experience, education, and abilities	34%
Dates of employment inaccurate by greater than three months	30%
Lies about why the applicant left the former employer	11%
False claims about a college degree, employers, or jobs performed	9%

SOURCE: HireRight, "Human Resources by the Numbers"; accessed 2012, http://www.hireright.com/Background-Check-Fast-Facts.aspx.

These reference checks should include speaking with prior clients who will talk about projects that had both positive and negative results. Even the best consultant will fail on occasion. Such reference checks are valuable because they give insight into how failures were handled and whether the consultant helped find a way to turn around the negative result. Likewise, anyone who thinks he has never done anything wrong or cannot list any weaknesses is probably delusional. If nothing else, a consultant should be able to look at a situation realistically and objectively consider his own abilities to solve a problem.

Availability

Almost 10 percent of executives surveyed for our study chose a consultant based upon availability. Be very careful when a key criterion for hiring is availability. Anything worth doing is worth doing correctly. If the decision to hire a consultant is based on real need, you must be willing to wait to get the right consultant. Taking the first available consultant might compromise the results you want. Although the available consultant may be fully qualified, the chances of the best person for the organization being available right when you need him are pretty slim.

The Selection Process

A sound selection process must be based on a well-thought-out needs analysis and a detailed request-for-proposals process. Using the right process is perhaps the most important step. The wrong consultant will not fix a problem, might make the problem worse, or could lead you down the path toward fixing the wrong problem.

When a formal request-for-proposal process is used, though, a thoughtful written proposal from the consultant becomes the key reason for selecting that consultant. The diligence with which the potential consultants perform the company research and show understanding of the project is a good indicator of how hard they will work when the project starts. If it is clear the consultants have read the request for proposals thoroughly, and ask appropriate clarifying questions, then they likely will respond with a rough plan of approach. The thoroughness of this response lowers the risk to the decision maker and makes selection more likely. Conversely, when a potential consultant refuses to "jump through the hoops" that make up the request for proposals process, but still wants a chance at the business, eliminate that candidate. These consultants may have a skilled sales force that can persuade the company, should they can get a foot in the door. Alternatively, they may wish to avoid the formal RFP process because it will display potential weaknesses that are hidden by effective sales skills.

Part of the candidates' proposals should include how much they will assist with project implementation, as well as total costs. Having these elements clearly defined prior to forming a contract builds trust in both the capability and integrity of the consultant.

A formal presentation by the potential consultants will also help build trust and credibility. It may, and often does, become the main reason for selection. It is a great opportunity for the consulting company to show past successes and share work references that can you can verify. The formal presentation is also the time when consultants can display the functional competence or experience you are seeking and also show why your problem is a good fit for their solutions.

Sometimes you will prefer consulting companies who offer a full range of services, or whose employees have specific qualifications. These services and qualifications can be outlined in the written proposals and formal presentations. The details of the consulting firm, such as size, location, and age, can also be outlined in the written proposals and formal presentations. Finally, remember that consultants you know and trust often recommend other consultants that specialize in different areas. These recommendations are worth considering.

Selecting the right consultant or consulting firm is very important, considering that the wrong one may cause delays or even failure. It is easy to make a wrong turn here. Hiring a seasoned team of professionals can, for example, lead to a poor result. You would think a group of four consultants with a combined experience of over seventy years in your industry would be very appealing to an organization looking for efficiency improvements. However, what if the consultants had not worked together before and had just formed the consulting company? This could bring greater risk to the project if the consultants start squabbling among themselves. Maybe their individual experiences led them to different consulting approaches. One part of the firm may be working on driving incremental changes that would lead to impressive gains while another part may be focused on showing results that may not be beneficial to the organization in the long run. The result is an unhappy customer and hundreds of thousands of dollars in consulting fees producing little or no tangible results.

One of the criticisms of larger consulting firms is that a principal consultant sells the project and then junior consultants work on it. Or, it may be less important to have a specific consultant on the project than it is to have a consistent approach and some level of guarantees for the project. In a small consulting firm of four owners, with a network of consulting acquaintances, the infighting can have catastrophic results. In a larger firm, this is less likely because any single consultant who is not performing to expectations can easily be replaced, with minimal impact.

The right selection of consultant depends largely on the project and your organization's culture. When we talk about building the consulting relationship in the next chapter, we will go into more detail about how to structure the relationships with various types of consulting organizations. For now, just realize that no one type of consultant is better than another. There is no formula for picking the right consultant every time. Nevertheless, there is a process that you should always use. Figure 7-2 shows the process steps associated with selection of a consultant. Each of these steps is discussed at length in the following sections. Again, the combination of the process and good instincts increases the chances of picking the best possible consultant.

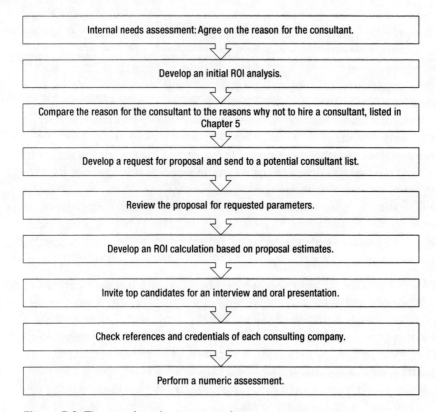

Figure 7-2. The steps for selecting a consultant.

Needs Assessment

When the decision is made to pursue a consulting relationship, the first step is evaluating why the consultant is necessary. Start by clearly defining the reason with the organizational leaders. This will aid in the process of selecting a consultant by ensuring that all of the potential decision makers and influencers look for the same result. The steps of the needs-assessment process are shown in Figure 7-3.

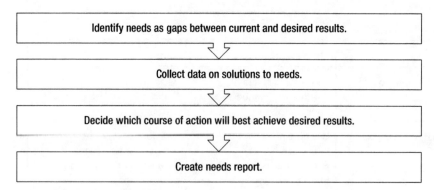

Figure 7-3. Needs assessment process.

The needs assessment is described in more depth in Chapter 9, but it needs brief attention here. A "need" is a discrepancy between the actual state and the desired state. Sales may be $1 million per year, but a company needs $1.2 million per year to break even. That gap creates a definite need. However, in that particular example, the root cause might not be inadequate sales; it could be many other things, from bad products to an inept sales force. Executives should be very careful to use the root-cause procedures discussed in Chapter 9. Many business problems are defined poorly and often in terms of symptom such as low sales, rather than the real problem. For example, an executive might say, "I need more resources." However, this is not a need. The real need may be that he needs more productive resources.

When trying to define a need, use all the important stakeholders as sources of information in assessing the situation. Employees may see a problem very differently from managers. Customers as well might view the situation in a different manner. It is important to try to gather as much data from all of these sources prior to proceeding. Some sample data-collection tools that can be used in this step are shown in Table 7-4.

■ **Tip** Many companies lack a skilled business intelligence person, someone who truly understands research methodologies and advanced statistics. Nevertheless, this is an internal skill that must not be sacrificed.

Part of this needs assessment—and many steps hereafter—involves developing incremental ROIs. Based on the data gathered up to this point, you can outline the ROI of the project and keep the analysis in mind as you proceed. This keeps project goals and activities realistic and also helps develop the numbers you need later for RFP purposes.

Table 7-4. Data Collection Tools and Sources

	Hard Data	Soft Data
Quantitative Sources	Performance Data Productivity numbers Budget analysis	Performance ratings Scaled surveys (1-5 disagree/agree)
Qualitative Sources	Document reviews Interviews Focus groups Expert reviews Multisource performance observations	Opinion surveys Individual interviews Single-source performance observations SWOT

The next step is to look at both the need and its possible solutions, and then try to determine if the options are feasible and realistic. These decisions should also be based on the data you gather.

The deliverable for this portion of the process is a document that shows the agreed-upon reason for the consultant and a list of goals associated with the project. This will help keep "scope creep" in check, as well as provide the clear expectations you will need to build the request for proposals.

The typical contents of a needs assessment report are shown in Table 7-5. This report helps, for two reasons. Not only does it serve as an outline to make sure that all protocols have been followed, but also it can be used as an internal company document when the time comes to sell the idea to employees. It is much easier to sell an idea if due diligence has been followed.

Table 7-5. Typical Contents of Needs Assessment Report

Needs Assessment Report
1. Executive summary
2. Introduction
3. Purpose, goals and objectives
4. Needs
a. Methods for identifying needs
b. Data used for identifying needs
c. Stakeholders involved
5. Actions considered
a. Methods for identifying alternatives
b. Data on alternatives
c. Criteria for comparing
d. Impacts, outcomes, outputs, and activities for each action considered
6. Data results
7. Decisions or recommendations
8. Implications
9. Appendix
a. Supporting data
b. Supporting tools and instruments

Develop the RFP

Once the reason for the consultant has been defined and validated, it is time to develop a formal request for proposals (RFP). This document is widely used when long-term contracts for goods or services are needed. A copy of a request for proposals is included in the Appendix of this book.

Key elements of a request for proposals are:

1. Introduction
    a. Purpose and Background
    b. Objectives and Scope of Work
    c. Consultant Qualifications
    d. Period of Performance
    e. Definitions

2. General Information
    a. Primary Company Contact for the RFP
    b. Schedule for the Decision Process
    c. Submission Process
    d. Revisions to the RFP
    e. Terms and Conditions
    f. Obligations and Rejections
    g. Insurance Coverage

3. Submission Requirements
    a. Format of Submission
    b. Necessary Information
    c. Information about the Consultant and Project Management
    d. Related Information
    e. References

4. Costs
    a. Identifications of all Costs (Budget)
    b. Computation of Costs

5. Evaluation
    a. Evaluation Procedure
    b. Notifications

The *introduction* tells potential consultants about the situation and what is expected. By developing a thorough introduction, all consultants will submit proposals to solve the same problems. In addition, a good introduction ensures, we hope, that the company receives proposals only from consultants who meet the minimum qualifications. By specifying the scope of the project and the anticipated length, there will be little question about responsibilities associated with taking on the project. Also, include definitions where necessary in the RFP. Even commonly used terms can be misunderstood, so defining them will minimize confusion.

The next section is *general information*, where you tell the consultants what is required to submit a proposal. By defining the primary company contact for the RFP, you can avoid confusion or promises made by unauthorized employees. Clearly defining a schedule around the decision process will help ensure timely responses while minimizing questions regarding where the proposals stand. Tell the consultants there will be little negotiation and that they should offer their best prices. That will eliminate the urge to quote high and try to negotiate to a lower rate.

The rules regarding the submission process ensure that all of the necessary information is submitted in the anticipated format. You will often find that information has changed since the initial request for proposals or that it was not correct in the original request. By noting that changes may be made, you manage expectations for the potential consultants. By defining terms and conditions during the request for proposal stage, the groundwork is set for the contract, which will be a necessary element of the project.

Negotiation during the proposal stage is easier because you have not emotionally committed to a consultant. You will have an easier time walking away from unfavorable terms in this phase of the selection process. The next part of this section tells consultants that the company is under no obligation to proceed with a contract and outlines how rejected proposals will be communicated. The final area in the general information section will tell the candidates what insurance is required to reduce the company risk during the project.

The third section outlines the actual *submission requirements*, including necessary information, consultant backgrounds, and references. This helps improve the quality of the submissions so that you do not have to request more information after the proposals have been submitted. The fourth section outlines the requirements around the *costs* associated with the project to ensure that nothing is left out to become a surprise later. The final section, *evaluation,* informs candidates of how you will evaluate and notify them of the results.

Evaluating the Proposals

Once you send out the request for proposals and start getting responses, you need to review the proposals to make sure the candidates have responded fully to the RFP. If the request for proposals was detailed and written well enough to relay the company needs, this response can be the first test of the potential consultants. In order for a consultant to be successful in your organization, he or she needs to be able to listen to your needs and take direction from you and others in the company when it is offered.

If the proposal does not meet the discrete and well-communicated requirements, then the consulting company is probably not going to work well with you, the internal project manager, or other employees. This is similar to the result of a series of interviews for a new employee. Often, interviewees will pick up necessary job duties and company culture cues during the interview process. If the interviewee does not relay some of these lessons learned in subsequent interviews with different people in the organization, then the interviewee likely does not listen well or is not able to put what is heard into context and adjust as needed. Likewise, expect any consultant to change the approach he or she normally employs based on the RFP and subsequent conversations with you. Failure to follow directions in a request for proposals is an indicator of potential problems later in the project.

There is one caveat to be mentioned here. Many consultants, especially those at large firms, have become highly skilled at selling themselves and are masterful manipulators. They have the ability to take what is written in the RFP and use it to imply that they are going to fix everything. You have to be very careful to evaluate proposals based on realistic, tangible action plans. If consultants use vague terms or clichés, or talk about their "proven methods," this is probably an indication of their inabilities. Be wary of any statements like, "I am going to take your weaknesses and leverage them. I will use your strengths to gain you a competitive advantage in the market place." They probably have no real idea what they are doing.

Check on Completeness and Adherence to Guidelines

Based on a review of the proposals, you should reduce the number of responses to a manageable few so as to move on to the quantitative portion of the evaluation. The number of proposals you will analyze will largely depend on the candidate pool and the quality of responses. Look for a minimum of three qualified candidates and a maximum of six. If you cannot identify three such consultants from the responses, send out a message to those presenting acceptable proposals saying you plan to delay the process. Then identify more potential consultants and ask them to provide proposals. Repeat this process until three satisfactory consulting organizations have met all of the project requirements. Also, if seven equally qualified candidates have submitted proposals, do not feel the urge to eliminate one just to get the number to a magical six. This is an initial evaluation stage and no real quantitative analyses have been done yet.

Calculation of ROI

The next phase of the project is calculating the return on investment for the project. You hope that the three to six proposals are similar in projected costs and benefits, although they may not necessarily be. Develop a consistent format for an ROI analysis similar to the one introduced in Chapter 4—you will also find one in the Appendix—to ensure that there are no formula errors in the calculations and no errors of omission. Once this format has been developed, it is time to input the proposal assumptions with regard to costs and benefits.

It is not uncommon to find errors in the proposals or to discover assumptions that are not necessarily clear. In these situations, have the RFP coordinator contact the consulting company directly to resolve the questions so that the calculations can be completed. By comparing the results of each spreadsheet, you should be able to spot which candidates ignored potential costs and benefits. Ask clarifying questions to solidify the cost-benefit analyses. The ROI calculations, coupled with any exceptions to the terms and conditions outlined in the request for proposals, should clearly differentiate any top candidates. However, do not eliminate a candidate unless the future cash flows do not turn positive within an acceptable amount of time.

Interviews and Presentations

Once all potential consultants have been validated by the ROI calculations, invite the acceptable candidates to the company for onsite presentations. Depending on the nature of the situation, presentations may start with the consultants spending their time evaluating the company and interviewing employees prior to the presentation. This is a good thing to allow because it shows whether the consultant is likely to be perceptive in the future, and it also reduces the risk that the consultant will try to implement a "standardized" solution that may not work in your unique situation.

The onsite visit needs to include the actual consultants who will be assigned to the project, if this is possible. By asking for this, you may avoid the bait-and-switch strategy often used by larger consulting companies, where a smooth, experienced salesperson sells the project and then fresh MBAs do the work.

Prepare a presentation of your own to show the potential consultants about the needs assessments you have done. Do the same presentation for all potential consultants. This will ensure that they all view the company from the same perspective. Following the company presentation and any observations made by prospective consultants, have the consultants present their services, history, and competencies. Then, they should explain their proposals and take your questions. Evaluate their answers based on their depth, soundness, understanding of your unique business needs, and precision. Again, look at vague answers very carefully.

The presentations from all of the candidates should help you reduce the choices down to primary and secondary ones. At this point, release the clearly unacceptable consultants from the evaluation process.

Reference Checking

After you have reviewed the presentations, request ten to twenty references from each candidate. A company with a solid client base and a history of success should be able to provide this many. Once the lists have been delivered, randomly select a few references from each and call them. This step is necessary to reduce the "only three references" bias. Anyone can come up with three references; that is not a very large number. Coming up with ten to twenty is much harder to do. You are not going to call all twenty necessarily, but it puts the candidates on guard that you are really going to check backgrounds well.

Come up with a predetermined list of questions to ensure consistent quality of each reference check. The questions absolutely must include something about ROI. Sample questions follow.

1. Were all expectations of deliverables met?

2. Did the work yield a solution to a problem or a solution to a symptom? In other words, was it a short-term solution or a long-term solution?

3. Were employees at all levels engaged in the project or did the consultant focus on leaders?

4. Was it worth the money?

5. Did you calculate an ROI and did they help you do that?

6. Was there a sufficient return on investment?

7. If you need a consultant in the future to work on a different problem, would you use this one?

8. What would you change about the project?

After the references have been checked, compile and compare the results. Verify all qualifications and certifications that play a part in the decision making. Unfortunately, some consultants may be untruthful about experiences and qualifications, so performing these checks is just part of the due diligence.

Numeric Assessment

Now that you have had the opportunity to review the proposals, conduct multiple ROI analyses, clarify the proposals, check references and qualifications, and meet the consulting team, it is possible to conduct a numeric assessment for each consulting candidate. Having a consistent format, as for the ROI, that includes categories for easy comparison is important. It should be developed using a ranking system and with weights associated with each category. Potential ranking categories are up to you, but they may include size of the consulting company, experience of the consulting team, cultural fit, consultant credentials, quality of the project methods, quality of the references, and even the consultant's reputation. This list is not exhaustive. You may come up with a completely different list.

The weights associated with the criteria will differ depending on the situation as well. Evaluate each consultant on a scale of from 1 to 10, with 10 being the most favorable. Multiply each weight by its ranking and take a sum of all categories. Figure 7-4 shows the calculation process for a simple consultant evaluation. The consultants with the highest composite score should become the primary choices. In this case, the best consultant, based upon the four outlined criteria and their associated weights, is Consultant 3, with a composite score of 7.7.

		Quality of the Proposal	Cultural Fit	Quality of References	Quality of the Presentation	Anticipated ROI	Total Score
Weights		0.15	0.1	0.15	0.1	0.5	
Scale 1 to 10							
Consultant 1	Rank	8.0	4.0	4.0	8.0	7.0	
	Composite	1.2	0.4	0.6	0.8	3.5	6.5
Consultant 2	Rank	5.0	5.0	6.0	7.0	6.0	
	Composite	0.8	0.5	0.9	0.7	3.0	5.9
Consultant 3	Rank	6.0	8.0	7.0	9.0	8.0	
	Composite	0.9	0.8	1.1	0.9	4.0	7.7

Figure 7-4. Consultant assessment.

Once you make your final choice, work on developing a contract with the consultant.

Ways to Reduce Risk during Selection

As discussed, there are many risks associated with hiring a consultant. Consultants seldom provide a truly independent perspective, and because of brand loyalty, most companies retain the same consulting firm for decades. Beyond the economics associated with a long-term relationship like this, you should avoid using consultants to meet a "survival skill" within your company, as described in Chapter 5. Companies often justify hiring a consultant because they want an independent perspective with industry knowledge. These long-term relationships keep this fresh perspective from happening.

Another key risk is that problems are not usually recognized with a consultant until the situation has reached a serious level. There is also the danger of losing proprietary information. The latter is a real and likely outcome of a consultant engagement, and should therefore, be considered prior to hiring a consultant. Even when competition and confidentiality agreements are in place, it is hard to prove that a trade secret or competitive advantage was leaked as a result of a consultant's work. In fact, ironically, this is a reason some businesses choose to work with consultants: to learn what others are up to. As business leaders, we hope that consultants will help apply the lessons they have learned in other businesses to our situations, even if we do not want them to share our own best practices. You have to realize that even the well-intentioned consultants will likely give away some secrets to other clients.

Another common risk associated with using consultants is that they apply cookie-cutter solutions. This is especially prevalent with larger consulting companies, who may have completed many projects and in the process have developed canned solutions they will attempt to apply to your situation as well.

Finally, again, there are no real means of evaluating consultants until you use them. There are no consumer reporting agencies or better business bureaus that track consultant qualifications and outcomes. Thus, in many ways, the selection process is always difficult and full of risk.

In sum, one excellent way of reducing these risks is to implement a standardized process for selecting a consultant. Another is to get that list of ten to twenty references for each candidate and check a random sample. As part of these reference checks, listen carefully to the happy former customers. As we pointed out earlier in this chapter, executives often do not have objective criteria to evaluate the effectiveness of their consulting engagements. In fact, the most common key to satisfaction with a consultant is merely having the consultant do what he is told to do, show up, and seemingly work hard.

In addition to the story mentioned previously, we have interviewed consulting customers who said that their projects were six months late and millions over budget, but that they were happy. Ask references if they conducted an ROI after the project's completion. If not, that reflects negatively on the reference's ability to objectively report on the consultant. It also reflects negatively on the consultant. If an ROI was not produced at the end of the project, whose fault was that? Did the customer neglect to do the analysis, or did the consultant neglect to provide the information for the analysis? A skilled consultant may be able to steer a customer into believing a return had been achieved, when in actuality no benefit was realized. If the customer has performed a return on investment, find out if the return actually translated into a bottom-line benefit.

There are many risk-reduction strategies in addition to reference checks. If only a couple of consultants are on the short list, visit their offices. If the team who will be doing the work does not show up for the onsite presentation, insist on meeting the team during this visit. If the consultant will be using any of his own resources, such as a lab, software, or equipment, inspect these resources during the visit. Ask some hard and probing questions to alleviate any fears, uncertainties, or doubts that still exist.

As part of the standardized selection process, ask the consultants about the project management process they use. You want to see that the consulting company has some well-documented, proven processes. The standardized process, as stated earlier, should include checking accreditations and degrees.

Ensuring that these are checked, and not taken at face value, helps reduce the risk. As mentioned, many resumes and proposals contain false information. The two biggest categories of lies are false education credentials and inflated past salaries.[3] Remember, you can buy a fake diploma or degree rather than earn it. If the regular work force has these types of dishonesties, assume that the consulting industry does, too. In short, buyer beware. A fair, transparent, and thorough selection process is your best way to select a consultant and improve your chances of success.

Summary

A robust and well-thought-out selection process is primarily aimed at risk reduction. This leads to picking the best possible consultant for meeting your current needs. It is common for businesses to cut corners in the selection process, due to the eagerness to get started with improvements and to obtain third-party help. Depending upon the scope of your project, however, hiring a consultant may be one of the most important decisions you can make. Follow the few steps of the selection process every time; skipping any steps will result in a hasty, possibly bad decision. The steps again are:

1. Perform a thorough and analytical needs assessment

2. Develop an initial ROI analysis.

3. Compare the reason for hiring the consultant to the reasons why you should not hire a consultant.

4. Develop a request for proposal and send it to a potential consultant list.

5. Review the proposal for requested parameters and selection criteria. All possible selection criteria follow. Before you use any one, consider its advantages and disadvantages.

6. Selection based on word of mouth or comments from colleagues

7. Selection based on cost/competitive bidding

8. Selection based on consultant level of experience in the specific area needing consulting

   a. Selection based on consultant level of experience in total years

---

[3] Karen Bush Schneider, "Resume Fraud: Little White Lies Aren't So Little Anymore," *The Greater Lansing Business Monthly*; accessed 2012, http://www.lansingbusinessmonthly.com/law-at-work/1325-resume-fraud-little-white-lies-arent-so-little-anymore.html.

b. Selection based on consultant level of experience in the same industry

c. Selection based on prior relationship (used the same consultant before)

d. Selection based on the consultant's education or accreditation

e. Selection based on the consultant's availability

9. Develop another ROI calculation based upon proposal estimates.

10. Invite top candidates for an interview and oral presentation.

11. Check references and credentials of each consulting company.

12. Perform a numeric assessment.

Once you have performed the steps and evaluated all options, you are prepared to make a sound decision that will bring you a positive outcome. The next chapter outlines forming the relationship once you have selected a consultant.

The Relationship
Building It and Maintaining It

If you give a man a fish, he will eat for a day. But, if you teach a man to fish he will buy an ugly hat. And if you talk about fish to a starving man, then you are a consultant.

—Dilbert

Once you have successfully built the business case for a consulting project and narrowed the choice to the top couple of consultant options, it is time to set the framework for the consulting relationship. A large part of the consultant-client relationship is set within this initial framework. The framework is built upon a combination of promises made by both the company and the consultant in the contract. Likewise, this is the time to set all metrics and timelines. You should also create outlines for meetings, resources, timelines, budgets, and all tollgates and other metrics. All of this is discussed in this chapter.

At this point in the relationship, there is only a modest amount of commitment to the project. Neither you nor the consultant has a lot of time, money, and emotion invested. This is, therefore, the perfect time to lay the groundwork for a successful relationship. During this period, the consultant (who is still hungry for the job) is willing to negotiate. In addition, you and your company have all of the power and at least two negotiating points: the best possible guarantees and the ground rules. As we will show in this chapter, most of the dissatisfaction that comes from a consulting relationship occurs because the initial framework was not carefully developed. Clarifying all the issues upfront reduces the chances of having a bad relationship.

Contract Development: Must Haves and Pitfalls

If the proposal from your top-qualified consulting candidate already laid out in detail the framework of the project and its terms and conditions, there is an inherent agreement on those terms. This is yet another reason to make sure that your RFPs and the consultants' proposals are very carefully constructed. But, whether or not due diligence has been performed up until now, it is imperative that the diligence is done at this stage. If you forget to include something in the initial contract, it is nearly impossible to hold the consultant accountable for it later on, when something you thought would happen does not happen.

Now that you and your colleagues have had the chance to evaluate the consultants and look for weaknesses, you can modify the terms based on the specific situation. For instance, if during your reference checks some customers said that the consultants were great but ended up over-budget and late, then it makes sense to include in the contract bonuses and penalties associated with staying on time and within budget. Such additions will depend on what your due diligence efforts have revealed.

Prior to releasing the alternative candidates from the selection process, build a contract with your first choice. For your first step, ask for a copy of the consultant's standard contract. The terms of the contract should not violate any terms outlined in your RFP. If the contract's standard terms are different from what is in your RFP, they will need to be changed. While consultants and clients can usually negotiate contracts that are mutually acceptable, sometimes you might find a show-stopper detail in a standard contract that the consultant will not alter. The consultant wrote the proposal based on the RFP's terms, so he or she should adhere to those terms when it comes to drafting the contract.

We would also like to point out another danger. People often find standard consulting contracts on the Internet and use them as templates. While this may be a time-saver—and we provide a template in the Appendix—be careful to examine every detail of the contract. Typically, disaster lies in the details, either things that were included that should not have been or things that were forgotten because everyone was anxious to get the project going. Timelines in contract templates, for example, are frequently vague or do not include milestones. Objectives, as well, are typically too vague to allow real evaluation along the way. Moreover, because bills for professional services are often aggregated, vague, and uninformative, they are of little use in controlling costs. Insist on detailed and itemized bills with receipts, where applicable, and write this into the contract.

Danger: Vague Contract Clauses for Expenses

Contracts often contain vague clauses that allow consultants to bill you for things for which you did not plan on spending money.

For example, take travel. Travel expenses should be laid out in detail for the entire project. Look at the range of airfares for the prior year and use this as a baseline for airfares during the project. In addition, consider such restrictions, such as booking travel two weeks in advance and always using a specific class, such as coach or business.

You can limit meals to a per diem amount and set restrictions on the extent consultants can entertain company employees. Hotel expenses should also be limited based upon the market in the area. For example, set the hotel budget to the median value for a nice hotel, not an expensive one. Likewise, set a weekly limit on car rentals, such that it encourages consultants to share a car. Spell out any other travel expenses that you are not willing to reimburse, such as alcohol, dry cleaning, or gym membership.

These kinds of restrictions are standard practice in many companies for full-time employees and should be used for consultants, as well. By setting the rules on travel and developing a budget based on the project timeline, it is possible to put contractual limits on these expenses. By the way, some companies negotiate weekly flat fees they pay consultants to avoid all reimbursement activities.

Nontravel expenses are not nearly as easy to control. These expenses include secretarial help, typing, editing, printing, copying, telephone, and other ancillary services. Again, outline in the contract the rules regarding these expenses. Ideally, you identified them in the proposal stage, but if not, the contract stage is your last chance to set them up.

In general, we recommend that the client incur as many of these costs as possible and demand itemized bills for reimbursement. It is doubtful that most consultants are trying to waste their clients' money; however, the truth is simple: When people are not spending their own money, they spend it more wastefully.

Eliminate expenses that seem unreasonable during this time also. If you do not, the consultants will likely overestimate their weekly expenses. Sometimes they charge flat fees for expenses that provide for additional margin. If the administrative expense associated with tracking the expenses is undesirable, you may, as mentioned, decide to pay a flat fee and allow the consultant potentially to make money off these expenses.

Although giving flat fees for travel or nontravel expenses is desirable from a predictability perspective, fixed-price contracts are typically bad for the client. In these contracts, there is usually a clause that allows unpredicted expenses to be reimbursed. In these situations, "unpredicted expenses" almost always occur, so do your best to eliminate such clauses. One reason you do the request for proposals is to encourage the consultants to give their best prices. This "best price," naturally, does not include a lot of buffer room. Make sure that your contract does not give the consultant the opportunity to add any buffer to his costs allowance or timeline.

Tip Establish the pricing during the RFP and do not change it during the contract negotiation. Make sure that there are no clauses that allow hidden costs to be added to the project.

Vague Staffing and Timeline Details

Make sure that a detailed roster of who will work on the project during each stage is part of the contract, along with detailed specifications of deliverables and their precise due dates. This level of detail protects both parties. So, the consultant should be happy to outline such things unless he hopes to extend the timeline to get more revenue. Consultants may also want to switch out less experienced, and therefore less expensive, personnel during the project.

Caution Consultancies may bait you with a smooth-talking and experienced consultant, only to switch that consultant out for a junior consultant. Avoid this in the contract stage.

Our advice is to take a "who, what, when" approach: Who will do the work? What will they do? When will it be done? Employ a Gantt chart, like those shown in Figures 8-1 and 8-2.

Figure 8-1 provides a more general look, but it allows the user to enter resource requirements at each stage. Figure 8-2 breaks down the project into very specific actionable activities for each staff member involved. Keep in mind that the staff requirements should include both internal (company) and external (consultant) staff requirements. This reaches the level of detail needed and also sets the basis for a detailed timeline. Just like ROI, no project should begin without a detailed workflow, budget, and resource timeline.

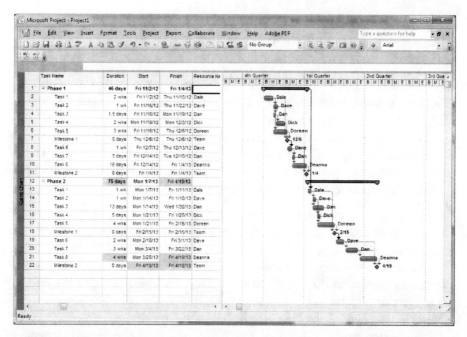

Figure 8-1. Overview Gantt chart.

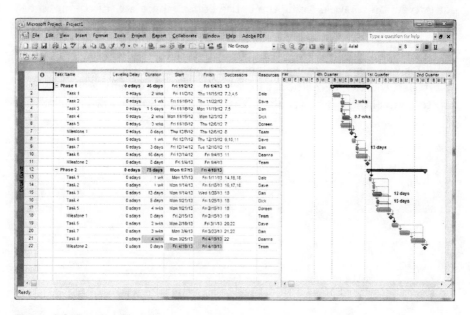

Figure 8-2. Detailed Gantt chart.

When developing the project timeline, incorporate some critical-chain project management techniques (CCPM) to ensure a successful project completed on time.

CCPM was developed because only 44 percent of projects typically finish on time. In fact, projects usually take well over twice as long as originally planned (222 percent of the original time period), and nearly twice (189 percent) the original budgeted cost. What's more, 70 percent of all projects fall short of their planned scope, and 30 percent are cancelled before completion. These results are mostly avoided through the use of CCPM. Typically, CCPM case studies finish 95 percent on time and on budget.[1] Figure 8-3 is an illustration of CCPM.

The power of CCPM lies in its strategy of identifying the "fluff" times, or padding, for each task, typically built into any project plan, and removing them. The timeline then becomes a clear view of what is possible with concerted effort. You then total the "fluff" times, cut it in half, and add it to the end of the project or to a subset of project chains, depending upon the situation. By monitoring the overall progress versus this buffer, the internal project manager can plan action when a third of the buffer is consumed by tasks behind schedule. When another third of the buffer is consumed, a plan can then be put into action to avoid losing the entire buffer. There are, of course, other methods than the 50 percent method for buffer sizing. There are also other methods for maintaining the chain or project buffers.

However you slice it, when developing the project timeline and agreeing on milestones, the CCPM method, based on the theory of constraints, may be a way to control the typical variability that causes delays in many projects.

---

[1] Steven J. Balderstone and Victoria J. Mabin, "A Review of Goldratt's Theory of Constraints (TOC)–lessons from the international literature," *Proceedings of the 33rd Annual Conference of the Operational Research Society of New Zealand, Auckland,* (1998): 205-214.

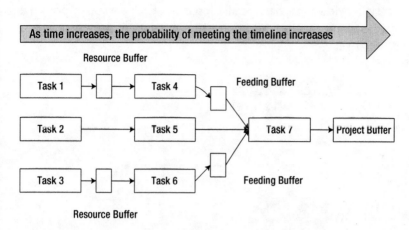

Figure 8-3. Example of calculating CCPM.

▓ **Caution** CCPM is not commonly understood by consultants who manage projects. If the consultant does not outline the project using CCPM, add your own buffer to the end of the project to account for the likelihood of being late.

Vague Objectives

To guarantee that the emphasis of the consulting engagement remains on the business objectives, if at all possible, designate a portion of the consultant's fees as a bonus to be paid only when an agreed-upon set of target metrics is realized. These objectives should take the form of a balanced scorecard.

A balanced scorecard format (Figure 8-4) follows certain guidelines. In this approach, the cost reductions or revenue increases that the consultant brings should not be the only measures of success. Other goals businesses often include are elements of customer satisfaction, employee satisfaction, product or service quality, safety, or anything else they want to see occur as a result of the consultant work. Lack of balance in deliverables can lead to unacceptable consultant behavior in getting to a single goal. For example, an overarching deliverable like "right sizing" the company may have unintended consequences, like poor service or quality.

Monitoring a balanced scorecard encourages ethical behavior, leading to real results. Operating with a view to a balanced scorecard will likely be a new experience for some consultants, especially since many companies do not even require an ROI calculation. Although, it is complicated, Figure 8-5 shows how one company is monitoring progress based on a scorecard approach. As you can see, each individual goal has specific initiatives. Each person responsible for the initiative is then constantly scrutinized in regard to his progress toward meeting that initiative.

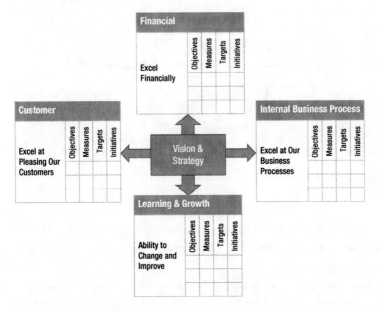

Figure 8-4. Balanced scorecard framework. SOURCE: Robert S. Kaplan and David P. Norton. "The Balanced Scorecard," *Harvard Business Review 76* (1996).

	Actual	Target	Variance	
Quality				
Internal Quality				
Internal Rejects	5%	2.50%	-0.025	☑
Improved Employee Training				
Cost of Quality	$7,500	$8,250	$750.00	▨
Six Sigma Process Improvement				
Employee Shift Changes				
External Quality				
Field Failure Rate	3%	2.75%	-0.25%	▥
Reliability Testing Improvements				
Improved Instructions for Customers				
Best Customer Satisfaction				
Customer Satisfaction				
% Satisfied with Sales	97%	95%	-2%	▨
Standardize Calls				
Customer Follow Up				
Solid Financial Performance				
Profitability				
Revenue	$100,000.00	$150,000.00	$50,000.00	☑
Sales Force Training				
Direct Marketing				
Balance Sheet				
Days Cash on Hand	80	90	10	☑
Vendor Terms				
Customer Satisfaction	97%	95%	-2%	▨
% Satisfied with Sales				

Figure 8-5. Balanced scorecard tracking.

Lack of Balanced Scorecard with Incentives

An operations executive was faced with a goal of increasing the profitability of a manufacturing operation to meet the financial goals of the organization. The strategy that he chose had multiple elements, as follows:

1. Reduce employee turnover from around 35 percent to around 15 percent.

2. Reduce energy costs by 15 percent.

3. Reduce safety incidents.

4. Improve machine efficiency through better equipment maintenance.

Because the goal was primarily financial, he brought in consultants who focused on financial goals instead of considering any underlying situations that might be causing the problems.

For example, the consultant was told that employee turnover was causing employee expenses to be too high; therefore, the company needed to cut turnover costs. So, this instruction meant that the consultants would not help maintain balance. Instead, they focused on the one financial issue associated with each objective. A more balanced view would have included employee and customer satisfaction, as well as quality improvements. This is why we have discussed the balanced scorecard to this point. All decisions should be made while considering what will be affected besides the primary decision driver.

In another example, the baseline for measuring the energy losses within the organization was not based on solid scientific principles or analysis of the company and its use of energy. Instead, as long as energy costs went down, that was good. No one cared why or how this happened, even if this meant turning off the air conditioner in the summer. While this move saved energy costs, it increased employee dissatisfaction and, therefore, increased the turnover the consultants were charged with reducing.

Next, although good preventive maintenance programs are a standard practice in manufacturing, no root-cause analysis was done to determine where poor maintenance was causing poor performance, which potentially could lead to unnecessary expenses. Maybe employee turnover was causing some of the manufacturing issues or vice versa. No one thought to link these items together.

Also, the consultant's improvement ideas were not implemented one at a time to verify their effectiveness, but rather, were implemented all at once. As a result, the improvements may have cost as much as ten times more than necessary to get the actual result. In this situation, one of the many changes that were implemented at the same time accounted for as much as 85 percent of the actual gains. When evaluated alone, it would have made sense to implement this inexpensive change and avoid all of the other changes that helped only incrementally.

Now let's look at the consultant's efforts in more detail. To improve employee turnover, the company at the consultant's suggestion implemented a bonus program based on internal quality rejects and the number of safety incidents. This also supported the initiative to reduce safety incidents. Although a performance-based bonus program was a good idea, the metrics used to drive performance incentivized employees to hide quality problems rather than solve them. This led to more external quality rejects and lower customer satisfaction, which, in turn, would probably lead to margin erosion and reduced customer loyalty, in addition to warranty costs.

Moreover, the incentives to reduce safety incidents did nothing to address the root cause of the safety problems. As with the quality incentive, the consultant and company assumed that employees were not trying hard enough to create a quality product in a safe environment. Although incident rates were reduced, actual injuries were not, which hurt employee productivity and morale.

While obviously much of the detail is left out in this case, the point is that the consultant was not incentivized to take a balanced approach—as happens in many consulting arrangements. Rather than focusing on the few measures that were used, this leader should have looked to maintain employee efficiency, monitor inventory, influence sales forecasting and labor levels, ensure external quality, and encourage ethical behavior in employees by asking them to identify and eliminate problems rather than setting goals on output metrics. If a full-time employee with a vested interest in company results can make poor decisions that are not based on a balanced approach, then you can expect a consultant who has fees to gain may and probably will make poor decisions if not forced to maintain a balance.

It is very easy to fix one problem and then create another. For example, what if too many customers are going to the competitor? So many times, your gut reaction is to lower prices. Then, you have to find lower-quality suppliers to maintain a lower price. What is the inevitable result? Quality decreases, customers complain and/or leave, customer loyalty falls further, and revenue drops. In other words, a downward spiral begins.

Just as executives cannot make good business decisions in isolation, neither can consultants. Factor a balanced approach into the consulting contract.

■ **Tip** Maintain balance in business and in life.

Vague Intellectual Property Guidelines

The commercial aspects associated with any project, such as intellectual property and confidentiality, are often the most fought-over sections of a contract. On one hand, the consultant who may have developed the intellectual property wants to maintain ownership for future use. After all, the consulting firm developed it. It was likely the brainchild of their efforts and work. On the other hand, the consultant is on the payroll of the client during the period the property is developed. So the company feels that it should own any intellectual property.

The reality is that both groups are correct. This is the root cause of why there is so much controversy. In the end, ownership of the intellectual property could go either way and should be dictated by the unique situation you are in and the initial contract. This decision could be used as an incentive to negotiate a different area of the contract. ("If you give us X, we'll give you Y.")

As for confidentiality, the reason it is a controversial topic is that the consulting business is all about sharing experiences learned with one client with each subsequent client. This is part of the value proposition for using the consultant and also what most clients want. (But not specific client secrets—sharing those can be a criminal act if a confidentiality agreement is in place.) Also, most confidentiality agreements are vague enough that there is not a lot of clarity about what constitutes a breach of contract. Such breaches of confidentiality, much like noncompete contracts, are hard to enforce unless real, financial damage can be proven.

Consultants do not like to sign confidentiality agreements that include anything outside of true trade secrets. Business leaders will want the confidentiality agreement to include as much as possible. The funny part of this is that seldom do either of these have anything to do with the success of the project itself. The fact is, it is pretty rare that contracts without them cause any real harm.

The CEO of Toyota realized this many years ago when people saw how great their production system was. Hordes of visitors ensued. One day, someone asked the CEO if he was worried if their trade secrets would get out. He responded, "They can take whatever they want. By the time they figure it out and implement it in their own factories, we'll be so far along to the next thing." In reality, most business executives who are concerned with trade secrets probably are not true market leaders. While you should work to protect your trade secrets, it is likely not that big of a deal, and readily can be fixed by simple clauses in the contract.

If you are concerned about confidentiality, by all means have a nondisclosure agreement between you and the consultant. But we would challenge you to look at what you are trying to protect and ask yourself if there is anything really special about it. If you need it, a confidentiality agreement example is included in the Appendix of this book.

Vague Deliverables

As mentioned, the contract needs to be specific in terms of "who," "what," and "when." To help facilitate this, it should clearly define the objectives of the work in the format of a balanced scorecard. Make sure the scope and work content are very clear, as well. Work out, in advance, what the consultant can do independently as part of the authority you give and when he needs to seek approval. How will approval be given? Is there a governance structure in the organization to manage the consultant? All of these areas are negotiable during the contract stage. The consultants probably have preferences they will share with you if asked.

At a minimum, you should appoint an internal project manager to work with the consultant and identify resources to support the project. In fact, you probably already know the resources required from your work on the ROI calculation. You should also create a steering committee, made up of major stakeholders, to monitor the progress, eliminate barriers to success, and make key decisions outside of the project team's authority. Set regularly scheduled meetings as part of the project timeline, with a basic agenda structured for each meeting. Supplement the agenda for each meeting depending on the current conditions of the project.

As part of the contract, specifically outline deliverables from both sides of the project (internal and external). The deliverables need to be discussed at every meeting and followed as was discussed in the earlier chapter. This way, you can monitor small goals. You will help ensure proper resources are being used, progress is being made, and the timeline is being followed. Less is left to be a surprise in the end.

Even though the consultant is a supplier to the organization, the organization has responsibilities to uphold to make the project successful. These responsibilities are better laid out in the contract than to be assumed by both parties. Along with defining responsibilities, the contract is a good place to validate the form of the consulting engagement.

Here is an outline of a consulting contract, including headings and subheadings. Not all of these sections are necessary in every contract. Likewise, specific situations might require additional sections. Review these items whenever you create a new consulting contract—do not just use the last contract as a template. (A complete template is in the Appendix.)

▓ **Note** Be clear on expectations and make sure that there is agreement on those expectations.

Contract Overview Outline

1. Construction of the Agreement
    a. Definitions
    b. Attached documents
    c. Precedence of documents
    d. Entire agreement
    e. Severability
    f. Waivers

2. Services
    a. Scope of services
    b. Responsibilities
    c. Deliverables
    d. Contract term
    e. Quality assurance

3. Resources
    a. Resources
    b. Exclusivity
    c. Resource substitutions
    d. Resource continuity
    e. Use of subcontractors
    f. Standard of care
    g. Cooperation with third parties

4. Commercial Terms

    a. Overall fees

    b. Rates

    c. Rate escalation

    d. Expense and travel policy

    e. Invoicing procedures

    f. Payment terms

    g. Audit rights

5. Intellectual Property and Confidentiality

    a. Intellectual property

    b. Personal data privacy

    c. Confidentiality

    d. Ownership of deliverables

    e. Regulatory requirements (Such as HIPAA)

6. Termination

    a. Termination by client

    b. Termination by consultant

    c. Notice period

    d. Transition assistance

7. Competition

    a. No solicitation of personnel

    b. Noncompliance

8. Guarantees

    a. Liability

    b. Warranty

    c. Insurance

    d. Indemnity

9. Other

    a. Dispute resolution

    b. Governing law

    c. Limitation on actions

    d. Force majeure

    e. Assignment

    f. Survival

    g. Independent contractor

    h. Escalation

    i. Notices

    j. Changes to agreement

Once the contract has been developed, vetted, and signed, it is time to tell the second and third choices for consultants that a decision has been made. This delay is part of the process because it is not uncommon to be unable to resolve key disputes in the contract phase. It is completely possible that, during the contract phase, the negotiations break down and the second or even third choice is called upon for contract negotiations.

If you cannot come to terms with the top three consultant choices, and all discussions end in contract disputes, it is likely that your expectations are unrealistic and that you should start negotiations over again. For this reason, among others, it is important to keep negotiations and the termination of negotiations amicable so you can possibly resume negotiations at a later date.

Necessary Meetings

As soon as a contract is signed, schedule the meetings involved with the project. Scheduling upfront ensures that everyone is able to put planned meetings on their calendars and guarantees that they are available. A few guidelines are worth mentioning here for whenever you schedule a meeting about anything. These unwritten rules (Table 8-1) make sure that the participants remain interested and committed to the project. They also make sure that participants do not get the idea that their personal time is being wasted.

Table 8-1. Holding Respectful Meetings

The Unwritten Rules
1. Never schedule a meeting during lunch hours.
2. Never schedule a meeting before 8:00 a.m. (Unless the parties all agree that this is their preference.)
3. Never schedule a meeting after 4:00 p.m.
4. Never invite participants if they are not needed.
5. Make sure you invite all required participants.
6. Never schedule meetings just because it is the thing to do (i.e., standing meetings).
7. Have an agenda with set objectives.
8. Do not schedule a meeting to review the same topics discussed in a previous meeting with the same participants.
9. Do not schedule a meeting about things that can be discussed or broadcast via email.
10. Never send out meeting invitations via outlook invites without previous discussion and approval.
11. Schedule all meetings to be no more than one hour. Anything more is a separate brainstorming session or working meeting.

Pre-Kickoff Meeting

Once the contract is signed, it is time to set the stage for the project. The pre-kickoff meeting may be the first meeting between the consultants and the internal personnel who will work on the project. Typically, this meeting has only a few attendees. The project champion or the executive team member who had the most to gain from the project will attend. The internal team leader will also attend with potentially a couple of other internal stakeholders.

From the consulting company's side, the project leader and subject matter leaders (i.e., marketing, operations, finance, business process, quality, procurement) who will work on the project may attend. It is important to make this meeting inclusive enough so that no one in the company feels that consultants are being brought in to do someone's dirty work. Things should be kept transparent and positive at all stages. See a sample agenda in Table 8-2.

Table 8-2. Pre-Kickoff Meeting Agenda

Agenda
1. Review deliverables
a. Make all team members aware
b. Discuss any risks
2. Discuss timeline including meeting schedules, project tollgates, and resource engagement schedules
3. Develop agenda for kickoff meeting

The first agenda item for this meeting is to review the key contract deliverables. During the contract negotiation phase, the deliverables and measurement methods were vetted and approved by all parties. So, the point of this pre-kickoff meeting agenda item is to ensure that all team members are aware of the contract terms. During this portion, it is necessary to evaluate risks to the project and develop strategies to avoid them. Because not all risks will be identified this early in the project, the risk category will be part of all subsequent steering committee agendas.

The second agenda item is to work on developing the next level of the project timeline. That includes meeting schedules, project tollgates not defined in the contract, and resource engagement schedules (times when each specific consultant will be onsite). This timeline is not meant to constrict the mobility of the consultant regarding the use of resources, but is rather, to set initial expectations.

The third agenda item is to develop the agenda for the kickoff meeting. This kickoff meeting agenda will include the introduction of key people, a general project introduction, and a discussion of the target audience. To prepare for this kickoff meeting, develop the organizational communication plan so that more expanded communication can be sent out via available channels immediately following the kickoff meeting. The reason for this is to avoid unnecessary and often potentially damaging rumors about the project.

The Kickoff Meeting

Whenever you start a large project or business relationship, hold a kickoff meeting. The kickoff meeting has multiple purposes. The first is to introduce the consultants to the rest of the organization. This may initially start by your presenting the problem statement and why the consultants were contracted to work with the organization.

Try to anticipate questions from those who will attend the kickoff meeting so you can answer them when they come up. This is something you and the steering committee might discuss during the pre-kickoff meeting.

The kickoff meeting should be led by multiple people in the organization, including the executive who is ultimately responsible for the project and the project leader. It is especially helpful to have the chief executive officer (or someone in a similar senior position) say a few words in support of the project.

The kickoff meeting is the first opportunity for the consultants to introduce themselves to the organization. If the selection process went well, and you hired the right consultants, the consultants should be comfortable speaking to the group and giving a quick review of their experiences and how they hope to help.

The audience for the kickoff meeting may change depending upon the size of the organization. The number of people present should be limited to a few dozen for each meeting so that workers are free to ask questions without feeling intimidated. Those in larger companies, where the consultants may be visible enough to cause disruption, may wish to consider multiple kickoff meetings. Although the time associated with these kickoffs can be expensive, this is a key step in the process because it offers transparency to the organization and encourages engagement.

Weekly Project Management Office Meetings

One easy way to doom a project is to not stay on top of the project, and not guide the project team toward successful results. That is why you need weekly project meetings. Key personnel at these meetings include the project champion, internal project leader, external project leader, and functional leaders being affected by the consultants' work. Let the consultants suggest the agenda for these meetings. If they are unwilling or unable, discuss an agenda at the kickoff meeting. Typical agenda items include current activities, past activities, risks to the project, barriers, and decision points. Later in the project, there may be the addition of analysis or review of project metrics.

Each project management office meeting should immediately precede monthly steering committee meetings.[2] Therefore, the project management office

---

[2] "Project management office" or PMO, is what consultants and experienced project managers call the project leadership team.

meeting may include preparation for the steering committee meeting. It is important to note that although the weekly meetings typically include a small group of key individuals, it may be necessary to invite others to join them on occasion to work through discrete project issues. For instance, if the overall project is an operations efficiency-improvement project, but an information technology need is identified, the leader of the information systems department may be brought into the weekly project management office meeting for a couple of meetings.

By holding these meetings, which typically take one to two hours per week, ensure that communication remains open and minimize delays to the project. During key points in the project, when more urgent matters are dealt with, more frequent meetings may become necessary. In these situations, daily or even twice-daily huddles may be scheduled to take the communication to another level of detail. These bursts of "huddle" meetings are not designed to be a permanent part of the project, but are intended to get the team past time-sensitive issues.

Monthly Steering Committee Meetings

All large projects should be led by a steering committee. The steering committee will include mostly top executives within the organization. Also, the internal project manager and the external project manager should be on this committee.

The steering committee meeting serves many purposes. Throughout the project, there should be planned tollgates to highlight when deliverables are due. These tollgates will be reviewed in the appropriate steering committee meetings. Any quantified improvements can be reported during the steering committee, as well. Because a high level schedule was developed during the contracting phase, the steering committee meeting can be a venue to discuss the schedule and ensure that everything is on schedule.

One of the downsides to a large consulting project is that it is nearly impossible to anticipate all of the project's potential changes and challenges. The steering committee has the authority to review requested changes and approve additional funds based on the business need. These fund requests may come from mistakes, unidentified needs, or a change in project scope. By ensuring that the process for these changes is formalized, it is easier to control the timeline and budget for the project.

As mentioned earlier, the steering committee is the group that will take corrective measures to address potential project risks. The regular steering committee meetings will always discuss project risks as part of the agenda, but in the case of a high-risk situation happening between steering committee meetings, you should call an emergency meeting to address the risk.

These are all of the necessary meetings for most projects—most of the time. Depending upon the project details, it may be necessary to hold other support meetings at different levels of the organization. These may include discrete subproject meetings, such as for implementing rapid changeover methods or validating data transmitted between IT systems. They also may be meetings held at a department or facility level in support of the project management office meetings. Likewise, training sessions and similar learning sessions might be required.

■ **Tip** Structure in the project management methods leads to less confusion and opportunity for mistakes. Take the time upfront to build this structure.

Metrics and Sustainment

Along with the need for an organized meeting structure, there must be a scoreboard for the project that is visible at various levels of the organization. The most important level is that of the everyday worker. Undoubtedly, since the kickoff meeting(s), there have been questions about the project and the goals. There may be fear mongering going on, with rumors of staff reductions or pay cuts.

All of the negative communication can be controlled by a thorough, proactive plan to highlight the positive, with a scoreboard as its centerpiece. Make it large and visual, and put it in a high-traffic area such as outside the cafeteria or near a time clock for hourly employees. To continue to get the attention of those employees, update it regularly. Some companies have installed flat-screen TVs in production areas with live, up-to-the-minute updates of productivity or revenue figures.

This is extremely motivating for hourly workers. It is similar to being on a treadmill and watching the calories-burned number tick upwards. As you run faster and faster, you can see the number of calories burned increasing faster and faster, thus making you move faster. It also helps the workforce realize its direct connection to results. In organizations where the employees work in multiple facilities across a large geographic area, it may be more practical to develop an intranet solution and post advertisements around the organization about the intranet scoreboard.

A sampling of these scoreboards is shown in Figures 8-6, 8-7, and 8-8. In this company, the boards are placed throughout the company, in work cells on the production floor, the break room, and from the ceilings in the hallways. They constantly rotate the various measurement statistics and information gathered.

Take a close look at these shots. You will see one showing employee feedback survey statistics, another showing cleanliness measures and statistics, and the third displaying a particularly poignant email from a very satisfied customer. These shots change daily, and all data is updated regularly. Employees see these and gain a sense of pride in their work and a realization that they make a difference to the company's bottom line.

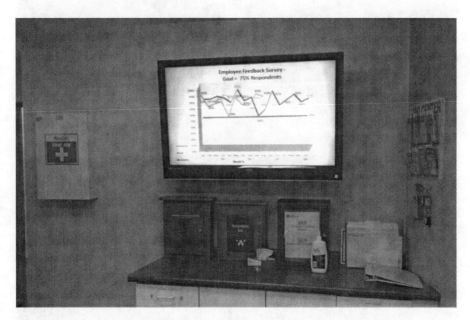

Figure 8-6. Live factory scoreboard #1—employee feedback surveys

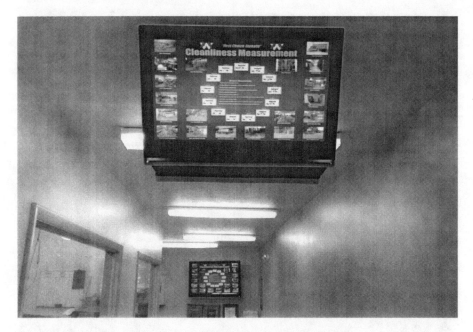

Figure 8-7. Live factory scoreboard #2—cleanliness measurement.

Figure 8-8. Live factory scoreboard #3—customer feedback.

To have useful information to display, you will need to develop metrics to measure the success of the consulting engagement during the relationship, as opposed to waiting for the final results. These metrics should relate to the audience. For instance, if the consultants work with a team to improve a discrete work area, then the scoreboard near that area should highlight the project for that area. In a factory situation, the project may be an efficiency effort for a work cell that is reported on a scoreboard for that cell. That project then becomes part of a factory-wide scoreboard that is the summation of all of the smaller, discrete projects. This scoreboard may also have a "Project of the Week" focus to highlight completed projects that led to efficiency improvements. That factory scoreboard then rolls up to a company or division scoreboard that includes all of the factories affected by the project. This is similar to the concept of Hoshin Kanri, as can be seen in Figure 8-9.

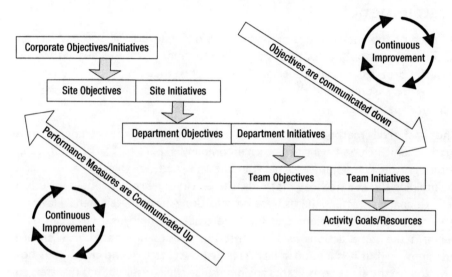

Figure 8-9. The principle of Hoshin Kanri. Source: Adapted from http://www.leanindonesia. com/wp-content/uploads/2011/03/3-HoshinPlanningProcess.jpg.

In these principles, the company sets goals for the project at the top level. Each subsequent lower level sets goals that support the level above, based on the direction from that upper level. The metrics for the project at the lower levels then measure progress toward the defined goals, and they then roll up into the metrics at the next level. This continues until, ultimately, the project level shows progress toward goals.

By implementing this structured goal-setting and metrics-reporting method, the project management office can ensure that the entire organization is pulling in the same direction. It is also much easier to ensure accurate and truthful information when metrics at the micro level are rolled up to metrics at a macro level. Thus, this makes it difficult for either workers or consultants to provide fake or exaggerated numbers.

The principles can then be translated directly into a balanced scorecard, as discussed earlier. Once again, this allows the workers and the leadership to see how every objective is being met and also ensures that the organization is taking a balanced approach in regards to the activities and objectives.

■ **Tip** Metrics and communication must be relevant to the audience, updated frequently, and easy to understand.

Sustainment

As part of the metrics strategy, you should define critical success factors (CSFs) based upon the contract goals. Define them with timelines associated with the progress toward those goals. Make sure that any results the project obtains are sustained and that the consultants have put processes in place to facilitate sustainment.

The preferred methods for the consulting industry to accomplish this sustainment include having an internal company expert to "carry the torch." Although this is helpful for understanding the methods that were used and maintaining the use of those methods, the consulting project should include a culture-change element that is necessary for long-term sustainment. Having a team of internal champions and full-time trained employees, who can now perform the same actions as the consultants, does not necessarily ensure sustainment (but it is a good start). This just ensures that the client does not have to hire the same consultants again because the consultant has transferred the skills and knowledge to the organization.

Another common strategy that consultants use is to say that training and audits are the sustainment methods. Training without good operational definition and ease of understanding standard processes is worthless. Furthermore, training typically is not sustainable because people naturally start to develop work-around processes immediately after the training is completed. As the company gets further from the project, the on-the-job training for new employees is based on the poor habits of veteran employees who do not have standard training methods available for them.

Further, audits are completely *not* value-added activities when it comes to sustainment. These activities are often necessary to monitor compliance to procedures that have been trained into the organization, but they merely identify problems and over time are subject to the same level of degradation as training.

The reason these are the preferred methods for many consultants is that they are easy to implement. By offering training and audits, the consultant relinquishes responsibility for the sustainment. If the improvements are lost, then the excuse is that the training was not carried through well, or the audits are not being performed. This is not to say that training and audits should not be performed, but rather, that they are not metrics. If they are used, set up separate metrics to ensure people learned from the training sessions. These are independent of other improvement metrics.

Most learning from training has completely dissipated after roughly six months if the skills are not used on a daily basis. Therefore, any effort toward training should be on a continual basis. A three-hour-a-week training session offered every third week for six months provides the same amount of training as a three-day intensive training session. However, the training that is spread out gives the learning a much greater chance of being absorbed, and a much greater chance workers will transfer the knowledge to their jobs. It also gives the trainer a chance to see what has been learned and not learned, and adjust the material accordingly.

Regarding audits, make monitoring key performance indicators part of the work and not an audit. By using these measures, it is easier to encourage continuous improvement after the project has ended. Metrics are not aimed at forcing compliance as is auditing. Instead, they are aimed at making the performance of the organization visible.

Metrics need to be as close to real time as possible and be directly affected by employee actions. Using metrics to drive internal champions and leaders to continue the work of the consulting project will help ensure sustainment.

Undermining the Consulting Project

Remember that about half of those surveyed for the study done for this book were happy with the consulting project even though only about 15 percent of them actually conducted an ROI calculation. One quick way to ensure failure is to define the project in terms of the work the consultant will do, and the product the consultant will deliver. In the survey results, the clients were happy because the consultants did what they promised to do. This is part of a consultant trap. Instead, the specific results you need must drive the project.

Defining the project in terms of the activities would be like measuring the company success through employee attendance and adherence to procedures, rather than through financial performance. Although a company want its employees to come to work and follow procedures, and wants its consultants to fulfill their promises, none of it matters if the company does not make or save money.

The next way to doom the project is to determine the project scope mainly by the subject to be studied or the problem to be solved. This approach has little regard for your company's readiness for change, a key ingredient in the success of the consultant engagement. By readiness for change, consider the ability, motivation, and sense of urgency that the company has to drive improvement. The project scope should be aimed at results that can be achieved by the internal capabilities of the organization.

Consultants will often promise amazing results from implementing one big solution to the main problem. Although there is, in fact, a rare situation where a company is doing one thing very badly that a consultant can fix, this is not usually the case. The most prevalent need of organizations is to work on developing processes to make smaller incremental improvements that build upon one another. This needs to be the expectation of the consultants from the beginning. If during the project a single solution to a problem yields big results, then that success is just a fortunate miracle.

Although the request for proposals and contract stages, as well as selecting a consultant and building a relationship, are important to ensure success, making the documents too rigid can doom a project. Successful consulting projects are driven by a team effort, where the internal and external teams work in concert, with shared responsibility toward reaching a common goal. If throughout the project, both sides focus on individual responsibility, then they will put more effort into documenting their actions to show adherence to their defined responsibilities, than to documenting actual results. Use consultants for brainpower rather than an extra set of hands. Dividing responsibility makes the team focus on task work instead of leadership work.

Critical Success Factors

There are a few simple things that you can do to ensure project failure. There are also some things that you can do—beyond what has already been discussed—to ensure success. In the survey, when business leaders were asked what led to success with a consulting project, a few key themes emerged. These included:

- The solution took into account the company's internal state of readiness.

- The project included prototyping new solutions.

- The project deliverables were clear.

- The consultant partnered with the project team throughout.

- The consultant was professional.

- The consultant understood the company's sense of urgency.

- Internal resources were considered first.

- The consultants emphasized a team approach.

- The project was governed well.

In this book, we cover the process of creating a framework and governance process for a consulting project. As can be seen in the list above, this is one of the themes that came out of our survey of business leaders. The method we have described so far is a proven way to ensure success, which is why we spent so much time explaining the process.

The other success themes have a central concept: build a team mentality with the consultants. If the internal and external people feel like a team, then they will take time to understand the organization's culture prior to implementing solutions. The team mentality also makes the consultants feel more ownership than if they had a supplier mentality. This ownership mentality will encourage change-management activities and validation activities, such as piloting solutions. Ownership will also encourage a sense of urgency toward meeting the deliverables set by the steering committee.

An independent survey of over 250 companies yielded other identified success factors, many of which have been addressed in this book (Table 8-3).[3] Not surprisingly, having a clearly defined need or problem makes it easier to define goals and strategies to meet those goals. This also makes it easier to have the required level of planning and structure that has been discussed. Clear planning helps ensure good time-management on the project, as well as efficiency in executing solutions.

Because companies bring in consultants to do things that the company does not feel it can do itself, it is expected that the consultant offers new ideas and knowledge to the organization. The number and quality of new ideas a consultant introduces leads business leaders to be more satisfied. This new knowledge can help the company define new strategies for future success. Remember, however, consultants should not be defining the strategy. Rather, they should help provide a fresh perspective that allows the company to develop the new strategy. This is an important point because strategy is a survival skill and should not be driven by a consultant. What the consultant should have is a clear strategy about their plan for the project.

---

[3] A. J. Vogl, "Consultants . . . in their clients' eyes," *Across the Board*, September 1999, pp. 26–32.

Table 8-3. Factors Contributing to Consulting Success

Factors contributing to consulting "success" from over 250 companies
• Competency of the consultant
• Clarity in need/problem formulation
• Number/quality of new ideas
• New knowledge provided
• Special planning
• New ways of thinking
• Level of planning
• Level of co-operational abilities
• Efficient management of time
• Planning capabilities
• Efficiency of execution
• Strategy formulation
• Problem-solving abilities
• Implementation success
• Follow-up
• Economy/budget awareness
• An emphasis on client results vs. consultant deliverables
• Clear and well-communicated expectations and outcomes
• Visible executive support (teamwork)
• Client readiness
• An investment upfront in learning the client's environment (not providing a canned solution)
• Overall success defined in terms of incremental successes
• Real partnership with consultants
• Inclusion of the consultants through the implementation phase

A lot of other factors concern the consultant's ability to "care" about the company. If the consultant has no regard for the company's funds, or resources, or timelines, there is a smaller chance of success. This sounds like common sense, but the consultant needs to consider himself a team player and be responsible for the internal success of the project.

One core competence that should be required of any consultant is the ability to work with others. Having the ability to cooperate and solve problems in a team setting improves the chances of success. In almost every case where these abilities are present, the abilities to follow up with people and to communicate well are also present. These skills, along with the new ideas and knowledge, are components of competent consultants, which almost certainly lead to client satisfaction. Competent consultants focus on client results versus consultant deliverables because they know that results will lead to satisfaction, and the client would rather have results than a checklist of activities. To drive these results, a good consultant considers client readiness for change through a thorough evaluation of the company environment and culture.

The presence of quality consultants leads to visible executive support that encourages incremental successes and celebrates them. Through this support and a real partnership with the consultants, you will set clear and well-communicated expectations and put measurements in place to show outcomes. Maintaining this relationship ensures the consultant will be included in the implementation phase and development of controls to sustain the gains.

The consulting industry is a big business with lots of variation in the quality of suppliers. What makes clients happy comes down to a simple formula. Figure 8-10 shows the consulting promise. If the entire industry followed this promise, then the industry would be growing even faster than it is.

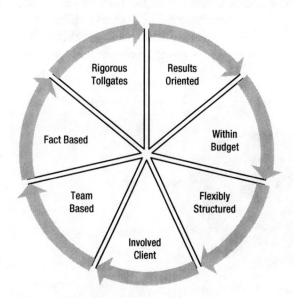

Figure 8-10. The consulting promise.

The techniques introduced thus far in this book are designed to support the consulting promise by setting you, the client, up for success. The proper selection of a consultant will align potential consultants with the consulting promise by offering proposals that are results oriented with a budget and timeline.

Questions of references during the selection process should focus on the items outlined in Table 8-3. For example, when conducting background checks, ask those references questions like, "Did the consultant have clear, tangible, quantifiable deliverables? Did the consultants set up incremental deliverables? Did the consultant take time to understand your unique issues prior to providing a solution?" These types of questions will more likely help you home in on qualified consultants. Setting the stage for a partnership with clear expectations as well as support facilitates a team environment in which the client is involved. The structure and governance designed into the project with supporting metrics leads to a fact-based consulting project that is focused on results in line with client capabilities and culture.

Survey Results for Client Satisfaction

Based on the survey that we described in the first chapter, we concluded that most executives were satisfied with their consulting experiences. This can be seen in Figure 8-11. When those who were not entirely satisfied were asked what led to dissatisfaction, the biggest response (mentioned by 14.75 percent of all executives) was that the consultant simply lacked the skills to get the job done. It is important to remember that there are no qualification requirements or skills assessments necessary to get a consulting license. In fact, there is no license. The ability to become a consultant is limited only by how well the consultant can sell his services.

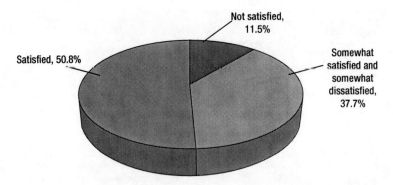

Figure 8-11. Survey results showing client satisfaction.

The second major dissatisfier for clients was that the project created no positive results. A full 9.84 percent of respondents said that after spending tens of thousands of dollars, the consultant did not actually show tangible results. This should not be a surprise, given that less than 50 percent of respondents even had a contract with their consultants. Without clear expectations of results, and without some protections for the client, and if no results are requested, it is unrealistic to expect results. Other areas of dissatisfaction might be expected, such as the project's costing too much or taking too long.

Unfortunately, 8.2 percent thought that their consultants overpromised, and 4.92 percent felt that the consultants actually lied to them about the results. This is not uncommon, and it is the major reason it is important to agree on a baseline and how that baseline is measured, prior to starting the improvements. Once you develop this baseline, then you can measure success at the end of the project. Of course, as discussed earlier, it is important to have a balanced scorecard for the project to ensure that one metric does not improve at the expense of others.

Figure 8-12 shows the top reasons clients were not satisfied with their consultants. The reasons not mentioned above, although small in scope in terms of survey results, reinforce some of the guidance we given about consultant selection and relationship building. Every one of these reasons can be eliminated, or at least the risk associated with these reasons can be reduced, by using the techniques described in this book. For instance, clear background checks and contractual obligations can improve the skill levels and results-related reasons for dissatisfaction. We hope the risk of having a consultant lie about results—or lie about anything else, for that matter—can be reduced drastically through thorough reference and background checks.

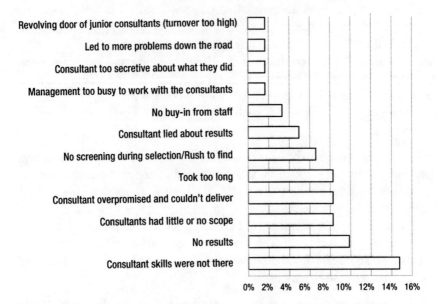

Figure 8-12. Percentage not satisfied with consultants, based on these criteria.

Having a plan for project governance and the internal resources to work with consultants eliminates anything else that would end up on this list.

The results of our survey represent the main reason for writing this book. Either most executives recognize these methods as effective, but do not take the time to follow them, or there is a lack of understanding. By following the processes discussed for selection of consultants and for relationship building, you will have greater satisfaction.

As can be seen from the satisfaction results, over 88 percent of respondents were at least somewhat satisfied, with over 50 percent completely satisfied. By a landslide, 52.46 percent of executives were satisfied with their projects because their consultants preformed the steps as originally outlined. This probably explains why there was such a high level of satisfaction. Being "satisfied" was simply a matter of the consultant's doing what he said he would do. In relationship to the Kano model, this should be a base-level satisfier, but is not a reason for total satisfaction. Figure 8-13 shows the basic Kano model.

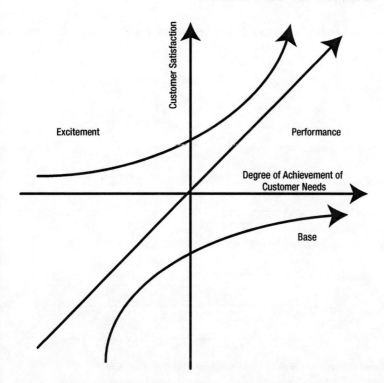

Figure 8-13. The Kano Model. Source: Noriaki Kano, Nobuhiku Seraku, Fumio Takahashi, and Shinichi Tsuji, "Attractive Quality and Must-be Quality," *Journal of the Japanese Society for Quality Control* 14, no. 2 (April 1984): 39–48 (in Japanese), http://ci.nii.ac.jp/Detail/detail.do?LOCALID=ART0003570680&lang=en.

Executives should base their satisfaction on the business results received and what was taught to or given to the staff so that the company can continue to have successes without the consultant. Getting tangible results on time and within budget is the performance quality element of the project. Because so many executives set their expectations at the base-quality level, consultants perform at that level. Just as any business selling a product or service must continually improve the product or service to meet customer expectations as they mature, consultants must accomplish more than showing up for work and doing what they are told to do. To be sustainable, the consulting industry as a whole needs to be results driven.

These survey results probably stem from the fact that many clients are not conducting an ROI analysis. Expecting an actual return on the consulting expense changes a leader's perspective on what will be satisfactory. If you are not conducting an ROI, how do you know if positive business results were achieved? Figure 8-14 shows the top reasons executives were satisfied with consulting work.

Percentage Satisfied Based on These Criteria

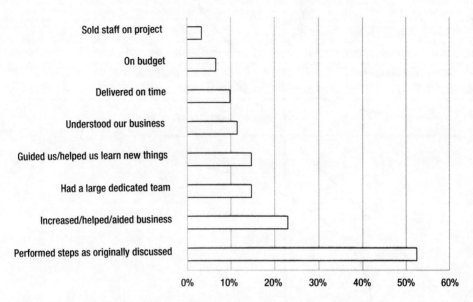

Figure 8-14. Percentage satisfied with consultants, based on these criteria.

Only two of these criteria provide actual value to an organization—helping the business and helping people learn new things. The misconception that "busy" equals "productive" needs to be corrected when evaluating consultant activities. This is the baby boomer view that if an employee spends a lot of time in the office, then he must be productive applied to a consultant. This view never was accurate when applied to employees and does not apply to consultants, either.

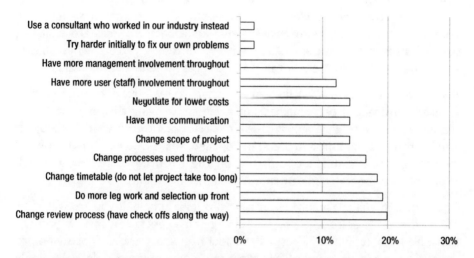

Figure 8-15. Factors regarding consultants that executives would change.

When the executives we surveyed were asked what they would change about the consulting relationship (shown in Figure 8-15), the top response was that they wished they had done more planning and had more control. Having a clear schedule with milestones and governance is logical for most business leaders, but because of many reasons—of which time is one—this often gets skipped. After a consulting project that has consumed large chunks of company resources yields no real benefit, there is regret that these steps were not taken.

The tollgates allow feedback points to possibly redirect the consultant or allow for learning moments. They allow you to catch mistakes before they become great. On a similar note, many executives wished they had done more legwork, trying harder to find the right consultant or setting up processes in advance. Executives also wanted lower costs and better timetables. Overall, many wished for more communication and involvement throughout the project.

Summary

Since the relationship between a consultant and a client is a short one, with clear outcomes that yield a return for the client and professional fees for the consultant, it is important to put all of the necessary steps in place to facilitate success. It is essential to have a thorough and comprehensive contract. The purpose of this contract is not to outline every possible aspect, with the threat of a lawsuit hanging over the future. Instead, the contract helps avoid some of the common pitfalls of the consulting relationship. By defining the project structure and developing the schedule of events that allow for open communications, along with ensuring that sufficient resources are available, you will reduce the risk associated with a consulting project. These basics should be specified in the contract and not presented in a vague manner.

If you calculate a return on investment, then you will have key deliverables focused on financial performance improvement. Having this expectation in place, and following through on those expectations throughout the project, you'll ensure a common understanding and team-oriented drive toward exceeding those goals. Metrics based on the balanced scorecard approach allow for incremental, departmental-based measurement.

The choice in building a consultant relationship is simple. If you are willing to put in the work upfront, through planning and expectation setting, you are more likely to see financial results and feel high satisfaction. Those who are not willing to put in this work are likely to be disappointed, unless their only satisfaction driver is having the consulting team show up and do exactly what they are told to do.

9

Options When Consultants Won't Do

Other Internal Possibilities Besides Consultants

The conventional definition of management is getting work done through people, but real management is developing people through work.

—Agha Hasan Abedi

When a company is faced with the need to change, has evaluated the consulting option and has decided against it, there are other options. That is because you can solve many business problems by looking for the solutions internally rather than going externally to a consultant for help.

In this book, we have provided information on the consulting industry, including some reasons when and when not to use consultants, how to select the right consultants, and how to structure the relationships. Yet many organizations rarely, if ever, use consultants, and they have continued to be successful. The problems that most companies face can generally be narrowed down to two root causes. The first, and most common one, is a failure to understand business strategy. There are many reasons for this. The primary one is a lack of overarching strategic vision, while the second is thinking about that vision as a fluffy concept and not understanding how to implement it.

Most organizations were founded on a vision of some kind, but over time, the market has changed or the core competencies have shifted, making it necessary to develop a new strategic vision. While visions should be enduring, not aimed at chasing trends and fads, they can over the decades become stagnant. By the time this happens, the founder of the business is often either no longer involved or does not have another great idea. This lack of vision leads to a general lack of direction. And that lack of direction, in turn, makes the company stagnant and less productive than it is capable of being.

The second root cause, as mentioned, is the implementation of that vision, particularly the ineffective hiring and control of employees. This is not limited to a specific level of employees; rather, it can affect the company on all levels. Strategy simply cannot be implemented effectively without the proper employees in place. When hiring and promotion practices favor aspects of a person's career that are not tied to his or her capabilities—like tenure with the company—it sets the organization up for trouble. Positions are filled by people who do not know how to do the job effectively. In processes that are stable and well designed, this is less of a problem than when companies undergo rapid change.

Further, the performance-evaluation processes used by many companies depend on a single view—the employee's supervisor, who may be misled into believing things about the employee that are not necessarily true. And the company's methods of motivating employees are often flawed, leading to behavior that is not desired by the company.

This chapter focuses on these key areas. Much of it resembles nuggets from a typical MBA program. But, while we present some basic, MBA-level information, our goal is to highlight some typical mistakes made when a company implements these MBA theories. Think of it as a presentation of timeless business skills as they play out in the real world.

For example, while many people are familiar with SWOT analysis, which we discuss, most tend to use this tool in an ineffective manner. Therefore, we show how to use these theories effectively, as well as how they are often misused. More important, we address how ineffective decisions lead to the unnecessary use of consultants. The key lesson: Business leaders need to lay a solid foundation, *then* use consultants to supplement certain areas at specific times.

Strategy

When considering business strategy, know that many firms do not truly understand their products and service offerings, how they relate to their customer base, and how the company's core competencies can establish a direct link to these customers. Many companies operate in firefighting mode. They do what needs to be done at the time and react to competitive moves. They frequently do not look at the overall picture in terms of how customers view them. They forget that their position in the marketplace is the customer's perspective, not theirs. They forget to constantly monitor that customer's view and make changes to influence it. Frequently, companies get themselves in the middle of a price war or in a hopeless quest to improve their bottom line, without considering the consequences of those activities on their customers and their customers' perception of the firm.

Much of what many large companies do on a regular basis regarding strategy constitutes throwing as much as possible against the wall to see what sticks. This ultimately erodes brand equity. Likewise, as mentioned earlier, many companies fall into a growth trap and grow for the sake of growing, without regard for internal or external factors.

Why Strategy Matters: In Commonsense, non-MBA Terms

To develop and implement strategies and tactics that will ultimately grow a profitable business, a company must understand its strengths and weaknesses. For example, a mid-size company was always known for making top-quality, American-made, durable products. Customers did not know the company's name, but they knew the products well. The company focused on top-quality products and assumed a good product would sell itself. There was no focus on overall strategy, customer understanding, or most important in this case, no attempt to build brand equity.

This company is an example of a company without a sound strategy. For almost two decades, the production/high-quality strategy worked. The company had a high-quality product with few competitors. But, things changed when the business environment changed and when the company was sold to new owners.

The new owners had one goal: getting the bottom line as large as possible. The company started to accomplish this by buying other companies in the same product area, in an effort to build paper equity. It did not invest in any form of sales or marketing (internal or via a consultant), nor did it invest any effort in improving the nonexistent brand equity. In an effort to boost profits, it started coming out with multiple new products a year. Whatever the owners could get out into the market, they did, without any quality marketing research. The company also started buying lower-cost and lower-quality parts for its products. This was all growth for the sake of growth. However, the company rapidly eroded its bottom line and caused a $15 million loss in one year.

What went wrong? What should the new executives have done?

There were many problems. First, the company had never marketed to the ultimate consumer, and it had never built brand equity, as mentioned. The production methodology of "a good product will sell itself" can get a company only so far. Eventually, the product matures and competitors enter the marketplace. So, at some point, the managers should have developed better sales and marketing strategies. Second, with the rapid-fire introduction of new products, the company cannibalized its existing brands and eroded much of its existing brand equity. The new owners did not ever think about conducting marketing research prior to any new-product development, nor did they conduct any cost/benefit analyses of the potential new products and launches.

There are more errors that could be explored. However, this typical example shows how companies get caught up in day–to-day operations and do not think about the overall picture. The really sad part is that, when the $15 million loss hit this company, the executives hired consultants to look at cutting manufacturing costs instead of addressing the real source of the loss. The consultants were able to generate savings in manufacturing, and these savings helped the company achieve a certain level of success. But as with all cost-cutting strategies, there is only so much that can be cut before the company cuts its own throat. The root causes of the company's problems have yet to be addressed, and until they are, the company is in danger of losing more money.

In short, you must assess the big picture on an ongoing basis, and especially when you are considering hiring a consultant.

Core Strengths

It is imperative for a growth-oriented business to recognize its core strengths and to build strategies around those strengths. This sounds like a cliché, and it is, but few executives actually understand what this means. To understand your company's core strengths, you must examine its internal resources and the external world that the company must navigate.

In terms of internal resources, consider tangible assets like equipment, facilities, patents, copyrights, distribution channels, and in-house-built technology. Intangible assets include brands, reputation, unregistered intellectual property, specialized skills, and relationships with suppliers and customers.

Counting and evaluating the tangible resources is easier than counting and evaluating the intangible resources. This is why it is helpful to rely on the balanced scorecard approach discussed in Chapter 8. The easiest way is just to step back and ask, "What does my company do best, and why do customers buy the products they buy?" Those two questions, if answered objectively, should reveal the company's core strengths. The key authors of the original core competency theory provide the following questions:[1]

1. How long could we dominate our business if we did not do "this" best?

2. What future opportunities would we lose without this core competency?

3. Does this competency provide access to multiple markets (providing the markets would be of value)?

4. Do customer benefits revolve around this competency?

Take Apple, for example. Customers buy iPhones. In fact, they stand in long lines to buy the newest iPhone. Why? For a couple of key reasons. It is not the product's quality, ease of use, cost, or other typical attributes that an executive thinks about when describing the product's strengths. Instead, for Apple, it is simply "coolness." The company has built its brand for decades as being the coolest, most innovative product on the market. Based on this, customers want Apple products. Once this loyalty and reputation is established, competitors find it nearly impossible to steal the company's core strength.

Many executives turn to consultants because they cannot answer the simple question: "What do we do best?" They see their profits declining and they focus their attention on the tangible details. However, as discussed elsewhere in this book, doing a root-cause analysis of the company's core strengths and internal resources is a necessity. (We show you how to do a root-cause analysis later in this chapter.)

But, while examining core strengths is important, it is also critical to understand the external market. Market forces change continually, and they include demographics, state of the economy, technology, culture, political environment, and unexpected events. While it is important to think about internal strengths first, keep in mind that your company cannot be all things to all people. Consider your core strengths with customers in mind:

---

[1] C. K. Prahalad. and Gary Hamel, "The Core Competence of the Corporation," *Harvard Business Review*, May-June 1990, pp. 1–15.

- What would customers think about this?

- How do customers view the company?

- What is likely to happen to customers that will change how they view my products?

The key here is a core strength or core value proposition. A core value proposition is essentially what the company can offer its customers that is of value. This is the company's promise to its customers and what its customers should expect. For a company to have enduring strength, that strength needs to be one that cannot be copied or would be difficult to copy. For example, it does not matter what technology Apple is marketing, whether it is the iMac of the early 2000s or today's iPads; Apple's strength is the coolness factor, not the brand itself. This strength transfers from consumer group to consumer group.

Too many executives hire consultants to do lots of market research or to generate new advertising strategies or to help launch new products. In reality, a company's core strengths should be so clear, so consistent, and so enduring that they remain stable despite changes in the marketplace. So, do your own market research so you will always understand what your customers' perceptions are. Do not make a decision without this research in hand. Remember though, research just provides information. It does not provide an implementation plan. The external information gained from marketing research may or may not require subsequent action.

Let's look at two types of companies that set up their strategies based on how they react to the market environment. One type of company is the *market-driven company*. It understands its competencies and how they relate to the market (the customers) it serves. Another is the *environment-driven company* that maybe does not understand its competencies as well, but instead adapts well to the business environment based upon its perception of it. Both types can be effective at what they do in the short term. However, the market-driven company is poised for the long term because of its understanding of its competencies and the market. The environment-driven company is good at keeping pace with changes in the business environment and in chasing market leaders. At some point, however, these abilities will fade and the company will no longer remain a force in the market.

Take, for example, JCPenney. It is having almost insurmountable problems because it cannot figure out what its key value proposition is and is merely reacting to the external environment. The company went through a massive rebranding strategy recently. Ron Johnson was brought in as JCPenney's new CEO in 2011, owing to his success with Target and the Apple Store.

He launched a large-scale "fair and square" campaign that included a changed logo, new look for the stores, and an everyday low-price strategy with no more sales. In June 2012, its stock tanked, going from $40 a share to $22 a share.[2] Shortly thereafter, JCPenney announced that Michael Francis, the retailer's president who was also in charge of marketing, merchandising, and product development, was no longer part of the company's management team. Customers seemed to be confused about the company's changes in pricing, leading to poor sales. As of November 2012, the stock was at $18 a share. The company is just guessing at what customers want and is throwing random strategies around because it thinks consumers are changing. Changing or not, what is the company's core strength? Why would a shopper be loyal to JCPenney? We really do not know. It has not established this in a way that is moving customers to spend more money at Penney's. Everything the company is doing is just chasing market trends, without even really understanding customers and without knowing who they are.

In order to maximize revenue, most companies try to be too many things for too wide a customer base. They constantly adapt themselves in the hope of "keeping up" with the pack and meeting the latest trend. The more sustainable model is the market-driven company that understands its place and maintains its market presence based on those strengths. These strengths have to be identified and understood before any actions are taken. Developing such a strategy starts with understanding the company and the market as well as possible. Until this is done, a company cannot make moves to react to the business environment. A consultant really should not do this step. Needing an overarching strategy is so constant, so enduring, so important that it has to come from within the company.

SWOT Analysis

One of the most popular and easiest tools for understanding your company is SWOT analysis (Figure 9-1). The acronym stands for strengths, weaknesses, opportunities, and threats. A SWOT analysis is commonly used in strategic planning. It helps with identifying the favorable and unfavorable factors, both internal and external. This analysis then serves as the foundation for setting future objectives.

Strengths are characteristics of a business that give it an advantage over other businesses. Weaknesses are characteristics that place the business at a disadvantage relative to other businesses. Opportunities are chances to

---

[2] Brad Tuttle, "More Troubles for JCPenney: Top Executive Departs Amid Sales Slump," *Time Magazine online*; June 19, 2012, http://moneyland.time.com/2012/06/19/more-troubles-for-jcpenney-top-executive-departs-amid-sales-slump/#ixzz29IUNsDT0.

improve the business in the current environment. Threats are elements in the environment that could cause problems for the business.

	HELPFUL	HARMFUL
INTERNAL	**STRENGTHS** • What are the advantages of the company? • What does the company do better than anyone else? • What unique relationships or resources does the company have? • What ability does the company have to produce its product or service at below industry standard costs? • What is the company brand value? • What is the company's experience level and what intellectual capital does it own? • Does the company fully leverage technology to optimize the business model?	**WEAKNESSES** • What could the company improve? • What aspects of the business does the company do poorly? • What do the company's customers see as its weakness? • What is the company's brand value? • What is the company's experience level and what intellectual capital does it own? • Does the company fully leverage technology to optimize the business model?
EXTERNAL	**OPPORTUNITIES** • What new technology-related opportunities can the company take advantage of? • Has a recent merger within the industry created an opportunity? • What mergers or deeper business relationships might help the company? • Are there legislative, political or cultural shifts that the company can take advantage of? • What particular niche segment of the company's existing industry could it fulfill?	**THREATS** • What obstacles does the company face? Does the company have debt or cash flow problems to manage? • Does the company's competition have a competitive advantage? • Are there legislative, political or cultural threats that the company is vulnerable to? • Are the requirements for the company changing? • What technology-related threats is the company vulnerable to? • Does the company have resource problems that will hold it back?

Figure 9-1. SWOT analysis.

It is important to note here that SWOT is not, in itself, a strategy or method. It is merely a tool for summarizing the research gathered about a company. It will not help you if you do not understand how to conduct market research. SWOT only reflects the information you put into it; remember the computer phrase, "garbage in, garbage out." If you are conducting faulty research, the tool will show faulty information.

If you have a competent market research department, then after the SWOT analysis has been performed, you can decide if your company goals are attainable with its current strengths and resources. If the objective is something you desire, then pursue it. Otherwise, select another goal and repeat the process of evaluation.

SWOT analyses are most powerful in a small group setting. This way you get diverse ideas and perspectives about the company and its environment. The team needs to ask probing questions to get to the real SWOT.

Consultants often come into a company and complete a SWOT as if this were a strategy. Yet anyone can draw a two-by-two box and write words in it. You need to be painfully aware of the competence of the research used to fill in the boxes, and even more aware of how to interpret the information.

The company needs to consider the environment and industry in which it operates. Factors here include the economic situation, legal requirements, regulatory requirements, the political situation, technology, nature, and society. The economic situation helps identify if the company is likely to be successful based on the purchasing power of its customers. Legal and regulatory requirements may limit the ability of the company to grow without further investment. Politics become especially important with international business. For instance, there are risks associated with being a multinational organization, and political risks are a big part of them. Analyzing technology, nature, and societal factors helps you understand your customers and your limitations. These are all fairly obvious variables, but some executives ignore or forget them nonetheless.

Competitive Analysis

Competitive analysis seems quite simple on the surface. It starts by figuring out who your competitors are, determining what they are doing, and then making sure that your company in some way is beating them in cost, quality, or differentiation. Although this seems easy, it is quite difficult because, with today's technology and small business approaches, the top competitor may not be the obvious big competitor. Rather, the summation of smaller competitors, who are more agile and hungry than the bigger ones, may be the serious contender. Normally, once companies grow too much, they overregulate themselves and lose agility.

The process to analyze competitors can be summed in three easy steps:

1. Who are the competitors?

2. What are the competitors doing? And almost more important, what will the competitors likely do in the future?

3. How is the business doing in comparison with its competitors? And, what should the action plan be going forward?

Step 1

Who are your competitors? Competition can come in many forms, including direct, category, generic, and budget competitors. To understand your competition fully, you must understand exactly why customers buy your products. What value does your product give them?

Imagine you are a large company like AT&T. Who are your competitors? A quick guess may produce answers like Verizon or T-Mobile. But what about Time Warner Cable, Vonage, Netflix, Hulu, Dish Network, Direct TV, and Apple? The key question is, "Why are customers using the product in question?" What intangible benefit does it provide? This is what determines why customers make the decisions they do. In this crowded mix of markets, the real story comes down to communication, connection to friends and loved ones, and entertainment.

Vonage has the clear advantage in the land-line market (lowest cost, reliable service), but that is a dying market. AT&T and Verizon are both doing well in the cellphone market. However, do people have actual loyalty to their phone company? Or will they switch companies in a heartbeat to get a lower cost? Cable companies have a clear advantage because they own the cable wires bringing the Internet into homes. No one needs cable TV anymore to be entertained, because of satellite and streaming options, but the Internet is necessary. However, once satellite or similar technology brings streaming video to everyone, and it becomes superior enough to beat cable in price and quality, cable loses. After all, entertainment is what matters, not having access to cable. If consumers can be entertained by streaming video, why would anyone need cable? Some of the above-named companies know this and have adapted, and some have not. Think about Hollywood Video. They apparently thought they were in the video business. As their bankruptcy shows, they were in the entertainment business. Their main competitors were Netflix and Hulu.

Marketing's job is to get consumers to take something simple and needed, like a new pair of shoes, and make them desire a certain brand. For instance, preteen girls may need new clothes that could be purchased at Walmart. But due to effective marketing, they desire clothes from a store such as Justice or Aeropostale. Marketers know this, so they define their products in terms of what consumers need rather than the technical aspects of their products.

General Motors did not understand this. The management of GM thought that it was in the transportation industry. If customers were all buying cars for mere transportation, they would all buy the cheapest, most reliable used car they could find. GM failed to carve out a differentiating advantage within this segment. In contrast, Honda has always aimed towards the same market segment, put focused heavily on enduring quality. In the luxury segment, BMW customizes its vehicles over 80 percent of the time because BMW understands that its customers are buying an experience rather than transportation. BMW recognized that it can sell this experience better than most of its competition. We know a CEO who is loyal to his BMW 7 series and gets a new one every two years. He does this because he likes to drive the car.

Consultants tend to sell myopia. They frequently come in and sell the idea of a benchmarking analysis and a SWOT. Rarely do they have the ability to think "outside the box" and identify correctly what customers are buying. Their argument is that, by performing the benchmarking analysis, the company can gain success. In fact, this is rarely the case. Companies need to understand why their customers buy their products or services, and this is a hard thing for a consultant to determine, especially when they provide a canned solution. If you cannot assess your company's total competitive picture, it is highly doubtful someone outside the company can, either. Business owners must ask themselves, "Why is a customer buying my product? What intangible benefit does it provide?" This moves you closer to a strategic direction. Competitive analyses and SWOT are the start, but some consultants end here, when it is appropriate to dig much deeper.

Step 2

Once your competitors have been identified, you need to understand what these competitors are doing and what they will be doing in the future. Michael Porter developed this formula in 1980 when he framed the questions that need to be asked.[3] These include: What are the competitor's goals? What is the company trying to achieve with its strategy? What is the company thinking about its current situation? What are the company's strengths and weaknesses? Based on answers to these questions, you also ask, How is the company's competition likely to respond or what are they likely to do? Porter's model is illustrated in Figure 9-2.

---

[3] M. E. Porter, *Competitive Strategy* (New York: Free Press, 1980).

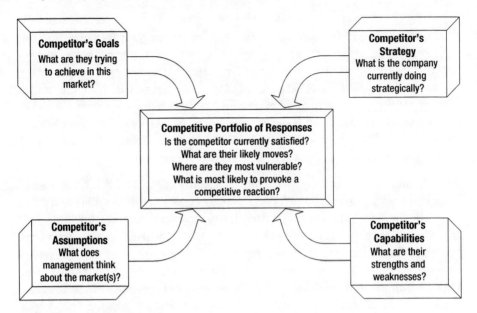

Figure 9-2. Competitor analysis.

These questions can be hard to answer—or easy to answer, depending on your situation. When a new microbrewery began in Pittsburgh, Pennsylvania, in 1986, the owner knew what strategies his main competitors would enact or continue. For example, Anheuser-Busch had built a large network of distributors with shelf space at many retail outlets. They were not about to give up this shelf space without a fight, and the microbrewer would lose that fight. Since Pennsylvania law states that all beer sales must go through distribution centers and restaurants, the restaurants become a more profitable outlet. So, the Pennsylvania Brewing Company took the direct marketing approach. The salespeople developed relationships with bars and restaurants. They attended community events, such as sporting events, to give out free samples. These direct marketing activities developed a loyal consumer base that grew the brewery.

Companies must understand their competitors. Anheuser-Busch did not seem to have a very robust strategy. Rising incomes and changes in the values of beer consumers made a market for a higher-class beer. So, use whatever resources are available to you, such as customer feedback, trade publications, or purchased databases, to understand your market, your customers, and your competitors.

Step 3

Once you have completely examined competitors and their likely future actions, link that information to your assessment of company strengths and weaknesses. Then, ask what your competitors are doing, what you are doing, and how you compare to them? Then anticipate and plan for the future. Forecasting is the key. To develop a strategic vision for the future, look at trends—how trends impact customers, how long trends will last, and how your company can work with those trends.

Compare your competitive and industry analysis to what you are doing now and what your goals are. Consultants tend to do these analyses and offer canned solutions for the next recommended competitive moves. An Ohio-based logistics firm (that is now bankrupt) used a sponsorship campaign as its advertising strategy because executives thought this was "the thing to do." The advertising campaign was with NASCAR because this was where its competitor advertised. The company thought that this would help increase their sales. However, doing this just because the competitor is doing it is not a good reason.

It is important to understand your company's unique strategic goals and its unique value proposition in the market place. Also, you must understand how your customers actually make their buying decisions and how these decisions will be made in the future. At best, a sports sponsorship may increase awareness, which may then, subsequently, increase sales if the target market comprises a huge group of fans. This example, however, is frequently the kind of failed advice consultants give. If a company has a reason to believe that the majority of its customers are NASCAR fans, and that NASCAR is a good image in their eyes, then the company may want to consider this possibility. If awareness is an issue, this may also be a good strategy.

In some mature industries, though, the recognition is probably already there and is not the problem. Brand image or loyalty may be a bigger part of the problem. Knowing who the competitors are and what they are doing is important, but the third and final step is to relate all that information to your company and to what you do best. This type of thinking is a survival skill in the strictest sense, even for the smallest business. A consultant cannot deliver this information unless he or she has a long-term relationship with the company and can conduct a complete internal and external assessment.

New competitors are likely to enter a market if it is attractive and there are low barriers to entry. In the words of Sun Tzu, "If you know the enemy and know yourself, you need not fear the result of a hundred battles. If you know yourself, but not the enemy, for every victory gained you will also suffer a defeat. If you know neither the enemy nor yourself, you will succumb in every battle." And, "In peace prepare for war, in war prepare for peace. The art of war is of vital importance to the state. It is a matter of life and death, a road either to safety or to ruin. Hence under no circumstances can it be neglected."[4]

You simply must know your company and your competitors, and be ready to "fight" at all times. Ask these three questions to develop a strategy.

- Who are our competitors?

- What are they doing?

- Are we doing it better than they are, at a lower cost than they are, or differently than they are?

Developing a Plan for the Future

Once these questions are answered, you are in a position to understand, strategically, what you can and cannot do. This also helps you understand what to do next.

The most basic beginning of strategy formulation is the understanding of internal core competencies and deficiencies, and the understanding of growth opportunities and threats from competition. Once this foundation work has been completed, you can define the company strategy and the strategic mission. The strategic mission helps define further strategy. It is the official statement that provides "the framework or context within which the company's strategies are formulated."[5]

In any strategic plan, there are short-term and long-term factors. With the situation analysis completed, you can see what the organization is capable of doing in the short term (zero to twelve months). Once you figure out the short term, you can develop the mid-term (twelve to thirty-six months) plan that will move you toward the strategic mission. Finally, you develop a long-term strategy that will take the organization five to ten years in the future. Thus, this can be described as a multi-generation plan (Figure 9-3). It is initially a simple representation of what is likely to be a much more complicated and detailed strategic plan later on. This stage is useful because, prior to putting

---

[4] Sun Tzu, *The Art of War*, trans. by Samuel B. Griffin, (London: Oxford University Press, 1971).

[5] Charles Hill and Garath Jones, *Strategic Management* (Boston: Houghton Mifflin, 2007).

in the work on a detailed plan, the strategy team can keep the overarching plan in view.

	Step: Fill process/ product voids	Stretch: Fill new Process/ products/ markets	Leap: Deliver productivity and value to the customer or end user
Vision: Long-term direction			
Process/ Product Generations:			
Platforms and technology: Necessary to execute the vision			

Figure 9-3. Multi-generation plan.

Figure 9-4 shows an overall strategy-development model. The key to this short-term, mid-term, and long-term strategy is always to reflect the company's value proposition: what value it provides the customer and how decisions could affect customer loyalty. Decisions should not be made in a vacuum or to chase fads. Strategies and missions are normally stable over several decades.

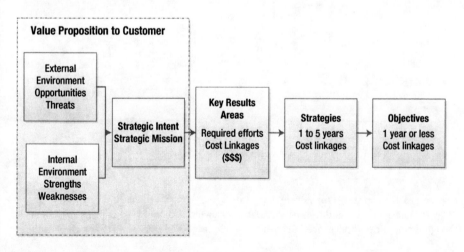

Figure 9-4. Strategy-development process.

Once the internal and external analyses have been completed, and have led to the strategic mission and multi-generation plan, it is time to develop more detailed strategies concerning the execution of the strategic plan. This can be done through detailed action plans or by using tools such as Hoshin Kanri (discussed in Chapter 8) to tie strategy to operational performance.

There are many tools available for development of company strategy (Figure 9-5), including simulation or modeling. There are many software packages with this technique, although inserting incorrect inputs and validations can lead to faulty results. Conjoint analysis is a statistical method that requires specific skills to perform, much like the simulation. These sophisticated tools are not as popular as some of the easier techniques that can be done within the organization, such as scenario development, win/loss analysis, financial analysis, and competitor profiles. It is beyond the scope of this book to go into all of these techniques, but an Internet search will yield plenty of information. Most of these methods are not as popular as the SWOT analysis because they are less widely known. But, they are simple enough and are good tools to use in the right situation.

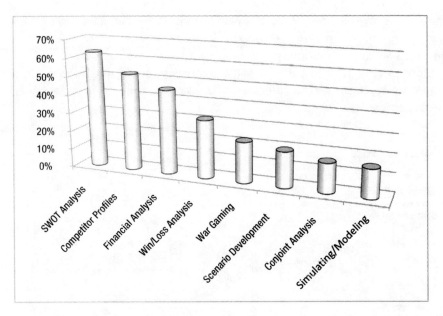

Figure 9-5. Top strategic-analysis tools (percentage of companies that use each tool)
SOURCE: Timothy Powell and Cynthia Allgaier, "Enhancing Sales and Marketing Effectiveness though Competitive Intelligence," *Competitive Intelligence Review.* 9, no. 4 (1998): 29–41.

Selecting and Evaluating Managers

Developing a strategic plan is an excellent beginning, but successfully implementing that plan takes great management and employees. In the next sections, we discuss how to hire a top-notch support staff, and how to evaluate the managers for the undertaking.

Finding the Candidates

Once you have accomplished the front-end work of strategy development, it comes down to people. The easiest way to fail in executing a well-designed strategy is to not have the right people implement the strategy. Another easy path to failure is not motivating those people to get the best performance possible from them.

The effectiveness of the average worker is a difficult measurement because most jobs are not tied directly to revenue, such as they are in sales or other countable divisions. One study has looked at managers overall and found that an astounding 90 percent of managers are ineffective.[6] And just look at salespeople: on average, 13 percent of a sales force delivers 80 percent of the company's revenue; 47 percent of salespeople admit to having no clue about their customers' biggest concerns; and 65 percent of sales managers focus on building volume instead of wooing profitable customers.[7] According to one consulting group, ineffective leadership costs businesses an average of 7 percent of annual sales.[8]

So, in sum, there exists the potential for financial disaster at most companies. Researchers Bruch and Ghoshal found that just 10 percent of the managers they studied took "decisive purposeful action" on a regular basis. They also found that 40 percent of managers were energetic but unfocused, 30 percent were prone to procrastination and had little focus and low energy, and 10 percent were lethargic, yet focused.[9] This obviously shows that having the right team members can make or break the company, as well as determine the successful implementation of the company's strategy plan.

Effective hiring is, therefore, the key. When implementing a strategic plan, do not look to a consultant. Rather, consider effective hiring as the answer. Recruitment problems arise because companies do not understand the

[6] Heike Bruch and Sumentra Ghoshal, "Management Is the Art of Doing and Getting Done," *Business Strategy Review* 15 (2004): 4–13.

[7] M. Bosworth and J. Holland, *Customer Centric Selling* (New York: McGraw-Hill, 2004).

[8] Ken Blanchard Companies website, accessed 2012, http://www.kenblanchard.com/.

[9] Bruch and Ghoshal, "Management Is the Art."

strategic hiring process. Just as forecasts are sometimes based on gut instinct, instead of analytical procedures and techniques, so too utilizing outdated tools of hiring will not bring you the good candidates. These old methods are simply not reliable or valid for predicting job success. A study found that the methods most commonly used to screen and hire candidates were actually less predictive of success than the flip of a coin.[10] Unfortunately, hiring practices have not changed significantly in the last thirty years.

Interviews, reference checks, and other mainstay recruiting tasks are fraught with biases and subjectivity. This problem is amplified by company policies concerning reference checks. In many cases, reference checks are sent to the human resource department of the former employers, where personnel will only affirm that the person was employed there and maybe a few things about the term of employment. You will find out little about the candidate's performance or his or her ability to work well in a company such as yours.

Interviews are often ineffective as well, due to the coaching that many candidates receive prior to an interview. Well-prepared candidates have a handful of canned experiences to cite and prepared answers to anticipated questions. Since most executives do not frequently interview candidates for leadership positions, the questions asked often are not creative or truth seeking. Although managers will not admit this necessarily, the outcomes of interviews often come down to first impressions and personality.

Interviews are well documented, with interviewers using human resource forms, but the questions are often so vague that the forms just satisfy legal requirements for avoiding discrimination. Even organizations that use sophisticated interview models to trick candidates into exposing flaws do not ensure that the right candidates are picked.

Table 9-1 shows typical hiring methods and their accuracy rates. Not much has changed in the hiring process, with the exception of use of the social networks and advanced computerized psychological testing. If we consider that a coin flip has a fifty-fifty probability, only a personality or ability test is more effective than a coin flip. Although there is slightly more validity when these methods are combined, the Hunter and Hunter study shows that new thought needs to be given to the hiring process.

---

[10] J. Hunter and R. Hunter, "Validity and Utility of Alternative Predictors of Job Performance," *Psychological Bulletin* 96, no. 1 (1984): 72–98.

Table 9-1. Hiring Methods and Accuracy

Typical Hiring Methods	Mean validity
Personality/ability test	.53
Job tryout	.44
Biographical inventory	.37
Reference check	.26
Experience	.18
Interview	.14
Academic achievement	.11
Education	.10
Age	-.01

One company found out that a commonly held belief about hiring—the value of same-industry experience—is a complete fallacy. The Gallup company found, when looking for customer service representatives for itself, there was a negative correlation between same-industry experience and success in the new company.[11] This is actually a common situation because same-industry experience typically makes people set in their ways and less able to think in creative ways.[12] Although this finding may not be true in all settings, it should be considered when making hiring decisions. Bringing in a fresh perspective may, in fact, improve overall performance.

Recruiting and hiring decisions are improved to 75 to 85 percent accuracy when position-specific, statistically validated job-assessment tools are used.[13] This is a great improvement over "barely better than a coin flip." When the Hunter and Hunter study was done, psychological testing was not as developed as it is now. Thirty years of improvements in testing have, however, provided more options for selecting the right candidates.

This is especially true for high-impact positions in which the emotional quotient (EQ) or business alignment may be more important than tangible job

---

[11] G. Phelps, "Creating Paths to Success," *Gallup Management Journal*, accessed 2010, http://gmj.gallup.com/content/286/creating-paths-success.aspx.

[12] Linda Orr, *Advanced Sales Management Handbook and Cases: Analytical, Applied, and Relevant* (New York: Routledge, 2011).

[13] H. R. Chally, *The Chally World Class Sales Excellence Research Report* (Dayton, OH: HR Chally Press, 2007).

skills. For these tests truly to be the most effective, however, they must be based on characteristics proven to matter for job success. They must also be statistically sound. This has become a growing industry for human resources, and there are many providers whose products do not meet either of these requirements. If a manager or human resource professional is sold a canned solution by a testing company, without adequate controls in place for the study, then he or she leaves the company open to having a failed new hire and of having wasted resources on testing.

These tests can measure many things, including personality traits, intelligence, decisiveness, energy and enthusiasm, results orientation, maturity, assertiveness, sensitivity, openness, tough-mindedness, emotional intensity, intuition, recognition needs, motivational needs, sensitivity, assertiveness, and even the ability to trust and the likelihood of deviant behaviors. If the position is one with a high impact, and also is hard to fill, then employ any available tools to ensure a good employee. Other forms of employment testing today are intelligence tests, knowledge tests for industry-specific needs, sales aptitude tests, vocational interest tests, and attitude and lifestyle tests. Many companies are also examining credit scores, drug tests, and nicotine tests to provide a measure of character. Smoking is now culturally unacceptable enough that this practice is being upheld in courts.

The newest test is the social networking test, which examine a candidate's "true self" as posted on the various social media sites. Many potential employees forget that the information they put on even the most "private" Internet sites is actually public and can be used to evaluate them as job candidates. A 2012 CareerBuilder survey reported that 37 percent of employers admitted they use social networking sites to research job candidates. Another 11 percent plan to start using this tool.[14]

This screening tool may visit both personal and professional networking sites. Of those who conduct online searches and background checks, 65 percent use Facebook, 63 percent use LinkedIn, and 16 percent use Twitter. Obviously, many of the companies that use these tools also employ other tools to evaluate those candidates as well. Companies feel it is necessary to use this method for all new hires so as to ensure that the candidates who show up for interviews are the same who show up for the first day of work.

Companies are using this "private" information to disqualify candidates on the basis that they posted provocative or inappropriate photographs or information. Indeed, 59 percent of companies have disqualified someone for this reason; 45 percent identified candidate who had posted content about

---

[14] CareerBuilder, accessed 2012, http://www.careerbuilder.com/share/aboutus/pressreleasesdetail.aspx?id=pr691&sd=4%2F18%2F2012&ed=4%2F18%2F2099.

their drinking or drug use. Candidates who badmouthed their previous employers, co-workers, or clients were disqualified by 33 percent of companies. Even candidates showing poor communication skills were eliminated by 35 percent of the companies. A staggering 28 percent found candidates making discriminatory comments. As mentioned in an earlier chapter, candidates lie about their qualifications; 22 percent of companies said that they disqualified candidates for this reason. About 20 percent disqualified candidates for sharing confidential information from a previous employer.

On the other hand, social networking sites can provide employers with positive information about candidates. Fifty-eight percent of companies using social networking sites have found profiles that provided a "good feel" for the candidate's personality and fit. Fifty-Five percent felt that the social networking persona conveyed a professional image. Fifty-one percent found profiles that supported the candidates' professional qualifications. Creativity was found in 44 percent of the company checks of the social networks. Positive communications skills were found by 49 percent of those companies. Other people posted great references about candidates 34 percent of the time.[15]

The truth is that many companies have bad hiring practices because they use the same practices they always have. Employers have to be more creative and must break free of assumptions when hiring (such as that within-industry experience is essential). They should employ testing when possible.

Selecting the Right Candidates

There are business courses, and even entire professions, that cover how to manage human resources, including employee relations, labor laws, compensation, privacy, and hiring. Our intent is not to replace those; rather, we want to challenge your thought processes regarding management's role in human resources. Figure 9-6 shows a simple process for hiring effectively, and we use that to illustrate the preferred method.

Prior to posting a new position, the manager hiring for that position must conduct a job analysis to identify the qualifications and must write a job description. This does not mean you should search on the Internet for positions similar to the one you have and copy the qualifications, as is commonly done. This job analysis starts with asking the question of what the business hopes to accomplish with this position. The answer helps you define what is needed to meet that goal. Depending on the situation, this may include past experience in doing what is expected or certain technical skills that are desired.

---

[15] Ibid.

The exception to this rule is when it is a commodity-type position that would not be considered an alternative to hiring a consultant. Unfortunately, businesses tend to treat every position like a commodity, with the possible exception of top management. You do a job analysis for all new hires expected to have an impact on the organization.

This step is normally difficult because if your company currently lacks the skill, you do not know how to describe that skill. For example, if a company is hiring a sales analyst to complete sales forecasts and customer lifetime value (CLV) analyses, it likely does not have someone doing that now. In fact, this is a new position for many firms. The manager ends up interviewing potential analyst candidates, having no idea what statistics skills are needed to conduct that CLV analysis. In short, the persons who can insert the most statistical terms into the conversation might win the job, even if they have no real idea what they are talking about or how to use these tools. Thus, if you do not have an incumbent to help you create the job description, then make sure that everyone interviewing the candidates understands the needs of the job. A consultant could help with this.

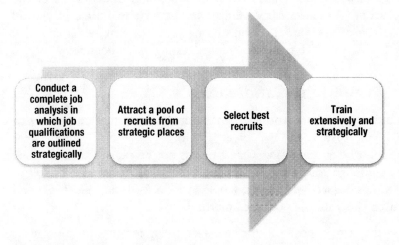

Figure 9-6. The hiring process.

After the job analysis has been done, and job description written, it is time to get the human resources department involved. They need to do a market analysis to determine the compensation. Even this stage should be done carefully. You should agree with the comparison groups that HR has chosen for the compensation study. If the comparison groups are not applicable, then you might overlook the right candidates or alienate them. Just as with products (but not necessarily consultants), the lowest-price option among candidates is often the lowest-quality option. Experience and education cost money; most times, these costs are well worth it to get a star employee.

Once the compensation package is vetted and approved, it is time to find candidates. Getting the right pool of candidates may be a difficult task, however. Often, top management roles are advertised on a regional or national platform. This approach should be taken for high-impact positions if another candidate pool cannot be reached. Candidate pool opportunities include trade organizations, headhunters, conference proceedings, publications, and professional networks. Depending on the type of position you are seeking to fill, there may be different options available to get high-quality candidates.

Once you have a good candidate pool, you need to reduce that pool to a manageable size. The minimum qualifications for the position can be filtered by the human resources team, but after that, you need to review the remaining resumes. The resume review should yield between three and six candidates for further review. If you do not have that many, go back to the previous step.

These remaining candidates will require some investment of your time and resources. The first investment is in proper testing to further reduce the pool to a primary candidate, a secondary candidate, and even a tertiary candidate, if applicable. Interview each thoroughly, and ask questions that will reveal both their knowledge and character. Ideally, one of these candidates will rise to the top, and you can make an offer, negotiate the terms of the new hire, and set a start date.

Training

As part of the onboarding process, you need to define the training needs. There will likely be needs common to all employees, as well as specific needs related to individuals based on their skills or experience. Do not ever conduct training without first identifying the objectives of the training, as well as how the effectiveness of the training will be assessed.

Once you have developed methods for delivering the training and evaluating the training, you provide that training as soon as possible following the onboarding process. Then you evaluate the training for effectiveness at timed intervals. This includes giving immediate feedback, midterm feedback, and long-term feedback. The goal of these evaluations is to assess the time at which the training becomes ineffective.

At that point, you offer the training again to current employees in similar roles, to refresh the skills they learned as new hires and to introduce new concepts and proven methods currently not used. Figure 9-7 shows a high-level view of the training process that all organizations should employ to improve the effectiveness of both leaders and high-impact employees.

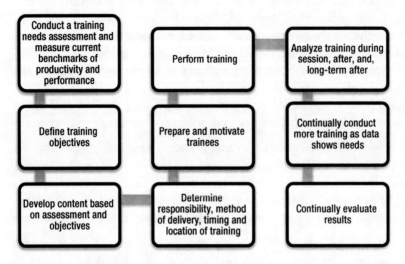

Figure 9-7. Training process.

Many businesses forget that training is an ongoing process. Studies have shown that almost all employees are most effective at year five. That is, it takes five years for them to get up to speed, learn the business, and start having a significant impact on the business! Then, generally after five years, average employees get burned out and have outdated knowledge—just as they are becoming really valuable. This is why, once the right candidates are selected, evaluated, and trained, you should cultivate a long-term training strategy and a training relationship between employees and the company.

Motivation

Training is part of the employment equation; motivating employees is, as well. What are the time-tested techniques for motivating employees to perform consistently at a high level? Let's look at a few.

Employees tend to perform better when they are given challenging goals that are SMART—specific, measureable, attainable, relevant to the position, and time bound. You also need a system to empower and reward employees frequently for their top performance. Do performance evaluations, and make them challenging but not punitive, unless a deficiency exists. By avoiding the punitive nature of evaluations, you will challenge the employees and they will more likely be honest about results because there is less fear of disciplinary action.

You must give employees, with high levels of talent the growth opportunities to nurture their development. This may look like assigning 70 percent of their responsibilities to job-specific tasks and 30 percent to stretch goals or projects outside of their specific jobs. All employees, either high performing or not, are motivated by different things. It is the manager's responsibility to figure out what motivates each individual employee, rather than taking a one-size-fits-all approach. By doing this, it is more likely your employees will be motivated to do their best for the good of the organization.

Part of this motivation strategy should include ongoing employee development. One example of this development might be paying 100 percent reimbursement of MBA tuition. Many companies are afraid of employee development because of the costs involved and the possibility of losing the employee afterwards. But, the truth is that employee development is always a key motivator, and the costs are likely recouped through the added abilities these employees bring to the job. Employers should not only provide money for employees to get certifications or degrees, but also provide time off work for the employees to attend classes.

Along with providing rewards and goals for employees based on their specific needs, managers need to avoid productivity killers, such as wasteful paperwork and unproductive meetings. Typically, employees experience the problems and inefficiencies in the organization. They are in a great position to provide effective solutions to these inefficiencies. So listen well.

Indeed, answers to challenges that an organization faces should easily come from within the organization. This is encouraged by providing the right skills, environment, and motivation to a carefully selected and nurtured workforce.

Evaluating Managers

Fifty percent of the time—and maybe as high as 90 percent—senior managers engage consultants to solve a problem because they have an incompetent group of managers who are unable to solve the problem on their own. Instead of evaluating the internal competence and getting rid of incompetent people, companies frequently turn to consultants to fix the problems at hand. More often than not, the problem is not fixed because the root cause is inept employees.

Not all managers are created equal. If you performed an analysis of personality types associated with management, you would find the full spectrum present, one end of that spectrum may hold larger portions of the population. Equally, managers have IQs and EQs that represent the entire spectrum. Therefore, if there is no strong correlation between intelligence and personality type and successful management, how should a company evaluate its managers?

Many companies follow the traditional models of regular employee evaluations and augment this information with performance specifications, such as adherence to budget and meeting productivity requirements. So, if a manager does what she is told to do, maintains her budget, and seems productive compared with current standards, then she is a good manager. Right?

No, not necessarily. A manager who simply follows the rules and meets performance standards is not a good manager. A good manager not only does what is expected but also reaches beyond the comfort zone when appropriate.

It is a good idea to add a 360-degree analysis to the budget adherence to help ensure balance. A 360-degree analysis is the process by which a manager is evaluated by not only their boss but also by her peers, subordinates, and customers. Through this analysis, the manager gets a balanced view of their performance, rather than only a top-down view.

Also, there should be an element of innovation in the way managers are evaluated. In an ever-changing business environment, maintaining current performance, or even trying to improve by just a couple of percentage points each year, will lead to loss of market share. Although personality type may not be an indicator of managerial capability, certain tests that show a manager's alignment with an organization may prove helpful. By performing these assessments, a company can measure its manager's values against the values of the organizational leaders, as well as future organizational values your company desires.

To address the skill gaps that many managers display, organizations implement evaluation methods to obtain a balanced-scorecard type of view of the manager. Part of this evaluation needs to include how managers handle improvement projects outside of their sphere of control, where persuasion skills are more important than authoritarian or relationship-management skills. This again helps build a well-rounded manager. And because the world is constantly changing, all managers must learn and improve, as do other professions, through continuing education.

Evaluating Company Performance in the Marketplace

As we discussed earlier, strategy is one of survival skills that companies should be able conduct internally. Like many of the other topics discussed in this book, we could write an entire book on this topic. There are general tools available to business leaders to evaluate performance. Many of these are strictly financial, while others are more industry specific. These tools can be used to benchmark your company against others in your industry. For instance, in the $6 billion plastics-molding industry, there are a few benchmarking tools used to compare the company against its competitors. Unfortunately, like many other industries, these benchmarking tools can prove unreliable and can lead a business to the wrong conclusions, as the data is self-reported and/or riddled with errors.

Trade journals and industry contacts help paint an accurate picture of where a company stands in the market. As the company fits into a tighter niche, the available data become less plentiful, although likely more useful. With the lack of applicable data, company leaders often resort to talking with customers about the competitors to understand the SWOT for other companies. Information on suppliers and pricing may be found around the bar with chatty industry acquaintances or at trade shows where industry leaders speak and mingle.

In the healthcare industry, group-purchasing organizations, trade organizations, alliances, and regulatory reporting agencies help with the comparative analysis. Companies such as Premier, the Advisory Board, Midas, or Thomas Reuters offer member organizations data on multiple facets of their businesses. These may include purchasing data based on available contract pricing or quality specifications. This helps the healthcare companies get the best possible pricing for the most consistent product available, with less guessing.

Along with purchasing information, the companies just mentioned provide valuable clinical-quality data about performance of their facilities and physicians. Because of the collaborative nature of these organizations, it is possible to evaluate the performance of one organization against others of similar size and services. By getting this information, you can drive improvement projects within an organization without the need for a consultant.

Hospital associations and the Centers for Medicare and Medicaid Services also aggregate data so that organizations can benchmark performance and compare it with performance standards and competition. These results cannot ever be verified because each database is proprietary and unique, however.

These are examples of two industries and the comparative tools available to the leaders in those industries. As discussed earlier, business leaders often look to consultants to bring in ideas from the outside as a way of driving improvement. But if you take the time to do your own networking and competitive analyses, or you empower an employee to do this work, you do not need to hire a consultant. Internal work likely would not only be a fraction of the cost of a consultant, but it would most likely be more accurate, due to consultant biases. For instance, companies that are leaders in their industries may not utilize consulting services often, so they would not be part of the information database that consultants would bring to a company considering hiring them.

Evaluating Sales Force Performance

Given that the sales force is primarily responsible for bringing the revenue into a firm, an accurate evaluation of the sales force is a requirement for any company. A *sales force audit* is a comprehensive, systematic, diagnostic, and prescriptive tool designed to assess the adequacy of a firm's sales-management process. It also provides direction for improved performance and a prescription for needed changes. To perform this audit effectively, it is necessary to have some established metrics in place. Establishing these metrics and performing the analysis are two activities that can be performed internally.

The first part of this process requires an evaluation of the sales environment. The necessary leading indicators for the sales force audit may vary depending on the type of company. For instance, in a value-added type of sales relationship, the number of customer visits or requests for proposals from existing suppliers may be statistically proven leading indicators of overall sales performance. In an organization where the sales strategy is not long-term relationship selling, as is the case in a business-to-consumer sale, then maybe just counting the number of customer contacts may be an effective leading indicator of sales performance. In some industries, customer contact time actually has a negative correlation with sales success. This is because there is so much strategic planning required prior to each sale that the degree and depth of planning is the most important criterion.

There is no cookie-cutter approach to analytics for evaluating *sales force performance*. There are, in fact, generally accepted methods of evaluation for lagging indicators, such as revenue increase, contribution margin, or organic growth with current customers. In most industries, idiosyncrasies associated with sales methods complicate the performance evaluation. Where possible, you do not want to count on after-the-fact metrics, but instead should strive to understand the actions that drive sales performance and measure those.

The sales force performance evaluation uses analytics to define the cause-and-effect relationship between sales force actions and resulting sales. In essence, you want to measure what actions each salesperson takes and what the resulting sales are. However, it may not be clear what inputs from the sales force create more profitable sales. By measuring all of the possible inputs, a skilled analyst can perform statistical analyses, like regressions, to see if relationships exist. This is necessary, again, because not all industries are created equal. Although sales techniques, such as SPIN selling, are universal in business-to-business sales, other actions that salespeople may not be present in an existing model.

Once these analyses have been completed, you will know what sales aspects must be measured as leading indicators proven to drive sales improvement. This is much more effective than setting goals, which are often based on magical thinking, and then waiting for the results in order to evaluate the sales growth. By looking at the inputs, the sales manager can intervene in sales activities and improve overall performance.

Sales volume analysis is another part of the sales evaluation process. This is a lagging indicator that serves more as providing data to build a model for leading indicators than as an indicator to drive performance. Any person who has spent a significant time as a successful sales professional will admit that increasing sales volume can as easily put a company out of business as it can improve the bottom line. Sales volume goals, unless controlled by a more balanced metrics approach, drive the wrong behavior toward margin dropping or even some unethical business practices. As with revenue or contribution margin, this is the score of the sale and not the goal. The goals of the sales force must be to refine the behaviors that will drive balanced sales, which will maintain or grow margin while ensuring the most ethical behavior.

Nevertheless, organizations must have an effective sales force analysis in order to generate the behavior models that the sales force can use to improve. Figure 9-8 shows considerations for the sales volume analysis. These considerations define what constitutes a sales volume analysis. How will the sale be defined? How will we measure the sales? Can the sales be stratified to see performance? Is there a way to compare to others? Where can the information be found? All of these questions seem simple—until you try to answer them.

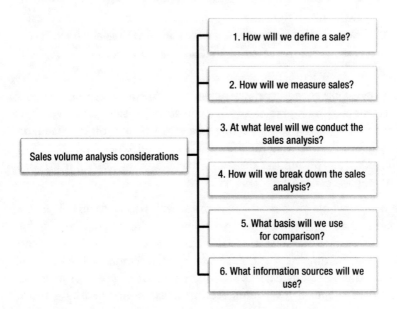

Figure 9-8. Key considerations for a sales volume analysis.

The rigor in defining what a sales volume analysis means should be applied to all business analytics, of course. This rigor yields a product that is a series of measurements that really matter to the business and can be proven to drive performance. There are many sources of sales information, including sales invoices, call reports, expense accounts, individual prospect/customer records, internal financial records, warranty cards, store audits, consumer diaries, and test markets. Each of these sources should be leveraged to build a reliable method for evaluating sales performance. Many of these sources can introduce bias into the overall measurement, however, so it is important to identify potential inaccuracies in the data.

A salesperson's performance appraisal is a systematic process for (1) establishing whether the salesperson's job behavior helps the company reach its sales objectives, and (2) providing specific feedback to the individual salesperson. Performance appraisals can help managers accomplish these goals. Compensation may be tied to performance, also. By reducing the sales metrics to the inputs to the sales process and the drivers of those behaviors, the business can change from a method that incentivizes salespeople to do whatever is necessary to get the sale to one that drives real growth and prosperity. These evaluations help identify skill gaps and needs for training. Through mentoring and follow through based on these leading indicators, it is possible to develop a world-class sales force.

Evaluating salespeople is challenging; there are many hurdles to overcome. Most salespeople work alone in the field, and they engage in a multitude of activities. Each territory has different potentials for growth and profitability, often making side-by-side comparisons unfair and leading to inaccurate evaluations. Also, sales potential may be influenced by the physical size of the competition. Depending on the customer makeup for the territory, some salespeople may be farmers while others are hunters. The farmers work to maintain relationships and accounts with loyal customers; hunters reach out for new opportunities. It is unfair—and a management error—to evaluate both types with the same metrics. Both types are necessary for a growing business, so the evaluation methods need to reward the actions of both types.

Overcoming Productivity Killers

An alternative to bringing in a consultant to drive better employee performance is to eliminate those actions that demotivate people and kill productivity. Many pop-culture examples display the common productivity killers. For example, the movie *Office Space* highlights how having stagnant management enforces non-value-added reports and activities that can demotivate employees. Although this is a great movie to show the inappropriate use of consultants, it is a great way to show how business leaders often make consultants necessary through their own poor actions.

Some employees are motivated simply by going to work every day; they see their contributions as valuable to the company, its customers, and society. Adding perceived unnecessary work to these employees' workload, however, kills productivity. For this reason, business leaders need to look at what they require from employees and question whether all those tasks add real value.

Productivity killers fall into a few general categories. The first is overextension—people working long hours or having too many responsibilities. This situation can be caused my many factors. Some employees are ambitious, highly driven, and overconfident. This leads them to reduce personal time or make promises they cannot keep. Others do not know how to say no, and spread themselves too thin. Even when employees do say no, a supervisor may compel them to perform a task. Overextension ultimately means tasks take longer to get done, and it is the reason employees burn out. The best antidote to overextension? Manage employee capacity and encourage reasonable workloads and work hours.

Another productivity killer is poor health. Loss of productivity occurs when employees do not take care of themselves. When you or others are not healthy, it is harder to be productive. Encouraging your employees to get enough sleep and to exercise outside of work can yield productivity increases during work hours. Like most things in life, maintaining balance is important. Too much rest or exercise can also have negative effects. Downtime during the day is also necessary to maintain balance. Encourage employees to take breaks, to rebalance and maintain optimal brain function. A healthy employee will be a more productive employee.

Similarly, poor diet may have an effect on productivity. This is ironic because many company functions include unhealthy food options such as donuts, pizza, or hamburgers. This food reduces employee energy levels and, therefore, productivity. Luckily, taking care of oneself leads to greater health. Commonwealth Fund survey data show that, in 2003, 69 million U.S. workers missed work days for sickness, equaling 407 million days lost.[16] Problems concentrating because of illness, or illness in the family, led to another 478 million days lost. Prevention is the key to reducing this problem. When an employee feels sick, the best thing to do is to give the employee time off to rest. This is in contrast to most human resource policies, which encourage employees to work when they are sick.

Pay attention to attitudes, as well, because they can lead to productivity problems. Employee attitudes are greatly affected by external factors, such as relationships, finances, and the kind of work being done. They are greatly affected by internal factors as well, such as bad management. A poor attitude may lead to procrastination or distraction. Being physically healthy is not enough to be productive. The mind needs to feel positive emotions and be free of bad stress and concerns. Companies can affect general attitudes by offering access to help for those who may be experiencing external stressors. Many organizations offer employee-assistance programs that are inadequate. If employee productivity and longevity are your strategic priorities, then you need to rethink the services you offer your employees.

The PricewaterhouseCoopers' 2011 Financial Wellness Survey showed, for example, that financial stress contributes to productivity loss.[17] In fact, this can be a big distraction, leading to folks managing their finances at work. Companies can offer reputable resources that assist employees in addressing financial issues. This is not to say that the organization should pay the employee's bills, but rather, provide financial-management tools they can use to get their affairs in order.

People tend to be motivated by doing work they enjoy. But if what they are doing is not motivating, it will drain their energy and enthusiasm. Improve

---

[16] Karen Davis, et al., "Health and Productivity Among U.S. Workers"; accessed 2005, http://www.commonwealthfund.org/usr_doc/856_Davis_hlt_productivity_USworkers.pdf.

[17] PricewaterhouseCoopers' "Financial Wellness Survey"; accessed 2011, http://www.pwc.com/en_US/us/private-company-services/publications/assets/pwc-financial-wellness-survey.pdf.

productivity by ensuring that your employees enjoy their work. Talk to them often about what is making them happy and unhappy, and work to provide solutions.

Interruptions such as email and phone calls also reduce productivity. Distracting use of smartphones, for example, should be eliminated. Rules for meetings can limit the use of cellphones and tablets. Encourage people to check email only a few times a day instead of constantly.

Productivity enhancements for meetings include: (1) mandating that meetings be scheduled in increments of fifteen minutes to allow travel time between meetings; (2) having meetings start on time and locking the door at the start time; (3) limiting the number of meetings during the day or number of days when meetings are held. Before every meeting, think about whether there is a purpose to the meeting and if everyone involved really needs to be there. Then, make sure there is an outcome and actionable takeaways from that meeting.

In a world where cubicles are prevalent, employers should consider designating certain times of the day as task times, when the office is a quiet zone. Discourage multitasking, a known productivity killer.

Although rules like these may seem a little ridiculous, they address some of the root causes of poor productivity. By setting some policies such as these, you can help maintain some minimum levels of productivity.

Note that not every company has every problem with these productivity killers. If a company wants to increase productivity in the office, a one-size-fits-all approach will likely not work. But, addressing some of the root causes can start with an internal analysis and follow with solutions based on group input. Some other tactics may be to spend time with employees explaining the time killers and the idea of value-added versus non-value-added activities. Most people, if challenged to map out how they use their time for two weeks, will realize that there is a lot of waste in the regular work schedule they can eliminate.

Simply encouraging employees to live more balanced lives, building policies around maintaining balance, and setting rules to eliminate wasteful activities during the workday will improve the productivity of most any company. These actions can be taken with minimal effort and without help of a consultant.

Root-Cause Analyses

Earlier in this book, we discussed root-cause analysis. One of the first skills that should be taught employees is the ability to analyze a situation and develop a root-cause analysis. Since organizations often bring in a consultant to fix a problem, building capabilities in root-cause analysis and corrective actions are keys to avoiding the need for a consultant.

There are several methods for getting to the root cause of a problem, including the Five Whys, the Ishikawa diagram, and the Eight Disciplines.

The Five Whys technique was developed by Sakichi Toyoda, and was used by the Toyota Motor Corporation to help it become the high-quality automobile producer that it is today. Toyoda believed that asking "why" five times in a row helps you get to the bottom of a problem.

There are two primary techniques used to perform five whys: the Ishikawa diagram and a tabular format. Figure 9-9 shows the tabular method.

Problem Statement: Describe the problem to be solved					
Why #1	Why #2	Why #3	Why #4	Why #5	Root Cause

Figure 9-9. Tabular Five Whys analysis.

A couple of examples of the Five Whys are below:

Example 1:

Problem Statement: Patients who show up on time for appointments end up starting their appointments late, leading to further delays and dissatisfaction.

1. **Why** are patients being started late?

   - Because the examination room is still busy with the previous patients.

2. **Why** is the exam room still busy?

   - Because the previous patients started late.

3. **Why** did the previous patients start late?

   - Because there were two patients scheduled for the same time.

4. **Why** were there two patients scheduled for the same time?

   - Because 15 percent of our patients do not show up for appointments.

5. **Why** do so many patients not show up for appointments?

   - Because our office hours conflict with other priorities those patients have.

6. **Why** are our office hours set as they currently are?

   - Because we had not previously identified this customer need.

In this example, we went further than the Five Whys because that is how long it took to get to the root cause. Without doing this analysis, the office manager may have been tempted to schedule fewer patients per hour, reducing throughput but increasing patient satisfaction. Instead, the real problem was identified as the need for evening and Saturday appointments. If the schedule was rearranged, the facility could possibly increase both throughput and satisfaction.

Example 2:

Problem Statement: Data collected for the efficiency project is not accurate.

1. **Why** is the data not accurate?

   - Because the start and stop times for operations in the process are the same.

2. **Why** are the start and stop times the same?

   - Because the operator entered the time into the computer system at the same time.

3. **Why** did the operator hit the times at the same time?

   - Because the operator was busy and didn't see why this data collection was important.

4. **Why** didn't he feel that the data collection was important?

   - Because nobody told him.

5. **Why** didn't anyone tell him?

    •   Because the company did not develop a good
        communication and training plan to explain the
        importance of good data collection.

Notice in these examples that, although it is called the Five Whys tool, the number of times you ask "why" will vary depending on the situation. Sometimes three whys will do while others many more will be necessary. The point is to keep asking Why? until a root cause is identified.

The Ishikawa diagram, also known as a cause-and-effect diagram or a fishbone analysis, is another method that can be taught to a person in minutes. With minimal experience, an employee with good critical thinking skills and in-depth company knowledge can be skilled in this method, which is the most common tool for root-cause analysis.

Figure 9-10 shows the basic format for an Ishikawa diagram. It allows the root-cause analysis team to focus on this single problem or output of the process and categorize potential causes logically.

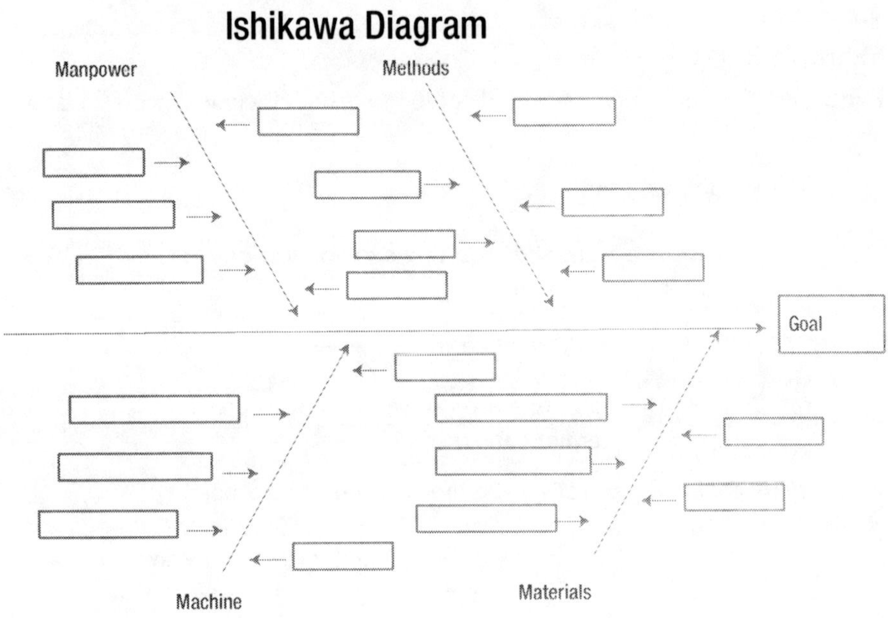

Ishikawa Diagram

Figure 9-10. Ishikawa example

There are many categorization methods used in an Ishikawa diagram. The first one is used primarily in manufacturing and is called "the 6 Ms," including the following. (Note that Measurement and Mother Nature are not shown in the figure, due to space constraints.)

- Machine
- Method
- Material
- Manpower
- Measurement
- Mother Nature

Some other categories may be used in certain instances, including Management and Maintenance.

When performing a root-cause analysis in marketing, the employee or team uses "the 7 Ps." The categories in this type of Ishikawa diagram include:

- Product
- Price
- Place
- Promotion
- People/personnel
- Process
- Physical Evidence

In a service industry, "the 5 Ss" may be used instead. But since the Ishikawa diagram has its roots in manufacturing, most training for using this tool is within manufacturing. Nevertheless, marketing and service types of Ishikawa diagrams were created because this tool can be used across industries. The 5 Ss include:

- Surroundings
- Suppliers
- Systems
- Skills
- Safety

The Ishikawa diagram is just one example of the root-cause analysis tools available. If the reason your organization cannot arrive at a root cause is that it lacks the skill set, do not hire a consultant unless your purpose is to teach your employees techniques such as Ishikawa, the Five Whys, or Eight Disciplines.

The branching methods used in both tools make it easier to get to the root cause of a problem. It is a simple root-cause analysis technique that can be taught to most people in a matter of minutes. It has been criticized for being too simplistic, and leading users to stop at the symptoms rather than drilling down to find the root cause of the problem. It is also limited to the current knowledge of the user, so it is necessary to have those with diverse experience handle the analysis. Nonetheless, it can be a powerful technique to eliminate problems.

Another great tool that can be taught to employees to improve performance is the Eight Disciplines approach to problem solving (Figure 9-11), or 8D. This tool is commonly used when a problem is identified and a corrective action is necessary.

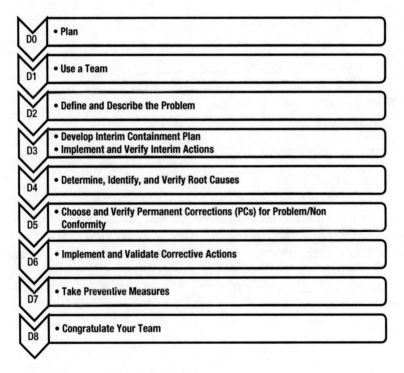

Figure 9-11. The "Eight Disciplines" steps.

Ford Motor Company developed this tool for team-oriented problem solving. The tool starts with identification of a problem. Once you have identified the problem, you establish a plan for solving the problem. You form a team of people with in-depth knowledge of the process or product that caused the problem. The team defines the problem with an in-depth explanation of who, what, where, when, why, how, and how many. Then you devise and implement a plan to contain the problem, so it does not get worse before you can eliminate it.

At first, you use a tool like the Five Whys to identify and contain a problem. The next phase is to a tool like the Eight Disciplines to verify the root cause of the problem. The containment action typically only addresses symptoms, so this next phase is important for a long-term solution. Many organizations stop their corrective actions at the containment phase. But, by completing all eight (or nine, a ninth step was recently added) steps, the team addresses the root cause and therefore, eliminates future problems. With the root cause identified, you develop potential solutions, prioritize them, and then pilot them through to ensure effectiveness.

In the manufacturing environment, some companies give short timelines for completion of an 8D. This defeats the purpose. A short time frame for containment is applicable, but the root-cause analysis and subsequent corrective action must be exhaustive and robust for the value of an 8D to be realized.

Once the solution is implemented and verified, the next step is to use the lessons learned to modify the controls in place, thereby ensuring that the same problem does not reoccur, and that it does not emerge in another area of the business, either. The last step is important: you congratulate and recognize the team. As with many other simple tools, there is a technique to doing a good 8D, but this skill can be developed within the company.

Commitment to using this proven method in conjunction with the Five Whys will lead to improved 8D results and thereafter in business performance.

Summary

This chapter demonstrated some commonly misunderstood and misused areas of business management that typically lead to the erroneous use of consultants. While the techniques and tools described here were by no means exhaustive, we hope they have provided insights into what must be done first, before a consultant is hired.

In the case of business strategy, you need a sound strategy that takes advantages of your company's value proposition and does not chase trends. You also need to ensure that you have a good-quality team to execute the strategy. Typical hiring techniques, in particular, are outdated and ineffective. You must use newer techniques and ideas to attract the right talent. Once you have the right talent, you use the right tools and techniques to evaluate and motivate your workforce. Rooting out ineffective managers is also key.

You also work to remove typical productivity killers. These actions include rethinking how things are done, such as frequency and length of meetings. It is our hope that the tools we present in this chapter—and in the book—will help you use consultants more effectively and efficiently only when you need them.

Tools

Information and Checklists for Managing Consulting Decisions

In this and the other three appendices, we provide the templates and forms you will need to work effectively with a consultant. Each tool is meant to be a guide to help you. But, keep in mind that the tools here and in Appendices B, C, and D do not substitute for legal advice when you are creating a contract for services or any other agreements. Have your attorney review all such contracts.

Appendix A covers:

1. Top Consulting Firm Strengths and Weaknesses
2. Top Industries Using Consultants
3. Top Consulting Industries
4. A Project Checklist
5. A Return on Investment Template

Top Consulting Firm Strengths and Weaknesses

These lists reflect our view of the top consulting firms, like Accenture, McKinsey, Boston Consulting Group, and other high-profile outfits.

Strengths

- Large organizations typically have plenty of resources available to support clients.

- Large firms have a reputation to maintain, so they will likely achieve a minimum quality level.

- There is significantly less risk of project failure due to the stability of the consulting company.

- When junior consultants run into roadblocks, there are seasoned consultants who can support them.

- There is a wider knowledge base to draw best practices from.

- The firm is likely to have experience in many industries rather than just one or a few, which may lead to better solutions.

- The firm has a wider pool of consultants to meet specific project needs. They usually have the right skills for each job.

Weaknesses

- Many large firms hire fresh MBA students to work with clients rather than use their seasoned professionals.

- A small client may not present enough business for a large firm to consider its needs a priority.

- The consulting company may be less willing to negotiate the terms of the deal. They tend to be more expensive.

- Large companies are often less nimble than small ones.

- Clients are more likely to get canned solutions instead of root-cause analyses and tailored solutions to those root causes.

- The consultants may think—erroneously—they know more about your industry than you do.

- The consultants may be less open to project-management office direction.

- Seasoned consultants may be better at spinning the results to look successful.

- There is less specialization than with some smaller consulting firms.

Top Industries Using Consultants

Who uses consultants? This chart shows.

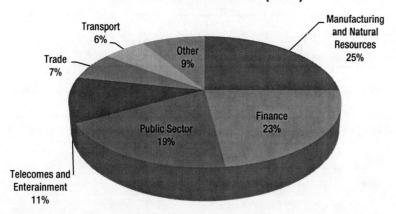

Figure A-1. End users of consultants in 2008 and 2009. SOURCE: Joe O'Mahoney, *Management Consultancy* (Oxford, UK: Oxford University Press, 2010).

Top Consulting Industries

Which areas do consults serve and to what extent? Here is a list.

Consulting Industry Areas	Percentage of Market Share
IT consulting	27%
Program/project management	20%
Operations	12%
Outsourcing advice	9%
Financial	8%
Strategy	8%
Business process re-engineering	7%
Human resources	7%
Other change management	3%

Figure A-2: Top consulting areas. SOURCE: *Datamonitor. Global Management and Marketing Consultancy, October 2008.*

Project Checklist

This list reflects the advice we have provided in the book. If you truly need a consultant and have planned well for the engagement, you should be able to check every box.

Do I Need a Consultant?	
	I have verified that I am not hiring a consultant to fill a survival skill.
	My need is a temporary one.
	I have identified a real return on investment for the project.
	I have included internal resource needs in the return on investment calculation.
	I have identified financing sources to pay for the consultant.
	I have met one of the following criteria: • I am too small for a full-time hire. • I have a skill gap to fill that can be trained. • I am doing this while I conduct a search for a full-time employee. • My own people and methods failed to find the root cause of our problem. • My need is a temporary one. • I need a breakthrough change that can then be sustained internally. • I need a highly specialized skill that is difficult to find. • I need an objective opinion.
	I have built a project charter (a statement of the scope, objectives and participants in a project).
	I have built expectations that include the needs of my employees and other stakeholders.
How Do I Find the Right Consultant?	
	I have sent out requests for proposals to at least six consultants.
	I have identified at least three fully qualified consultants who are capable of doing the work. These were qualified based on the criteria outlined in Chapter 7.
	I have negotiated for the best deal with my preferred supplier while maintaining relationships with the top two suppliers in case of a breakdown in the original deal.

How Do I Enable Success?	
	I have negotiated a contract that meets my project goals.
	I have introduced the consultant to the organization and given employees the ability to ask questions while providing relevant information.
	I have negotiated the ground rules with the consultant and the project-management office team.
	I have set up a rigorous and well-defined project-management meeting schedule.
	My project has tollgates and a Gantt chart that defines the responsibilities.
Was My Project Successful?	
	I validated my return-on-investment assumptions.
	The celebrated gains actually resulted in an improvement on the income statement or balance sheet.
	My employees have adopted the change and are supporting its sustainment.
	I have a sustainment strategy that ensures continuity extending long after the consultant has left.
	I have performed an after-action review with my trusted team members.
	I have celebrated success and rewarded employees for their hard work with the consultant.

Return on Investment Template

Perhaps the most important action you can take prior to hiring a consultant is to do an ROI analysis. This template will help you do just that.

Return on Investment Calculation	
Project Name	
Project Manager	
Date of Analysis	
Consulting Company Name	
General description of benefits: This project includes increasing revenue and reducing costs to turn around company performance.	

BENEFIT DRIVERS	Quarter				
	Q0	QI	Q2	Q3	Q4
Revenue Increase					
Capacity Increase					
Cash Flow Increase					
Cost Avoidance					
Capital Expense					
Fines/Fees					
Cost Reduction					
Labor Costs					
Material Costs					
Reduced Time Spent Handling Complaints					
Total Benefits[1]					
Implementation Filter[2]		85%	90%	95%	95%
Total Actual Benefits[3]					
Costs[4]	Q0	QI	Q2	Q3	Q4
Total[5]					
Benefits	Q0	QI	Q2	Q3	Q4
Quarterly Benefit Flow					
Cumulative Benefit Flow					
Discounted Benefit Flow	Q0	QI	Q2	Q3	Q4
Discounted Costs[6]					
Discounted Benefits[7]					
Total Discounted Benefit Flow	Σ of Q1-Q4				
Total Cumulative Discounted Benefit Flow	Σ of Q1-Q4				

Cost Detail	Q0	Q1	Q2	Q3	Q4
Consulting Fees[8]					
Travel Expenses[9]					
Personnel Costs[10]					
Project Management Costs[11]					
Capital Expenses[12]					
Supplies[13]					
Total Costs[14]					
ROI measures					
Discount Rate[15]	3.75%				
Net Present value[16]					

Notes:

[1] This is the sum of all of the benefits listed above.

[2] Implementation filters are meant to reduce the expected benefits by a percentage.

[3] This it the "Total Benefits" reduced by the implementation filter.

[4] This worksheet only shows four quarters; as many quarters that are necessary can be added. This could also be adjusted for month or annual calculations.

[5] Equals the sum of all costs listed below.

[6] This is the costs discounted using a time value of money calculation.

[7] This is the benefits discounted using a time value of money calculation.

[8] Charges from the consultant.

[9] Travel expenses for the consultant.

[10] Internal company costs for personnel working on the project.

[11] Costs of the internal project management team.

[12] Capital expenses anticipated for the project.

[13] Supply cost estimated for the project.

[14] Total of all costs. Duplicate these figures above for the "Total" under "Costs."

[15] This is the discount rate used for the time value of money calculation. Remember to divide the annual rate by the number of periods used in the spreadsheet. In this case, since there are four quarters in a year, we divide the estimated rate of 14% by 4 so our rate is 3.75%.

[16] This is the current value of all of the benefits minus all of the costs using the estimated discount rate.

Requests for Proposals

This appendix is a sample request for proposals (RFP), which you can adapt to create a document that consultants will then use to create their proposals. It is not meant to be a one-size-fits-all document. Rather, it outlines some basic considerations for an RFP. Specific industries may require more or different language in any of the following sections. If your procurement staff is not familiar with an RFP, you should reach out to an expert for legal and procedural advice. Have your attorney review the RFP prior to releasing it.

Request for Proposals (RFP)

RFP NO. _____

Project title: _____

Due date for Proposal: _____

Only emailed proposals will be accepted.

Introduction

Purpose and Background

Provide information on why you are issuing the RFP. What is the project? Is it replacing something? What's the problem to be solved?

Objectives and Scope of Work

What will success look like? What is within the authority of the consultant to effect?

Minimum Qualifications

What minimum qualifications are required of the consultants, including degrees, specific skills, or experience?

Period of Performance

This contract will begin on _____ and end on _____. The company has the sole right and discretion to extend this contract.

Definitions

COMPANY The [company name] is the company that is issuing this RFP.

PROPOSAL A formal offer submitted in response to this solicitation.

PROPOSER Individual or company that submits a proposal in order to attain a contract with the company.

REQUEST FOR PROPOSAL (RFP) This is the opportunity for the consultants who would like to work on meeting the company's needs to provide the best price, using their approach, to meet this need.

General Information

RFP Coordinator

All communications between the Proposer and the company will be with the RFP Coordinator:

Name _____

Email Address _____

Mailing Address _____

Physical Address for
Delivery _____

Phone Number _____

Fax Number _____

Any other communication will be considered unofficial and nonbinding. Any communication regarding this RFP with any other company member may result in disqualification for the Proposer.

Schedule

Request for Proposals sent _____

Question-and-answer period _____

Last addendum to RFP sent _____

Proposals due _____

Proposal evaluations _____

Finalist interview _____

Contract negotiation _____

Notification to unsuccessful
Proposers _____

Begin work _____

The schedule may be modified by the company at any point.

Proposal Submissions

The proposal submission deadline is: _____.

Proposals must be emailed to the RFP Coordinator in a Microsoft Word or PDF file attachment. Any delays caused by the company's email servers will result in a deadline extension. Any delays caused by the Proposer's email servers will not be considered a reason for an extension.

Any proposal not submitted by the deadline will not be accepted or reviewed.

RFP Revisions

The RFP Coordinator will send all revisions to the entire, active group of Proposers. This may be done at any time prior to the contract being executed.

Review Period

The company may take up to [XX] days to review all proposals.

Responsiveness

Although the RFP Coordinator may disregard minor administrative discrepancies, it is understood that any RFP response that is not complete based on the RFP specifications will not be considered valid.

Most Favorable Terms

The Proposers are encouraged to supply the best offer in both cost and time, since there will be no second or third offers requested. Any proposal will be considered part of the contract file.

Contract and General Terms and Conditions

The general terms and conditions associated with this RFP are the standard terms and conditions for the company. Any exceptions to these should be noted as part of the response. After the RFP response, there will be no allowance for changes in general terms and conditions.

Proposal Costs

The company is not responsible for any costs incurred by the Proposer preparing this proposal.

Contract Obligation

The company is not required to enter into a contract because of this RFP.

Commitment of Funds

The company is not obligated to pay any costs incurred prior to the execution of the contract.

Proposal Contents

Proposals must be In English, as described below, and in the following order:

1. Cover letter, signed and with Certifications and Assurances
2. Technical proposal
3. Management proposal
4. Cost proposal

Proposals must provide information in the same order as presented in this document with the same headings.

Cover Letter

The cover letter must be signed and dated by a person authorized to legally bind the Proposer to a contractual relationship—that is, the president or executive director. The cover letter must include, by attachment, the following information:

1. The contact information of the business or individual with whom contract would be written (name, address, phone, email)
2. The contact information of the company officers
3. Legal status of the Proposer
4. Federal Employer Tax Identification number or Social Security number
5. Contact information of identified consultants to be used on the project
6. Any conflicts of interest applicable to this contract, including personal and business relationships

Technical Proposal

The technical proposal includes the following:

1. *Project approach.* Shows a clear understanding of the project and explains how it will be approached. Includes methods to be used.

2. *Timeline/Gantt chart.* Includes milestones and key decision points for the company. It is preferred that critical chain project management (CCPM) methodology be used.

3. *Resource requirements.* Includes required resources and support that the company will be responsible for supplying.

4. *Performance measurement.* Explains what the measures of success will be, including how the measurement system will be validated and how the baseline is established. This should include formal signoffs for the company to review at various project milestones.

5. *Risks.* Includes mention of risks to project success. This should be comprehensive list, but may be a living document, such as a failure mode and effects analysis (FMEA). (If you are not familiar with FMEA, we recommend you purchase a book on the subject, as it has many purposes besides just risk reduction.)

6. *Deliverables.* Includes what will be delivered in addition to standards for proper performance.

Management Proposal

Project Management

1. *Project team.* What is the team structure?

2. *Project management.* What methods will be used to ensure adherence to timeline and budget while maintaining quality? How will the triple constraint be managed?

3. *Team qualifications.* Identify all team members, their qualifications, their roles, and if there is a prior relationship with the company.

Experience of the Proposer

1. *Experience.* Explain any experience the Proposer has had in dealing with issues to be addressed by this RFP.

2. *References.* Include references for all projects completed in the last five years. This list should include customers with good and

bad experiences. The Proposer will have the ability to explain poor relationships to the company.

Cost Proposal

Identification of Costs

Include a full budget, including expenses and personnel. The personnel portion must include Proposer personnel costs and expectations of the company personnel.

Evaluation and Contract Award

Evaluation Procedure

Proposals will be evaluated against the requirements outlined in this RFP. The Proposer may be asked to clarify the proposal during this evaluation. The company will award the contract to the Proposer whose proposal is deemed to be in the best interests of the company.

Oral Presentations

Finalists may be requested to present their proposals on site. Any promises or clarifications made during this presentation will be considered binding as part of the contract.

Certifications and Assurances

1. I/we declare that all answers and agreements made in the proposal are true and correct.

2. The prices and costs have been put together independent of any other Proposer or company resource.

3. This proposal is good for 60 days from submittal.

4. I/we understand that all costs incurred preparing this proposal will not be reimbursed and that all proposals belong to the company once submitted. Furthermore, I/we claim no proprietary right to the content therein.

5. I/we agree to the terms and conditions contained in the RFP unless otherwise stated in the proposal.

6. I/we have not attempted to keep other potential consultants from submitting a proposal.

7. I/we grant the company the right to contact all references contained in the proposal, including those who may have not been pleased with performance.

8. I/we agree to comply with all applicable federal and state laws prohibiting discrimination against persons on account of race, sex, color, age, religion, national origin, disability, or any other reason.

Check below to note if there are any exceptions being made to the terms in the RFP.

☐ I/we have no exceptions to the terms of this proposal.

☐ I/we have taken exception to some of the terms of this proposal and have attached an addendum outlining these exceptions.

Signature of Proposer

Title   **Date**

Sample
Consulting
Contract

This contract is for your reference only. You must seek legal help when drafting your own contracts. Your state and local laws, as well as your needs, will require a contract drafted specifically for your unique situation.

Sample Consulting Contract

This Contract is between [Insert Company name] ("company") and the company below ("proposer.")

Proposer Name:

Address:

City, State, Postal Code:

Phone:

Email:

Purpose

The purpose of this contract is to [fill in].

Scope of Work

Services will be provided as outlined either in the attached Proposal from the proposer and the Request for Proposal from the company, or in a detailed outline of the work to be done.

Exhibit A, which outlines the General Terms and Conditions, will be used in addition to the applicable option above to define the overall scope of work.

Contract Period

This contract will be valid starting on [start date] and will end at the completion of the deliverables outlined in the Scope of Work.

Payment

The Proposal submitted by the proposer outlines specific fees and rates. Any deviation from this Proposal shall be included as Exhibit D to this contract and be signed by the company. All payments will be reviewed by the company project manager for accuracy prior to being made. Any disputes over payments may be addressed by the project steering committee. Any disputes not settled in the steering committee will be dealt with using the dispute process in this contract.

Billing Process

The method for billing and acceptance may vary depending upon the nature of the project. All time-based billing will include a detailed time sheet of activities to justify the expenses, which are to be validated by the company project manager. All expenses, in addition to the time-based billing, must include itemized receipts and also be considered applicable expenses as part of the RFP agreement and all company policies.

Contract Management

Proposer Contracting Manager	Company Contracting Manager
Contract Manager Name Proposer Company Name Company Address City, State, Postal Code *Phone:* *Fax:* *Email address:*	Contract Manager Name Proposer Company Name Company Address City, State, Postal Code *Phone:* *Fax:* *Email address:*

Assurances

All applicable current federal, state, local, and company laws, rules, and regulations will be followed in the execution of this contract.

Order of Precedence

If there are any inconsistencies in this contract, the inconsistencies will be resolved by giving precedence in the following order:

- Special terms and conditions outlined as part of this contract.
- Exhibit A – General Terms and Conditions
- Exhibit B – Company's Request for Proposal
- Exhibit C – Proposal from proposer
- Exhibit D – Deviations

Approval

Only a written amendment signed by both parties shall alter, amend, or waive this contract.

Those persons signing below have warranted that they have the authority to execute this contract and agree to the execution of this contract through this signature.

Proposer	Company
Signature	Signature
Title Date	Title Date

General Terms and Conditions

Definitions

1. "company" is the [insert company name], or any of the officers or other persons authorized to represent that company.

2. "proposer" is that company providing services under this contract including all employees of the proposer.

Advance Payments Prohibited

There are no advanced payments authorized as part of this contract.

Amendments

Only amendments to this agreement signed by both parties can be made.

Assignment

This contract is nontransferable.

Attorneys' Fees

If any litigation takes place as a result of this contract, each party will be responsible for its own legal fees.

Nondisclosure

The proposer agrees that all agents of the proposer shall adhere to the standard Nondisclosure agreement used by the company.

Copyright Provisions

Any Materials produced as part of this contract are "works for hire" and the property of the company as defined by the U.S. Copyright Act. IF U.S. Copyright laws do not consider the materials to be "works for hire," then the proposer hereby irrevocably assigns all right, title, and interest in Materials, including but not limited to all intellectual property rights, to the company as of the creation of said materials.

Any printed or digital materials produced and including recordings and films will be considered applicable Materials. The company reserves the right to create, keep, or transfer copyrights, patents, and registers related to these materials.

Any materials provided to the company by the proposer which are pre-existing and not produced under the contract are hereby granted to the company for use in a nonexclusive, royalty-free, irrevocable license (with rights to sublicense others). The company may reproduce, distribute, modify, and publicly use all materials that are preexisting. The proposer warrants and represents that proposer has all property rights necessary to grant the company aforementioned licensure.

Disputes

Either party may request a dispute hearing. All disputes must go through a mediation process prior to any further litigation. All disputes must be clearly outlined, including the positions of both parties.

Governing Law

All interpretations of this contract shall be evaluated in accordance with this of [insert state] state laws. All actions shall be in the Superior Court for [Insert court].

Licensing, Accreditation, and Registration

The proposer shall comply with all applicable company and government licensing, accreditation, and registration requirements necessary for this contract.

Overpayments and Assertion of Lien

If the company mistakenly overpays or makes errors in payments to the proposer due to this contract, the proposer will repay the company, including interest. If the proposer fails to repay, the company may put a lien on the proposer real property or require some other security acceptable by the company.

Privacy

All personal information obtained by the proposer or proposer's employees will not be released or otherwise made known to any unauthorized party without the written consent of the company. The proposer shall implement appropriate safeguards to prevent unauthorized access to this information.

The company may monitor, audit, or investigate the proposer for appropriate use of personal information. The proposer shall ensure that all personal information is properly destroyed at the end of the contract period.

The proposer is responsible for any damages related to any unauthorized use of personal information. Failure to comply with this privacy portion of this contact may result in immediate termination of this contract.

Records Maintenance

The proposer shall maintain proper records of this project for a period of [xx] years following the date of final payment. These records will be considered property of the company to be maintained at no cost by the proposer. The company may access these records at any time and at no additional cost.

All records that are related to any litigation must be retained regardless of age until the litigation is completed.

Right of Inspection

The company has the right of inspection of the proposer's facilities and records related to the work done under this contract.

Severability

If any specific portion of this contract is illegal or invalid, the other portions of this contract will remain valid.

Site Security

While working on site with the company, the proposer's representatives will comply with all company procedures.

Subcontracting

No subcontracting will be allowed without the expressed written consent of the company.

Taxes

The proposer is responsible for tracking and paying applicable taxes for all activities and personnel involved in this contract.

Termination for Cause

If the proposer fails to meet the conditions of this contract, the company has the right to request a corrective action. In the event that a corrective action is not done to the company's satisfaction within 30 days of request, the company reserves the right to terminate this contract. Any costs incurred by the company due to a termination for cause will be the responsibility of the proposer. This may include direct costs and indirect costs associated with replacing the proposer.

Termination for Convenience

The company may at any time end this contract and only be liable for services rendered at the time of termination. Terminations are to be in writing 10 days prior to final termination.

Termination Procedures

Once a termination has been put in place, the proposer must:

1. Stop work under the contract as specified.
2. Place no further orders for materials or services.
3. Allow the company to take possession and pay for open orders and services.
4. Complete any work that is not part of the termination in a quality manner.
5. Protect all company property that is in the possession of the proposer.

The company reserves the right to withhold reasonable payment until all commitments of the proposer have been met.

Treatment of Assets

1. All property provided by the company remains the property of the company. Any property provided by the proposer and reimbursed by the company as part of this contract will be considered the property of the company.

2. Any property provided by or paid for by the company shall only be used in the execution of this contract.

3. Any loss of damage to the property of the company resulting from negligence on the part of the proposer will result in the proposer's replacing, repairing, or paying the fair market value of the property.

4. The proposer is responsible for notifying the company if property is lost, destroyed, or damaged.

5. All company property will be surrendered to the company by the proposer prior to the end of this contract.

6. Proposer's employees or agents must also abide by this clause.

Waiver

No waiver from this contract is considered a modification of this contract or its terms unless stated in writing and signed by an authorized company representative.

Sample Nondisclosure Agreement

Here's a sample nondisclosure agreement you can use as a guide. But remember: Your situation is unique, so it will not fit every case. As always, have an attorney familiar with intellectual property law and state and local laws review the agreement before you use it.

Nondisclosure Agreement

This Nondisclosure Agreement is entered into by and between the "Disclosing Party" and the "Receiving Party," in order to prevent unauthorized disclosure of "Confidential Information" as defined in this agreement. The parties and their employees agree to enter into a confidential relationship with respect to certain Confidential Information.

Confidential Information

"Confidential Information" shall include all information or material that has or could have commercial value or other utility in the business in which the Disclosing Party is engaged. In addition, any personal information or information protected under law, such as HIPAA, will be considered confidential even if it is not identified explicitly as confidential. Information that is transmitted orally will be noted as confidential in writing by the disclosing party within 2 days of disclosure. Any written confidential information should be marked as confidential by the disclosing party.

Exclusions from Confidential Information

Information that is publicly known at the time of disclosure or becomes publicly known through no fault of the Receiving Party is not considered confidential information. As well, any information discovered or created by the Receiving Party before disclosure by Disclosing Party is not considered confidential information.

The Receiving Party may disclose information if it receives written approval by the Disclosing Party.

Receiving Party Obligations

Receiving Party shall keep the Confidential Information in strictest confidence for the sole and exclusive benefit of the Disclosing Party. Receiving Party shall restrict access to Confidential Information to only those who need the information to provide service to the Disclosing Party. Any person receiving this information from the Receiving Party must also sign a Nondisclosure Agreement at least as restrictive as this agreement. In order to use the disclosed information for any other purpose, the Receiving Party must obtain written permission from the Disclosing Party. At the request of the Disclosing Party, the Receiving Party must return any written or electronic records of the Confidential Information.

Time Periods

This Nondisclosure Agreement stands in place until the Confidential Information covered by this agreement is deemed to be no longer confidential.

Relationships

This agreement does not imply that either party holds an interest in the other's organization.

Severability, Integration, and Waiver

If any part of this agreement is deemed to be illegal, the remainder shall remain in effect. This agreement supersedes all prior agreements and cannot be modified without written approval of both parties. Failure to enforce any part of this agreement does not imply that this agreement shall be rendered void.

Disclosing Party

By: _____

Printed Name: _____

Title: _____

Dated: _____

Receiving Party

By: _____

Printed Name: _____

Title: _____

Dated: _____

Index

I

CPSIA information can be obtained at www.ICGtesting.com
Printed in the USA
LVOW130100140213

320037LV00005B/181/P